M000304849

What about me?

Louise Michelle Bombèr is qualified as both a teacher and a therapist. She has worked with individual pupils, classes, whole school settings, teachers and support staff across both the primary and secondary phases. She has provided consultations and training for education, social services and health. She currently works as an Adoption Support Teacher for Brighton & Hove in an advisory capacity and as an Attachment Support Teacher Therapist for The Yellow Kite Attachment Support Service To Schools (theyellowkite.co.uk) which offers a range of services advocating for and supporting pupils in care and adopted, in a freelance capacity. She also works privately as a child and adolescent therapist and as a clinical supervisor for therapists working out in schools. She has developed a seven day course for education staff supporting pupils with attachment difficulties that she runs with local authorities, charities and independent organisations.

There are now Attachment Lead Teachers and Attachment Lead Key Adults in numerous schools. She facilitated an arts project and exhibition (*Walk A Mile In My Shoes*) which gained media interest and opened up a much needed dialogue in the community regarding the impact of abuse and neglect and the need for increased inclusion within schools and the wider community.

Louise is the author of *Inside I'm Hurting* (Worth Publishing 2007) and contributed a chapter to *Teenagers and Attachment* (Worth Publishing 2009). Her curiosity, passion, experiences and trainings have enabled her to get alongside vulnerable pupils in schools in creative ways, enabling them to make the most of all that education has to offer.

What about me?

Inclusive strategies to support
pupils with attachment difficulties make
it through the school day

Louise Michelle Bombèr

worthpublishing.com

First published 2011 by Worth Publishing Ltd
worthpublishing.com

© Worth Publishing Ltd 2011

All rights reserved. No part of this publication may be reproduced, stored in a retrieval system or transmitted in any form, or by any means, electronic, mechanical, photocopying, recording or otherwise, without the prior permission of the publishers, nor be otherwise circulated without the publisher's consent in any form of binding or cover other than that in which it is published and without a similar condition being imposed on the subsequent purchaser.

Printed and bound in Great Britain by MPG Biddles, King's Lynn, UK

British Library Cataloguing in Publication Data
A catalogue record for this book is available from the British Library

ISBN 9781903269183

Cover and text design by Anna Murphy
Front cover image: © Image Source/Getty Images
Illustrations p.178 and p.260 by Molly-Rose Murphy

Adele McNally
November 2011

For Jonathan

Acknowledgements

I would like to acknowledge the following people, without whom this book could not have been created. Thank you so much for the part you have played in *What About Me* coming into being.

The special tribe of children and young people that I have been privileged to walk alongside in school over the years. I continue to learn from you.

The young people who participated in the arts project, *Walk a mile in my shoes*. Your art work says it all. I hope I can represent you well in all I do.

Sam Taylor, Experience In Mind and Young Minds for their support and valuable contributions.

It has been fantastic to come alongside some exceptional key adults supporting some very vulnerable pupils over a number of years: Adam Haddington, Ann Gibbs, Beryl Elms, Carol Clark, Geddy Mc Naughton, Jane Hindle, Jenny Ansell, Julia Jefferson, Julie Hickey, Jody Mason, Kate Walmsley, Marieke Wilcox, Rowena Leaney, Sarah Cumming, Sarah Turner, Sue Rooke, Vanessa Hoskins, Yvonne English.

Gillian Luckock, Karen Devine, Sharon Donnelly and my social work colleagues at the Adoption & Permanency Team in Brighton & Hove. I have been very fortunate to work for a service and authority that advocates for and facilitates support for children and young people to be fully included within the school context.

Words cannot express my appreciation for my trusted clinical supervisor Penny Auton who is one of those unsung heros. I continue to have utmost respect for her in all she does and advocates for. I am so grateful to Dr Paul Holmes for introducing me to Penny. Her expertise, authority and humour have both developed my professional practice and grounded me over the last years, leaving me her gifts of courage and wisdom.

A special thanks to some extra special people: Kerry Twistleton of Moulsecoomb Primary School; Jane Mc Naught Davis of Cradle Hill Primary, Lesley Torn of Cardinal Newman School, Clare Langhorne, Vanessa Hickey and Carol Clarke of Downs Park School who continue to inspire and encourage me on by demonstrating in all they do that inclusion can be a reality and not just idealism.

For all the adopters that I have met in England, Wales, Scotland and Ireland who have shared their personal stories with me; stories of courage, perseverance and hope. Your words have shaped this book. I hope so much that I have said and done enough to make a difference in your child's life at school. For such a time as this ...

Thank you to Felicity Aldridge at CAMHS and to Dr Leslie Ironside who have both been so supportive of my work and have contributed significantly to my understanding of the pupils whom I support by sharing their expertise with me.

Judith Coad and Joanne Alper from Adoption Plus for honouring the necessity of this type of work out in schools and for all the creativity you bring in integrating different models of support in order to enable the children in your care to be all that they can be. It is a pleasure and a privilege to work alongside you.

A special thank you to Chris Walsh who has just retired from ACE in Brighton & Hove for believing in me and giving me so many opportunities, for trusting my passion and for trusting me with the responsibility for some very vulnerable pupils over the years.

Dr Kim Golding: I'm so glad of your invaluable contributions in this pioneering area of work. It has been a privilege to read your books, to consider your findings, to hear you speak and to work alongside you.

A special thank you to Alan Burnell from Family Futures for contributing his developmental trauma flowchart for us to use within this book, to deepen our understanding of the significant impact of relational trauma and loss. I would like to acknowledge my respect for Marion Allen for her involvement in raising the profile of these pupils within education too. Thanks for your ongoing support of my work.

Thank you to Sue Darby, Sarah Guy and the Children In Care team in Brighton & Hove for all of your support of this work and for all that you do citywide and beyond to honour this special tribe. I look forward to continuing working together with you.

I want to thank the following significant people who are engaging with very innovative work amongst this population and have contributed to some of the thinking in this book: Colin Newton – Inclusive Solutions: Jan Banks – Thrive: Glenda Barratt – Compass Childrens' Services: Phyllis Booth – Theraplay: Dan Hughes – DDP.

Ben Dew, Vicki Melville Reed and Sarah Relf for your invaluable administrative support and friendship along the way, in preparing this book and in the creation of Yellow Kite! You are all amazing.

For very close and trusted friends Ali, Jacks, Jules, Sarah and Lainey who have remained faithful, loyal and committed to all of who I am and all of what I am about and believe in. I couldn't have done this without you.

Martin Wood of Worth Publishing – who has beavered away behind the scenes to enable this book to be birthed into the world. I could not have asked for a more inspirational editor than Andrea Perry who has also become my dear friend. Andrea has an extraordinary gift of realising and releasing the potential of those around her.

And finally and most importantly to my best friend and partner Jon whose gentleness and strength have contributed to my becoming more of the person I was intended to be and to my understanding … may I never stop learning and becoming. Life is a journey, not a destination: thank you for being alongside me. The chorus in Alexi Murdoch's song *Wait* says it all!

Foreword

Schools are frequently judged in terms of results; value added learning and league tables. However, perhaps the true measure of a school is how it teaches its most vulnerable pupils. Children who have experienced developmental trauma are not well equipped for school and learning. Providing positive experiences of education for these children not only leads to learning and enhanced cognitive development but also to emotional growth, social growth and resilience. These children will grow into adulthood better prepared to face the challenges involved in finding career, romantic and parenting success. This will not only benefit these developing young people, but also the generations that will follow them. Meeting the needs of vulnerable pupils thus also makes a contribution to building stronger societies.

In *What About Me?*, Louise Bombèr writes about the importance of inclusion; helping developmentally traumatised children belong to and have success in their school. It is my opinion that this requires a re-focussing on child-centred education, throughout the school system. Too much focus on curriculum directs attention away from the individual child with his or her unique needs (Doddington & Hilton, 2007). As we explore the needs of developmentally traumatised children, the dangers of losing the focus on the child become apparent. *What About Me?* places children firmly at the centre, in our minds, in our hearts and in our schools.

Child-centred education, although not without its critics, has been a rhetoric that has permeated our education system since the time of Rousseau (see Darling,

1994). He proposed an education system founded on our understanding of children and the individual child: '... *education should be designed to reflect the nature of the child ... Child-centred education is not just a respecter of childhood, but a respecter of individual children and their differences'* (Darling, 1994, p.3).

If we are to meet the needs of developmentally traumatised children, we must go further still. It is not just the learning needs of the children that need to be central to their education, but also their social and emotional needs. Darling goes on to suggests that: *'The child-centred answer is that if the school is to be made to fit the child rather than the other way round, the curriculum should be determined by the child's needs and interests.'*

In the 21st century we are learning that this is not enough. In particular, recent advances in neuroscience are highlighting the essential role of relationships for the healthy development of the brain, the foundation for all development. Schools must take this message seriously. Szalavitz & Perry (2010) point out that modern education methods are leading to a decrease in opportunities for healthy relationship interaction; yet if the need for relationship and the emotional safety of the child are not a focus of the school, then many of the children will not reach the calm or alert state in the brain so necessary for learning. *What About Me?* provides practical advice for meeting the conditions necessary for learning and development so clearly articulated by Bruce Perry and other leading neuroscientists.

Schools will only truly fit the child when their holistic needs are met; including the need for safety, relationship, and support for emotional regulation. This provides the foundation for the development of the child's ability to explore, reflect and learn. When these needs are met children will have resilience, and the resources to benefit from the education that surrounds so much of their childhood. Understanding the needs of the child in school means understanding what the child needs socially and emotionally, as well as cognitively.

When we do not take this lesson to heart we are not just failing to teach the child, we are also developing children who feel ineffective and no good in the world; children who make sense of the failures of the adults by attributing it to deficiencies in themselves. Two examples will illustrate my point.

Rebecca, a young adult, reflects with me on her early school experiences. She remembers an episode in Primary School. The teacher asked her if she would like to read the prayer that morning. She answered with a polite *"No thank you"*, and found herself in trouble. The problem was, she tells me, that she didn't understand about rhetorical questions.

Gary, a young boy struggling in high school, tells me that he is the naughty one in the class. Frequently in trouble, he now answers for any of the misdemeanours that the teacher questions the class about. He knows it must be him, even if he can't remember doing it.

Both of these young people, in their different ways, are attributing difficulties to their own failings. To avoid taking this view of themselves through life they urgently need adults who can understand their individual needs, and can provide appropriate support to meet them.

In *What About Me?* Louise builds on her previous book *Inside I'm Hurting*. She provides a wealth of practical advice and support for teachers, and education staff; essential wisdom for those who truly want to understand and meet the needs of children who have been traumatised by their early experience. As Louise emphasises, supportive practice and the importance of relationship underpin the successful education of all children, but most especially the children socially and emotionally disadvantaged by their early parenting experience. Truly, as she eloquently points out, social and emotional needs are as important as academic needs. When we understand challenging behaviour as a communication instead of a nuisance, we can build strong relationships with the children; relationships that offer the opportunity for healthy dependency, the *'stepping stone to healthy interdependence' (p.86)*.

Readers of this book will find a treasure trove of practical strategies alongside sensitive understanding of the needs of developmentally traumatised children in school. I wish such wisdom had been available for the Rebeccas and Garys that I have met over the years. I am glad it will be available for them in the future.

Dr Kim S. Golding

June 2011

REFERENCES

Darling, J. (1994) *Child-Centred Education and its Critics* Paul Chapman Publishing Ltd: London

Doddington, C. & Hilton, M. (2007) *Child-Centred Education: Reviving the creative tradition* Sage Publications: London

Szalavitz, M. & Perry, B. D. (2010) *Born for Love* HarperCollins Books: New York

NOTES ABOUT THE BOOK

1 To protect the confidentiality of individual children, carers or professionals, names and autobiographical details have been altered in every case quoted. Any case examples written are composite and drawn from a number of similar examples known to the Author from her experiences over many years of working with children and adolescents.

2 To simplify the text, the male gender is used on occasion to represent the child who has experienced trauma and loss, and the female gender to represent educational staff. No prejudice implied by this.

3 To simplify the text, the terms 'child' and 'pupil' have been used on occasion to represent both children and young people. The strategies described are relevant to both primary and secondary phases, unless stated otherwise.

4 To simplify the text, the term 'parent' is used on occasion to represent those now providing the primary care for children with attachment difficulties. This term will therefore include birth parents, adoptive parents, foster carers, family and friends.

Contents

Introduction   **1**

The effects of developmental trauma   **17**

1   Here I am – Meet and greet   **31**

2   On the lookout – Safety   **43**

3   Settling to learn – Taking on the curriculum   **61**

4   Who's in charge? – Practising dependency   **83**

5   What's next? – Moving from one activity to the next   **97**

6   The temperature's rising! – Stress   **109**

7   Out and about – Playtimes and break times   **135**

8   Where am I? – Out of the ordinary   **147**

9   I'm starving! – Lunchtime   **157**

10   Don't look at me like that! – Body matters, PE and beyond   **169**

(continues …)

Contents (continued)

11   It's all over! – Reparation   **183**

12   But I'm different ... Celebrating difference and diversity   **207**

13   Will I stay or will I go? – Moving on again   **223**

14   School's out! – The end of the day, weekends and holidays   **233**

15   But what about me? – Staff care   **245**

16   And us, the parents/carers? – Home/school partnership   **259**

17   Final words   **275**

Signposting   **279**

References   **283**

Index   **288**

Introduction

We need to create environments – in our schools, in our workplaces and in our public offices – where every person is inspired to grow creatively. We need to make sure that ALL people have the chance to do what they should be doing, to discover the element in themselves in their own way.

(Robinson 2009, p.xiii)

Sharing a vision

Since writing *Inside I'm Hurting* in 2007, I've had the privilege of meeting many education staff and adoptive, foster and birth parents at conferences all round the country. I've been asked to the events to speak on the impact relational traumas and losses have on pupils in the school context, and to share practical strategies which support these pupils to settle to learn. I've discovered that most education staff are still only just beginning to receive information regarding attachment theory and developmental trauma. In some regions, the principles are already integrated into practice, but in other areas, there is very limited knowledge even of the basics. I constantly meet a real thirst for information and ideas: a momentum of curiosity seems to be building pace, as well as the willingness to engage. At long last, mainstream school developmental checklists, and guidance for their use, in both the early settings and in the primary and secondary school contexts, are being developed by, for example, team members in the Integrated Service for Looked after and adopted children (ISL) in Worcestershire, UK, led by Kim Golding. There is growing recognition of the need for this understanding to be formalised into mainstream practice.

Use of these checklists seems to be the next step we need to take, building on everything we've learned from the effectiveness of nurture principles from the Nurture Group Network and the success of the Boxall Profile (1998) (used within Nurture Group practice within many schools). Many staff are starting to actively use attachment principles as a framework for making sense of the behaviours they observe; but we're still in the preliminary stages of ensuring that these principles are genuinely integrated into our school life, and seen as a core requisite for all education practice.

I believe this theoretical framework and the latest research and practice needs to be spread further afield; it is from this premise that I have written *What About Me?* Let's be radically pro-active. Let's ensure that *all* education staff know about these critical issues and findings. Let's include the pupils who respond so differently to what we usually expect. Our systems have been set up with the assumption that the pupils entering school would have received sufficient, good enough care for them to understand and make the most of education. But it's increasingly obvious that this assumption is simply not true. We are going to have to adapt our ways of being in and 'doing school', in order to reflect the reality of the communities in which we live. Each life is valuable. Every child matters. These are truths, not clichés.

When we have pupils who have experienced developmental trauma in our classes, teachers often feel disempowered, because these children and young people can seem practically impossible to reach and to teach. In the midst of so many other growing demands, every professional working in education needs access to practical and effective strategies that can be implemented easily. Many people are very aware that there's a problem, and recognise that these pupils are not yet in a place to learn, but what to do to actually help? Staff in schools simply don't have time to wade through dense theoretical literature in order to try and tease out what will work right here, right now.

On my visits around primary and secondary schools carrying out assessments and providing advice, I am often asked, *"What would 'attachment support' look like on a typical school day?"* This is the question I have set out to answer within the pages of this book. By exploring and explaining what helps to create an optimum environment in school, I've designed the book as a guide to support education staff to get alongside our pupils, at each point of the school day, so that they can settle to learn. This is where we need to start. I've aimed to complement and build on the thinking and strategies included within my previous book, *Inside I'm Hurting* (2007) and the chapter I contributed to *Teenagers and Attachment* (Perry (Ed.) 2009).

What About Me? will support you to further your inclusive practice in the area of attachment difficulties and developmental trauma. I will be assuming a basic understanding of attachment theory and principles, which are explored in detail in both *Attachment In The Classroom* (Geddes 2006) and *Inside I'm Hurting*. Together we will examine the different areas that need to be reflected on in order to maximise the possibility of all our pupils settling to learn.

I am hoping that the ideas in this book will start to be integrated into the inclusion policy of many schools. We need a shared ethos and vision, and we need to take up corporate responsibility. All of us, every member of staff, in whatever role in school, should know what to do and why we are doing what we are doing. Key adults play a significant part in this work, in terms of their relationship with a particular vulnerable pupil; but every member of staff needs to be on board to enable genuine attachment support to be fully given.

Before we begin our journey together though, I want to set the scene by examining the specific difficulties our pupils face, and to look at some new perspectives that will help us really get to grips with how they might experience school and the 'mismatch' going on. Then I'll explore some issues to do with the financial climate we're in. Despite the current difficulties, I believe we can't afford to compromise the significance of having key adults involved with this group of pupils; I think to do so would be unethical and irresponsible. We can't escape the reality that *relationships matter*, nor would I wish to: so we still need to find ways of facilitating strong, healthy relationships within our school systems. I will outline some fundamental principles which can encourage us all to be part of the solution; and finally, I will invite us all to be history makers! School doesn't have to remain the same. Let's all be part of shaping a new way of doing school. The time is nigh!

The specific difficulties our pupils face

As we consider together the nature of the work to be done in our schools with pupils who have experienced relational trauma and loss, I'd first like to map out the problematic aspects of the current situation by thinking about: who these pupils are: the mismatch between their needs and what our schools currently offer: their adaptive responses: the need for 'translation': and our starting point for interventions.

Who are they?

For the last ten years a growing number of us have been concerned about a group of pupils out in our schools. These are the ones who are at risk of being misinterpreted, misunderstood and, at worst, excluded from the very places that could offer them opportunities to learn that life can be very different from their early experiences: what Winnicott described as 'second chance learning' (1964) .

These children and young people are currently identified in a number of different ways in our schools: we give them labels such as 'pupils at risk': 'vulnerable': 'in need': 'looked after and adopted': yet really, they belong to the very same tribe. They all have something fundamental in common. They have all experienced multiple relational traumas and losses, or what is now being referred to as 'developmental trauma' (Van der Kolk 2009) (this description is currently being reviewed in the States as a possible new category for Psychiatric Diagnosis classification in the DSM V, and

I will use this term throughout this book). Developmental trauma can come about as a result of having experienced or witnessed, amongst other things, physical abuse, severe neglect, sexual abuse, domestic violence, multiple placement moves, emotional abuse, deprivation ... all within the child's close, early relationships with parents and carers in their homes. This list is harrowing, but not exhaustive.

We must never underestimate the level and intensity of emotional pain and grief these particular pupils carry with them. The brain is a historical organ, storing up all that's gone before in both a sensory and cognitive format. We will never know the entire detail of what was experienced by any individual pupil. We are a sum of what we have experienced – no matter what our age. The pupil's body itself has stored the evidence of what he has lived through, in its entirety. The impact of developmental trauma is significant; in fact, the earlier the trauma and loss, the more extensive the consequences usually are. This is contrary to what most understand within the education setting (the common belief being that if a child is taken out of an abusive setting early enough, then there will be hardly any impact) so this misunderstanding needs to be challenged for the benefit of many pupils out there.

So, for example, many staff seem puzzled by the adopted child who was removed in their first six months, adopted at three, and is now twelve and struggling in their secondary context. They may believe that now the child is adopted, he should be fine. They may even question the parents' concern, wondering what all the fuss is about, maybe even considering them to just be an over-anxious family.

We need to be aware that what the child's brain should have learned in the first days, weeks, and months, when it was growing at its optimum rate, will now take much longer, as the brain has already slowed down considerably. The timing of developmental trauma is also significant, as different systems (hormonal, behavioural, emotional, perceptual, relational and so on) are being laid down like building blocks in the brain, at different stages of life. Please watch 'The Wall' produced by Adoption UK on their website *(see Signposting p.282)*. It's a wonderfully clear, if distressing, illustration of how this happens, and the consequences when this process doesn't happen at the appropriate time. The impact of developmental trauma will be mapped out in the next short section. You'll see that it's not just a case of a pupil merely 'having a sad story'. The consequences are substantial.

The good news is that there are brain growth spurts and the possibility of healing. However, there are no fast tracks. The journey towards adaptation and recovery is long. There is plasticity in the brain, meaning that it has the ability to adapt in response to new experiences. In the right environment, there is therefore capacity for much change (Gopnik et al, 2009; Greenfield, 2001). Each and every relationship has the power to confirm or challenge everything that has gone on before. But the benefits inherent in healthy relating take time.

The mismatch

I believe that our best starting point is from understanding that some of our pupils haven't yet experienced what so many of us take for granted – safety, security and stability. These conditions are fundamental to our well-being and our ability to grow as human beings. These particular pupils are interpreting things very differently to the majority, and we must never overlook or dismiss this. It's not a matter of *"Just get over it"* as some cynics might comment when they overhear discussions regarding vulnerability. This isn't mere sentimentality, but based on hard-hitting research. These pupils' understanding of themselves, others and the world is communicated through many of the behaviours that are presented within the school context and beyond. It's easy for us to notice their hyper-vigilance and other maladaptive responses.

The majority of pupils entering the school gates have experienced what Winnicott described as good enough care and so have relatively secure attachment styles. Schools are also operating as relatively secure systems, so there is organised safety, predictability, routine and trustworthy staff. Securely attached pupils have a particular way of viewing themselves, others and the context that they are in; they generally assume safety, and can relax in confidence. However, the pupils we are focussing on in *What About Me?* have a totally different 'internal working model' *(p.27)*: they do not assume safety, and they cannot relax but must stay constantly hyper-alert to threat. I will be exploring this in more detail in the next chapter. So there are bound to be conflicts, because we're so used to using the 'lens' of secure attachment in school whereas these pupils are viewing the world through a 'lens' of insecure attachment. There is a very definite mismatch going on.

Adaptive response

Many of the ways in which these pupils now interact with us, their peers and the learning context are adaptive responses learned in order to cope with very challenging and often dangerous situations outside school. Let's never lose sight of the fact that although they are unhelpful now within the school context, these adaptive responses serve or have served our pupils extremely well, in terms of survival. The brain organises itself in such a way to prepare for the long haul of a life full of stress, if this is what has been experienced before. If the brain hadn't responded in this way, many of our pupils might not even be alive or functioning in any kind of capacity today. A young child is dependent on the responses of the adults. He doesn't have the developmental capacity to do anything else.

In the classroom or school context these adaptive responses can significantly interfere with our pupils' ability to settle and learn. They are at risk of missing out yet again, but this time due to their own defences rather than because of the lack of nurturing experiences possible and available. Though it's often masked and we may have to be very sensitive to pick it up, there can be an undercurrent of fear and panic behind many of their behaviours – whether their insecure attachment style is avoidant, ambivalent or disorganised. These children and young people are not yet in a place to receive what is being offered, if they are merely left unsupported.

The need for translation

But rather than being afraid of the conflicts that will inevitably arise because of this mismatch, we need to view them as possible catalysts for growth and new learning. A key element of our work needs to be that of *translation*. We are in a prime position to introduce our pupils to the world of secure attachment by providing the stepping stones they will need to interpret facial expressions, gestures, tones of voice, posture and activity more accurately … I think of this as translation.

A minority of these pupils may just about navigate their way through the complexities of a secure school system without us even knowing their background and the extraordinary experiences that they carry deep inside; but they are the exceptions. I would argue that the majority of those who have experienced developmental trauma will need us to get actively involved and to advocate for them within a system that is really alien to everything they have experienced and learned. We need to provide support so that these pupils can really access everything that is on offer to them.

Our starting point for interventions

Why might these pupils be at risk within our schools? Because at present, we still don't understand clearly enough what is really going on behind the behaviours that we encounter. We interpret what we see through an incorrect lens. Then we intervene with an approach that can often result in us being punitive, however good our intentions were – in an attempt to pull these pupils into line. We continue to use the traditional behaviourist approaches still regularly practised in schools, and yet they don't seem to make much difference with these specific pupils. If they do make a difference, it seems to be short-lived. However well they work with children who've had 'good enough' care experiences at home, these interventions can prove inappropriate or inadequate with the pupils we're focussing on. Sometimes they can even exacerbate existing stressful interactions, meaning that the risk of exclusion of these particular pupils actually increases.

> Trying to teach or discipline them with conventional educational methods is not different to attempting to communicate to them in a language they don't understand or relate to. (Glasser 2007, p.227)

Glasser goes on to state that inclusion can work, but not without leaps within school philosophy. We need our classrooms to be willing to be therapeutic as well as academic if we are really going to be able to help our pupils who have experienced developmental trauma settle to learn. Glasser boldly states that these are the prerequisites for change. It may not be what we thought we'd be doing when we trained to be teachers, but this joined-up approach is what is needed in order to move these pupils on into higher level functioning. And surely, that's the core aim of our work. Glasser challenges us to consider,

> Why not do a great job instead of one that is less than successful? There is almost nothing that cannot be accomplished in six or seven hours a day.
>
> (p.234)

For many years we have seriously misinterpreted what is actually going on in our classrooms, and set off with interventions that came from an inaccurate starting point. This isn't because as education staff, we intentionally set out to cause difficulty! Far from it; education staff don't train to work with children and young people unless they actually like their pupils and want to support them. The vast majority of our profession haven't had any core training in the area of trauma and loss. But now this information is available. More and more people are having that training and are increasing their awareness of the effects of trauma on a child's global development. We are responsible with what we know. Access to the latest research and knowledge base is crucial for all of us at this time, and creating new ways of working a natural consequence.

We can't merely observe these pupils from a distance, feeling sorry for them or overindulging them in an attempt to alleviate the unbearable pain that we can experience in response to what they have lived through. These pupils need compassion – not pity. Compassion reaches out to touch, and must offer the possibility of something different, something new. As I have mentioned, *every* relationship has the powerful potential of either confirming or challenging everything that has gone on before. So we need to prioritise the vehicle of 'relationship' within school.

> We are shaped by other people as well as by what we breathe and eat. Both our physiological systems and our mental systems are developed in relationship with other people.   (Gerhardt 2004, p.10)

> Different relationships and changes in life circumstances can promote cognitive re-evaluation.   (Taylor 2010, p.38)

The current financial climate

If there has ever been a time when inclusive practice should be maximised, it's now. Having to deal with financial cuts means that schools have to be prepared to include increased numbers of vulnerable pupils. Residential units and specialist support services are no longer viable options for many authorities. But it's my belief that what we really can't afford is to continue with antiquated ways of 'doing school' or merely focussing on the academic curriculum. So what makes an inclusive school?

The emotional literacy and availability of the staff team is key. This sets the tone for the work. Staff need to tune in to and have empathy for the pupils in their care by acknowledging their vulnerabilities and differentiating for their nurture needs, before worrying about the academic curriculum. We can have the best procedures and policies in place and plan to the nth degree but if we lose a sense of their humanity – we might as well give up.

(Chris Walsh (2010) – former Vice Principal of ACE & Head of the EBDS primary school, Brighton & Hove)

More and more staff are recognising that imposing further consequences and sanctions is not the way forward. If we do continue to behave in this way within our schools, then we're going to see increased numbers of pupils disengaged, outside education, on the fringes of society with little other option but to find themselves involved in addictive behaviours to try and soothe away their pain. This route can all too easily lead to a life of crime or serious mental illness.

This would obviously present an even greater cost to our communities – and not just financially. It would be crazy not to consider the cost of employing one key adult – a teaching assistant or mentor – as an alternative to the unbelievably high costs involved in supporting pupils estranged from mainstream life through both school and home placement breakdowns.

As a matter of urgency, we need to have these pupils on our radar at every level of influence. Education must catch up with social services and health, who are leading the way in integrating what research has clearly shown to be the impact of developmental trauma on the brain into their everyday practices.

Some staff express concern about funding implications, especially for key adults. I need to clarify that there are only some pupils for whom 1:1 full time support will be necessary, and this is usually when there are considerable health and safety concerns. The majority will need bursts of regular, intermittent support throughout the school day and week. This is what I call 'flexi-support'. There is no reason why current, delegated funding for pupils with additional needs can't be managed differently. We have become accustomed to allocating support in half/whole hour blocks, when actually, these pupils respond best to flexi-support and integrated ways of working, coupled with being actively 'kept in mind'. A regular and active presence communicates this. There are so many other options for support provision mapping than the way in which it is frequently practised at the moment. Let's have a go at doing things differently.

> Schools, local education authorities and others should actively seek to remove barriers to learning and participation.
> (Inclusive Schooling: Children with Special Educational Needs (2001))

If we are truly going to embrace inclusion in its fullest sense, we are going to have to start re-focussing our attention onto the *quality and duration of key relationships*. I believe we have been distracted by putting too much emphasis on tools rather than the people (that is, the key adults) using the tools. Now is the time to identify the best possible matches between support staff and pupils: to be explicit about our commitment to these relationships: and to ensure that key adults are provided with adequate support, so that they can endure the long haul.

> Inclusion is about the quality of children's experience; how they are helped to learn fully in the life of the school.
> (Removing Barriers to Achievement (2004))

The significance of the key adult

The role of the key adult (the teaching assistant or mentor's role) also needs to be taken more seriously than it is at present. My sense is that historically, their role has been regarded as inferior to other roles within the school environment. Because of the difficulties of many pupils in our schools, the role has changed dramatically in the last ten years or so, as these staff members have responded intuitively to a fundamental need – that of providing consistent, good enough care in the form of a close relationship for the pupils in their classes. Yet the systems in place around their contracts are antiquated. We are losing many excellent staff because of their current employment conditions. Let's challenge ourselves to change our attitudes about this work, and really reflect their value in our structures. We'll need to re-evaluate terms, conditions and status in view of the level of expertise these staff are now contributing. Let's really value the professionalism that they employ, in relating to and supporting some truly vulnerable pupils within our schools, in the effort to keep them included. Without key adults, this work of settling pupils who have experienced relational traumas and losses to learn is impossible. Perhaps we need to introduce a whole new career structure for this role in order for it to be properly embedded into school life? Any policy changers reading this, please do consider such an option, for the benefit of education!

We need to be mindful of the risk of key adults themselves becoming marginalised in this kind of work. It's crucial that key adults are not left alone with the sole responsibility for their key pupil, but that school management and leaders ensure corporate responsibility through their different roles. Sometimes other teaching staff don't understand the type of work that's underway. Unfortunately I have known some very skilled key adult workers who have ended up feeling criticised, rather than supported at times of difficulty. If the rest of the staff are not genuinely on board in terms of their understanding regarding inclusion, *then isolation of the key adults is a real risk*. Let's not let this happen. Let's make sure that we work as well as we can together, letting go of blame and stopping ourselves from being judgemental, especially of those who are most closely involved with these pupils.

Being part of the solution!

Thankfully, school really can provide an alternative. School offers the opportunity of an alternative way of being, relating and doing. Since the pupils are not usually in a place to work this out on their own, we adults need to become actively involved to notice differences out loud and to make connections for them. Explicit messages of safety, security and stability are essential – they are not additional extras. In fact, unless the *attachment system* is genuinely attended to, then the *exploratory system* won't kick in to its full potential. The exploratory system is needed in order to take the risks required in the process of learning *(and see p.44)*.

> Humans are evidence-seeking creatures. We understand social relationships by processing the information we receive in our social exchanges and environment: evidence that things are one way and another.   (Taylor 2010, p. 41)

You will notice that most of the strategies I suggest in the following chapters are basically bringing into the foreground that which is usually left unsaid. The most important lesson that I have learned within this work is the need to be explicit. It is what I'd call one of the golden keys to really making an impact in the life of a pupil presenting with attachment difficulties and developmental trauma.

School needs to act as a surrogate secure base in order to contain our pupils' anxieties; to facilitate compensatory relationships and experiences. This will contribute to building resilience.

> Recovery means that the child is able to live a fulfilling life regardless of the problems and difficulties faced, that they come to experience 'earned security' by acquiring a coherent account of their attachment experiences and are more able to integrate their thinking with their feelings. Recovery happens in relationships.   (Taylor 2010, p.100)

It is not appropriate to move these pupils about in the name of 'fresh starts' or merely because staff are becoming tired. Increasing the number of significant transitions for these pupils can cause further difficulty, and so moves need to be kept to an absolute minimum. Let's protect these pupils from further transitions as a matter of priority. Consistency is essential. Let's work towards increasing stability. This isn't to imply that this work will be easy. It is definitely not for the faint-hearted. A robust and secure sense of self is necessary – as well as regular staff support.

I need to emphasise that all the strategies described in this book are intended to be used within the context of a relationship between a pupil and their key adult. These pupils have been wounded within relationships, and so it makes sense that a positive experience of 'relationship' is necessary in order to facilitate the process of adaptation and recovery. Relationships take time. There are no short cuts. From my experience out in both primary and secondary schools, at least two to three years commitment is necessary from senior management within schools, in order to see consistent change. Time invested into providing a true, genuine relationship with a pupil such as this will reap major long term benefits. Over time, they will learn significant relational capacities through the powerful experiences they share together. We only have to think about everything that happens in the development of a young toddler in relation to their parent or carer giving 'good enough, consistent care', to understand the power of relationship.

Within this book, you'll find examples of strategies that can be run in parallel to both Nurture Group and Theraplay principles and strategies. I strongly recommend making contact with these two specialist, professional organisations *(see Signposting, p.280)* as their approaches and theoretical bases are invaluable for pupils who have experienced relational traumas and losses.

There will be times when it will be important that we invite outside agencies in to provide specialist advice for the pupils with whom we work. However, I believe that there is so much more we could be doing before the specialists need to come in (I'm sure I've made some already over-stretched services very happy by saying so!).

Some very basic measures can easily be implemented now. I would even go as far as to boldly say that if we use some of the tried-and-tested strategies outlined in this book, we may not even need to make a referral on at all. I strongly believe that many pupils presenting with attachment difficulties can be well supported in our schools, with some basic structures in place.

Obviously there will be exceptions to this, and in those cases, more specialist advice must be sought. Please note that this book is not intended as a diagnostic tool but as a means to increase understanding so that we can support all our pupils appropriately.

Making history

If you are truly committed to inclusion, I'd like to invite you to join me on a journey through a pupil's day at school. There are many attachment-friendly opportunities out there and I'll be exploring some of these from first thing in the morning, to the end of the school day and beyond. Not only will we be considering the pupil in all this, but staff care will be an important chapter, towards the end of the book but just as significant. Let these ideas inspire you on to be creative and come up with some more. Once you know the presenting difficulty and what we are aiming to communicate, you will be freed up to develop your own individual plans and strategies. You know the pupil you have in mind and the culture of your specific school.

My hope is that over time, individual development plans will be created that take into account the impact of developmental trauma, so that targets and support provisions are appropriate and actually do support the pupil to settle into their learning, rather than exacerbating existing difficulties.

> What is required is not more of the same. If we are to reach the unreached and include the excluded, more must mean different.
>
> (Sir Christopher Ball, in Claxton 2008, p.24)

The effects of developmental trauma

Before we get started on our journey through the school day, exploring possible inclusive principles and strategies, I believe it's important that we take a short detour. Our detour will enable us to reflect on the impact of relational trauma and loss upon specific areas of development, described now collectively as 'developmental trauma'.

First, we'll take a look at a flowchart that provides an overview of the possible areas that are likely to be affected. Then I'll describe what we might observe in our pupils' ways of being in school in regard to the difficulties they may be experiencing in their executive functioning, affect regulation and psychological development. Finally, I'll reflect on the wide range of specific problem areas that have repeatedly shown up for these pupils in the school context. Grasping the gravity of all of this will, I think, not only aid our understanding and empathy for the pupils who we support in our classrooms, but will also mean that we won't be able to view additional support as a luxury any more, or as simply an excuse for bad behaviour, but as the *necessity* which it actually is.

The flowchart on the following page has been reproduced with the kind permission of Alan Burnell of Family Futures Adoption and Adoption Support Agency. It very clearly presents the areas of a child's functioning that are likely to have been affected by developmental trauma. To read the Trauma Tree, start at the bottom of the page. As you progress up the tree, it becomes clear that the impact and effects of trauma on brain development and physical development are intertwined.

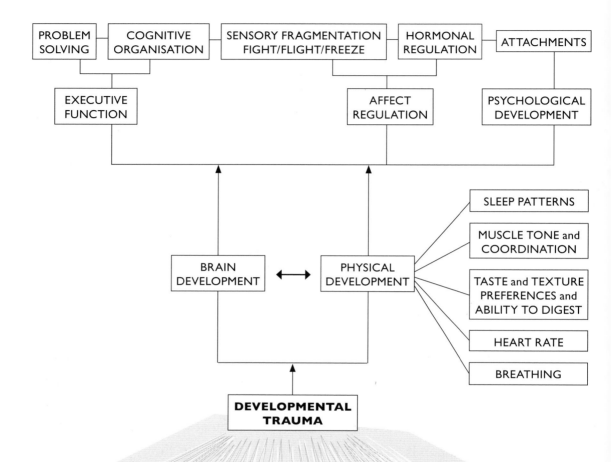

| PROBLEM SOLVING | COGNITIVE ORGANISATION | | SENSORY FRAGMENTATION FIGHT/FLIGHT/FREEZE | | HORMONAL REGULATION | ATTACHMENTS |

EXECUTIVE FUNCTION

AFFECT REGULATION

PSYCHOLOGICAL DEVELOPMENT

BRAIN DEVELOPMENT ↔ PHYSICAL DEVELOPMENT

SLEEP PATTERNS

MUSCLE TONE and COORDINATION

TASTE and TEXTURE PREFERENCES and ABILITY TO DIGEST

HEART RATE

BREATHING

DEVELOPMENTAL TRAUMA

The Trauma Tree's 'roots' are in the
prolonged neglect, deprivation, loss, abuse, violence, upheaval
or any combination of these that the child has experienced in his or her early
childhood, fundamentally affecting the development of brain, body and the
relationship between them.

TRAUMA TREE

© Family Futures 2011

As we go through an average school day in the life of a pupil who has experienced relational trauma and loss, looking at how to meet the challenges the day presents in an attachment-friendly way, it will be important for us to keep these difficulties in mind; so it's a useful chart to refer back to. We will also need to remember that while a certain level of stress can be helpful in making us feel and stay alert, the stress experienced by these particular pupils is way above the usual thresholds.   So their performance and learning is often severely compromised.

This section goes into more detail for each of the areas highlighted on the Trauma Tree to ensure that we are clear about possible difficulties. Please note that in all the following features, there are many examples I could have used! I've selected some common areas of difficulty that I frequently encounter on my visits to both primary and secondary schools. There are obviously examples included that could have other possible causes too, rather than or as well as the ones outlined. Nothing is clear cut when we are observing or relating to human beings. We are complex. The examples used are merely intended to give us clues as to what to look out for, to encourage and cultivate a curiosity about the pupils with whom we work, to start us off in our reflective practice. It's the overall pattern of difficulty and needs, plus our knowledge of the pupil's difficulties, that will give us the best understanding.

Executive functioning

This involves the pre-frontal cortex of the brain. Various researchers have described executive function as a set of cognitive abilities that control and regulate other abilities and behaviours. These can include:

- an ability to initiate, organise and stop actions
- an ability to monitor, evaluate and then change behaviour as appropriate
- an ability to plan future actions when faced with new or different contexts
- an ability to anticipate what might happen and to adapt
- an ability to form concepts and to think more abstractly

Some of the specific difficulties we might observe or notice in the classroom could be:

Initiating

Pupils having difficulty starting off a piece of work or a task unsupported or without prompts. *For example*, the pupil staring into the distance whilst the others have already written a paragraph. Or the pupil who doesn't seem to have any ideas of her own to start up new project work in class.

Using working memory/recall

Pupils having difficulty remembering what is known or was learnt recently. Difficulty in doing more than one thing at once.
For example, the pupil only able to remember the first or last instruction on a complex a list, or unable to listen and make notes at the same time.

Planning and organising

Pupils having difficulty bringing order to concepts or working out how to do a given task and carrying out plans. Difficulty problem-solving and prioritising.
These pupils often get distracted or confused in completing tasks, especially longer term projects, or get bogged down in unimportant detail.

→ *Organising ourselves*

Pupils having difficulty being in the right place at the right time.

For example, the pupil arriving late to his form group or his next lesson,
or the pupil missing a crucial deadline with her homework.

→ *Organising materials*

Pupils having difficulty organising what is necessary for particular contexts or
constantly losing things.

For example, the pupil turning up at PE without kit, or the pupil who comes
to Maths having lost her calculator for the third time this term.

Making transitions (shift)

Pupils having difficulty shifting attention or transitioning between one focus, task,
topic or place to another, or responding differently when the context/routine changes.

For example, the pupil may still be at his desk whilst the rest of the class are lining up
for assembly or the pupil may become very agitated when there is a change of plan,
she has to work with a new teacher, or when the class goes off-timetable.

Monitoring and evaluating

Pupils having difficulty being aware of their need to check back or check out the
impact of her effort, action, behaviour on herself and others.

For example, the pupil rushing through a piece of work and thinking it's complete
when it's not, or the pupil unaware of how his wild and agressive behaviour is
alienating other children.

Exercising emotional control and managing frustration

Pupils having difficulty in both expressing and regulating their emotions.

For example, the pupil may laugh uncontrollably or lash out at another pupil when
feeling frustrated.

For further information, please visit help4adhd.org/faq.cfm?fid=40&varLang=en
www4.parinc.com/Products/Product.aspx?ProductID=BRIEF

Inhibiting inappropriate behaviour

Pupils having difficulty in blocking out distractions or controlling their impulses. These pupils don't look before they leap!

For example, the pupil goes over to another group and interrupts them mid-task or the pupil asks the teacher a question loudly in the middle of silent reading.

Affect regulation

These are some of the difficulties I've regularly come across in schools with respect to affect regulation.

States, sensations and feelings

Pupils having difficulty knowing what is going on in their bodies, and therefore responding inappropriately or in an unhealthy way.

For example, the pupil running about in a t-shirt in the snow unaware that he is cold despite goosebumps, or the pupil not eating any lunch despite her tummy growling, clearly hungry.

Self-soothing

Pupils having difficulty knowing what to do when they have a need or feel uncomfortable, wobbly or dysregulated; often engaging in actions that make them feel worse rather than better.

For example, the pupil who feels like he doesn't belong, running offsite and engaging in risky behaviour or the pupil who starts hurting herself when she is upset.

Comfort levels

Pupils having difficulty knowing the boundaries of comfort. These pupils often walk a tight line between pain and comfort, inappropriate and appropriate touch.

For example, the pupil who pulls his trouser belt so tight it leaves a mark or the pupil who masturbates at her desk.

Over-sensitivity to sensory touch

Pupils having difficulty receiving accurate or appropriate signals from the different sensory receptors on their bodies.

For example, the pupil who feels like he is being strangled when the top button is done up on his shirt or the pupil who becomes hysterical when she gets paint on her hands.

Dissociative responses

Pupils having difficulty remaining in the 'here and now' – accepting who they are and experiencing and owning their personal feelings and responses. An avoidant strategy to manage a *sense* of being overwhelmed; yet this is quite often an over-reactive response to the 'here and now' context.

For example, the pupil who turns into a wild cat when he feels uncomfortable in the Literacy class, clawing at his peers, or the pupil who uses a different voice to her usual voice when she is feeling anxious.

Being able to settle

Pupils having difficulty sitting still for extended periods of time.

For example, the pupil fidgeting at his desk, up and about, out of his seat, rocking on his chair or wriggling around on the carpet.

Hypo/hyper responses

Pupils having difficulty responding in a modulated way – either remaining unmoved or responding in an over-reactive way.

For example, the pupil who sits and stares or falls asleep during the music lesson despite the class using instruments or the pupil who starts break-dancing in the middle of a quiet classroom of pupils working through a maths worksheet.

Psychological development/ Ability to form secure attachments

These are some of the areas pupils appear to have particular difficulty with:

Following the lead of the teachers/support staff

Pupils having difficulty trusting the motives and intentions of the adults.

For example, the pupil not following instructions to line up for the next class or the pupil running off after being asked to stay close by an adult during break.

Relationship difficulties

Pupils having difficulty knowing how to make and keep friends.

For example, the pupil running up to his peers poking them to try and connect, or the pupil jumping around being the class clown in order to gain others' approval but the others being irritated by this, keeping a distance: or the pupil being possessive over a friend, unaware of how to give her friend space or how to engage with her.

Emotional and social age

Pupils having difficulty responding in an age appropriate way due to not having negotiated or consolidated necessary developmental tasks yet.

For example, the pupil aged 11 happily playing with cars and trucks alone, or the pupil aged 14 rolling down the mud bank repeatedly at lunch time.

Control

Pupils having difficulty relinquishing control to another pupil or adult.

For example, the pupil who is adamant that she will sit where she wants to despite the seating plan, or the pupil who always has to have the last say when instructions are being given out.

Over-reaction to experiences/events

Pupils having difficulty engaging in an appropriate modulated response to everyday occurances or low level stressors.

For example, the pupil engaging in a full-blown rage in response to someone brushing past him in the corridor, or the pupil covering her ears whilst other pupils are communicating with their talk partners during a history lesson.

Heightened levels of anxiety

Pupils having difficulty being at ease in themselves and with others.

For example, the pupil who scans their classroom constantly or the pupil who is preoccupied by the visitor in class today, watching his every move whilst he carries out a classroom observation.

Toxic/pervasive shame

Pupils having difficulty processing usual forms of discipline without falling apart, due to a sense of feeling that they are fundamentally flawed or a mistake.

For example, the pupil who leaves the classroom swearing after his name is put on the board or the pupil who trashes the classroom after the teacher gives her a stern look. Over-reactive responses are commonplace.

Permanency

Pupils having difficulty realising that they can still be kept in mind or connected to, despite separation.

For example, the pupil who keeps talking to the teacher or shouting out in class – anything to be remembered, to stay connected.

Constancy

Pupils having difficulty realising that someone is capable of feeling different feelings at the same time or using different parts at the same time and yet remaining whole.

For example, the pupil who thinks the teacher must hate him now as she was upset by his behaviour, completely oblivious that she still likes *him*, just not his behaviour.

Panic/fear

Pupils having difficulty acknowledging or sharing any vulnerability or sign of helplessness, in particular to adults. Often bravado, but can also be more visible.

For example, the pupil who rages or behaves in such a way as to keep others at a distance and yet in other contexts communicates fragility; or the pupil who trembles and cries when the teacher addresses the class telling them they must all do much better in future.

Trust

Pupils having difficulty relinquishing any control to an adult – even in very ordinary circumstances, not trusting them to know what they are doing.

For example, the pupil who won't allow an adult to see the work he's doing or comment on it, or the pupil who jumps in to sort out a fight between two older and stronger pupils despite there being a senior manager nearby.

Mixed up motives and intentions

Pupils having difficulty reading others and their social interactions; often concluding that others are out to harm them in some way. Assuming the worst.

For example, the pupil who thinks that a boundary put in by the teacher communicates that the teacher must be out to harm him, or the pupil who catches someone glancing at her shouting, *"What are you looking at?!"*

Fear of abandonment

Pupils having difficulty experiencing relationship withdrawal as anything other than a form of punishment.

For example, the pupil who stands at the door of the Inclusion room knocking constantly after being asked not to enter for a moment, or the pupil who follows staff around the school building.

Feeling unsafe

Pupils having difficulty experiencing safety in the classroom or Inclusion room that is actually set up as a secure base for the pupil.

For example, the pupil hiding somewhere in the school or the pupil running out of a lesson and climbing up the nearest tree.

Once we start developing a comprehensive perspective of the way in which these different areas of difficulty inter-relate, we'll have a far more accurate starting point (then we've been previously using) in terms of making sense of how we see our pupils behaving day to day in our schools. From this viewpoint, we'll then have a much better idea of the most appropriate intervention to use with the pupil we are working with – whatever their chronological age. What is most important is their *starting point*.

Internal working model

We also need to be very aware of how these pupils view themselves and others. They view the world from the perspective of their early experiences (as we all do), so it's essential that we don't misinterpret their interactions with us by making assumptions about their perceptions and responses.

Geddes (2006) has written extensively about this area as to why the pupils in our care see themselves the way they do and why they do what they do. Her writings on this subject make essential reading and are a backbone to all the strategies we will be exploring later. Pearce (2009, p.36) supports others' findings by describing very clearly the pupil's view of themselves and others. A pupil with insecure attachment difficulties will have 'negative attachment representations' (as outlined below) which form, as Bowlby (1980) described it, an unconscious 'internal working model' based on the pupil's past experience of problematic relationship to himself and the world.

I AM	OTHERS ARE
Bad	Unreliable
Unlovable	Unresponsive
Unsafe	Uncaring
Undeserving	Unsafe
Impotent	Don't understand me

Most of our pupils coming to school will have relatively secure attachment representations or internal working models, because they have received 'good enough' care in their early years. They see themselves as good enough (lovable, safe, deserving and so on), and other people as trustworthy, responsive, caring (and so on). The pupils we are concerned with have not received good enough care. They view the world through the 'lens' of insecure attachment and so will interpret everything that goes on (or rather what they perceives goes on) through this lens. So it's very clear that the two 'lenses', or filters through which the two groups of pupils view the world are very different; hence the urgent need for translation work in our schools.

Opposite are some of the particular challenges these pupils have to face in our schools, challenges that we don't usually consider in any depth. We need to bear them in mind so that we can provide 'translation' throughout the school day, and repeatedly introduce them to the world of secure attachment.

Whilst lengthy enough, this list is not exhaustive, and reminds me again that we really mustn't simply leave these pupils to their own devices to sink or swim, only reacting when problems (inevitably) occur.

With everything that we know about our pupils' difficulties, caused by past relational trauma and loss – everything on this list really is a *big ask* for them. Let's never under-estimate the scale of the daily challenges they have to face. No wonder these pupils are not always completely focussed on our agenda in school! They need to know that they are not alone, and that there is at least one significant person in their school context who knows the score and who is genuinely interested in what is happening for them.

The 'Big Ask' – everyday challenges in school

- Separating from their primary carer/s
- Being in a restricted space with many others
- Sharing the attention of someone important to them (parent, teacher, mentor, best friend and so on)
- Understanding the motives and intentions of school staff
- Understanding the motives and intentions of their peers
- Trusting adults at school
- Following the lead of an adult
- Relinquishing control
- Knowing they can remain connected and kept in mind, despite separation
- Being expected to organise themselves

- Being able to relax into their environment
- Being able to settle to learn
- Having an integrated view of themselves
- Taking the risks necessary in learning
- Knowing how to repair relationships when things go wrong
- Having the confidence to go off and explore
- Engaging fully with their exploratory system
- Understanding 'who' they are in terms of their identity formation
- Coping with having missing pieces in their own personal story, for example, no baby pictures, big memory blocks and gaps …

- Moving between different spaces, staff, expectations and learning styles
- Moving from having one class teacher to having 12 to 15 members of staff involved with them at different times through the school week
- Negotiating adolescence
- Making and keeping friends
- Managing sensory overload
- Managing stress
- Managing peer pressure
- Managing uncertainty
- Managing self-consciousness/feeling different
- Being able to express what's going on internally (psychologically and physically)
- Being able to respond appropriately and in a healthy way to their needs
- Being able to ask for help
- Resolving conflict

So, holding our pupils, their internal working model and their need for relationship 'in mind', let's now begin our journey through a school day, reflecting on how we can be and what we can do, say and create, so that we can be fully supportive of every pupil who has experienced relational trauma and loss.

> Current policy directions that ignore the centrality of relationships are deeply damaging many students, causing them to physically, psychologically and emotionally withdraw from a meaningful educational experience at school ... the work of teaching is profoundly relational in nature.
>
> (Smyth 2007, p.222)

Let the inclusive revolution begin!

Chapter 1

Here I am!
Meet and greet

Having the capacity to care and to attune to individual children has now become the responsibility of care-giving settings beyond the family.

(Read 2010, p.5)

PRIMARY PHASE

Ben arrives in the playground where his key adult Jake meets him and walks him through to his classroom. Jake has been employed to begin his day from 8.30am.

SECONDARY PHASE

Lena arrives at the Inclusion Department where her key adult Ann meets her individually. Ann has already had an opportunity to settle herself into the day so that she can give Lena her full attention.

In terms of preparing pupils to settle to learn and make the most of all the opportunities on offer to them at school, the beginning of the school day is the most important part. In this chapter I'll be looking at the role of the primary classroom and the secondary school Inclusion Department. I'll be suggesting that having some mini-rituals (simple sequences of activity) to set the tone of the day can be of real benefit. These will include allowing the pupils to scan his or her environment, which I'll talk more about in Chapter 2. I will highlight the importance of routine, by outlining how we might communicate with our pupils on meeting them at the beginning of their day; looking at the importance of welcome, engagement, preparation, and being 'kept in mind'. Finally, I'll review the implications for Ben and Lena – our two case pupils who we will be following throughout this book.

WHAT WE NEED …

"Key adults to meet and greet and act as a link"

Headteacher, primary school

To have the greatest and most significant impact, we need to offer each pupil who has experienced relational trauma and loss an individual approach. What they need is boundaried time together with their key adult; we'll call this 'meet and greet' (by 'boundaried', I mean uninterrupted). For primary aged pupils, the meet and greet can take place in the classroom whilst the rest of the class are in the process of settling, or in a small room en route to the classroom. Not only does the key adult become very significant for primary pupils, but so does the actual space of the classroom. Over time this becomes the 'safe space' or 'secure base' – the place to return to. For secondary aged pupils, meet and greet can take place in the Inclusion Department ten/ fifteen minutes before they are due to go to their form room for registration. A room in the Inclusion Department can be set up to become their 'safe space' or 'secure base'. Over time, this space becomes very significant to secondary pupils as well, the place they can feel confident to return to.

A secure base, that is, a physical, protected, boundaried space retaining consistent focus and function, *and* a key adult, are essential for our pupils to be able to return to or 'check in' with in between experiences or tasks. This specific provision would usually be more familiar with a much younger child. However, it is also necessary for pupils who have experienced developmental trauma whatever their age, given that we know that their developmental age is frequently well behind their chronological age.

Of course it's especially helpful if the key adult is actively present from time to time in the designated base/area, attentive and attuned, ready to engage with their key pupil.

It is important to be aware that open-plan formats are not that helpful for these pupils. Let's recognise how that kind of arrangement might be experienced by someone who has little or no trust, is suspicious of others' intentions, doesn't believe confidentiality exists and needs to constantly check out where threat might be coming from. What we're trying to do is communicate safety, security and stability; so let's be sensitive to the need for spaces that convey those feelings.

Please also note that both the room and an adult are necessary 'vehicles' through which to communicate these very fundamental messages. Giving explicit messages of safety will be explored further in Chapter 2. Some secondary schools have one or two support staff 'on duty' in their Inclusion Department rooms so that a constant 'presence' is communicated. This is good practice, and is especially helpful for those specific pupils who need the experience of someone 'remaining' that they can check in with from time to time.

Because of their heightened hyper-vigilance, some pupils will need time to scan their environment before being able to settle. If you notice this, then do get alongside your key pupil and say something like, *"You're having a good look around. Let's check out the room together"* (and see Chapter 2). Commentaries like this communicate to the pupil that you have acknowledged him and what is important to him. It also gives him the

WHAT HELPS US ...
"School being fun and people who don't hurt you"

experience of someone being alongside and joining in with him. This is especially significant for those pupils who had to manage very stressful situations in their home contexts all alone, or may even have had to cope with something difficult that very morning, before coming into school. I will write further guidance on this below, whilst describing the key components and tasks of a 'meet and greet'.

TASK I ▶ WELCOME

The first task is the welcome. Prepare yourself emotionally to greet your pupil. Think strong! Being pleased to see the pupil is crucial. Be mindful of your proximity, eye contact, facial expressions, posture, tone and pace of voice. Once a relationship has been built up you may want to also use brief touch to connect with the pupil (on his arm or shoulder) if he is comfortable with this. Overemphasise your pleasure to see him, using all necessary means of communication! When I say overemphasise, I don't mean going over the top in a superficial way. I mean using positive and animated facial movements that are sincere. This will be powerful for many pupils, as they may well be more familiar with being surrounded by blank or hostile faces in other contexts and relationships. Smiles and healthy, appropriate touch are 'the most vital stimulus to the growth of the social, emotionally intelligent brain' as Gerhardt (2004) describes, drawing on recent brain research. Ferguson (2011) also writes about touch being a necessary but often missing element when relating to children and young people.

Concentrate on giving your key pupil your full attention, as there are likely to be other distractions around. The child or young person you are working with will notice if you don't seem 'present' and focussed on him. Yesterday may have been a difficult day, but today is a new day with so many new opportunities for growth and learning.

Some pupils may need to be directed to a breakfast club at this point. Many of our pupils won't have eaten before leaving home. Ensure that you check this out. Breakfast is best served and eaten within a small, quiet and calm setting, for example, within the Inclusion Department at a table especially set up for this purpose. It's especially helpful if key staff can join in with this too – not merely as observers, but actively participating in the meal. We need to be making the most of every opportunity to co-model (demonstrating explicitly by our actions what is appropriate and healthy) as this is such a powerful means of communication, especially for these pupils who learn far more by seeing, doing and sharing than by being told *(see Chapter 3).*

During the welcome it may be necessary to draw attention to the pupil's uniform, if this is part of the school's culture. Personally, I don't believe we should be too rigid in our approach concerning uniform, as this really isn't necessary and can often lead to pointless control battles. There will be more important issues to address. Our first and paramount priority is to honour the fact that the pupil is in school, despite the school environment often being so alien to what he is familiar with.

That being said however, I also believe that for this particular group of pupils, uniform can be a really helpful means of reinforcing the message that they *belong*. So many of these pupils feel on the periphery, as if they are already excluded, and so to hear the explicit messages, *"You belong here"* or *"We missed you"* can be especially powerful. Wondering aloud about their use of or lack of uniform is often a good way in to start helping these pupils to really have a sense of belonging and mattering within their school community. I know of an example of good practice within a secondary school whereby a spare set of uniform is kept in the Inclusion Department for one boy, not as a punishment but as a tool to communicate that this pupil belongs and that they want him to belong.

TASK 2 ▶ PRE-SCAN

It is generally more helpful to support a pupil to scan his environment with his eyes rather than doing so by moving about. However, at the beginning of the scanning process, you may need to be more active, especially in the early stages of building relationship and trust, but just be aware that too much moving about and checking may dysregulate the pupil, especially if it's done quickly. So if possible, locate a position in class or within the Inclusion Department which provides a full view of the room. Try and seat yourselves alongside each other, quite close, against a wall or in chairs with strong back support. This will enable the pupil to feel grounded. Engage in commentary as above. Over time, the amount of time necessary for this pre-scan will reduce. Eventually the pupil will no longer need to do this so actively. He will gradually start to internalise a sense of the room being safe, stable and secure as he becomes more familiar with the space and with you.

TASK 3 ENGAGEMENT

The next task involves making connections with the pupil. Invite him to let you know about last night and the journey to school. Show interest through active listening. Give eye contact and summarise back what he shares explicitly and implicitly. Aim to be accurate, but don't worry if you don't get it exactly right, as engaging in a clarification process is always helpful and reinforces the sense that you are genuinely interested. For example:

KEY ADULT

"Oh, so you went to the shop to try and get that skateboard you wanted but it didn't work out. Sounds as if you got really frustrated. Then you went back home, ate a huge pizza and watched a film before falling asleep at 10. You nearly didn't get up in time as you didn't hear your alarm! Luckily mum came in and woke you. You're feeling a bit grumpy this morning as you're still a bit tired but you know that once you get going you'll be OK".

You'll notice that this key adult added a hopeful comment at the end of her reflection. We can only earn the right to do this if we have spent a lot of time with the pupil and feel that we've started to get to know them. Most pupils will appreciate you having a go at reading their minds or stepping into their shoes to see things from their perspective. However, be mindful that some might find this approach intrusive, so still have a go but soften your approach by saying, *"I'm guessing/wondering ..."* and adding that *"I may not have it right, but I am really wanting to understand things from your point of view".*

TASK 4 ▶ TRANSITIONAL OBJECTS

Be curious about whatever your pupil has brought in from home to show you. Communicate interest. Objects from home have important value. They need to be placed carefully in a special box that has a lid, or in a personal tray. It's important to provide a boundary for things that are brought into school (as represented by the special box and its lid), or else the pupil will not learn about the need for containment. Without this essential boundary, some pupils have been known to bring in bags of gear which then dysregulates them further! In the primary phase this container is sometimes referred to as a 'treasure box'. In the secondary phase, it can be helpful if pupils have their own special tray within the Inclusion Department in which to carefully store special items.

Make a point of saying that you will take steps to ensure that items with special significance are honoured by being kept safe and remaining in the same place. It's important that these objects are not moved around or interfered with. From experience, I know pupils can become very upset if they return to find their items moved or damaged. Keeping objects safe and in a consistent place will communicate care and demonstrate memory and organisation, which we'll explore further in Chapter 3.

TASK 5 ▶ PREPARATION

The fifth task involves preparing the pupil for the day ahead. Most primary school teachers and some form tutors go through the day's timetable with the whole class but an individual approach is best with these specific pupils. Owen & Wilson (2006) observe that improved time perception can reduce anxiety and provide a feeling of control over life events. So anything that supports time perception is going to be fundamental within our work. Use an individualised, visual planner or a journal to look at the day ahead together. It can be helpful to have the pupil actively participate in some way, for example, moving subject cards into the correct position on their individual timetable. Use connector descriptors in your dialogue such as *'before'*, '*after*' and '*next*', to support the pupil you are working with. Being able to point to where a pupil is on their journey through a school day can help them begin to develop a concept of time.

We can encourage self-reflection by asking the pupil to 'scale' their interest in the numerous individual subjects ahead, and to scale the effort levels they anticipate. Take a note of any subject or relationship that might require additional input today. The dialogue that you have together is going to be quite informative – giving you clues as to how the pupil is doing and how he or she perceives the challenges and opportunities of the day to come. So it's important to listen really well so that you don't miss important clues as to what might be going on inside him!

> Not only must we be skilled at communicating with the child, but we must also
> be skilled and patient at unravelling their communication with us.
>
> (Taylor 2010, p.44)

Remember these pupils may well be interpreting what's going on and what's going to happen very differently to how we might read a situation. In particular, be mindful that motives and intentions are very easily misinterpreted. Mix this with a low sense of self-worth and you have a recipe for disaster. There could be many occasions where you may need to be a mediator; to be a human bridge to another member of staff, another pupil or lesson in order for your pupil to have a settled day. This sensitive attunement is a real investment in supporting the pupil to be in a position to settle into their learning.

Being kept in mind

At the end of the 'meet and greet', the key adult must remind the pupil that she will continue to keep him 'in mind', as they may separate at this point. Inform your pupil when you'll see him next. We often forget to tell pupils when we'll be back, and yet this is the most important information we can give at these times – during attachment focussed support work. To fully internalise the value of the relationship we are making with them, these pupils really need support at times of transition, between periods of togetherness and separateness. They really need to know that when they are out of our sight, they are not out of our minds; for example,

KEY ADULT

"I'll be wondering about how you are getting along in Literacy.
I look forward to hearing all about it when I see you in period 3".

Many of our pupils will need visual clues in addition to verbal statements to support them with this. It may be that a post-it note, a memory card or a note in their book or planner would be helpful. We explore this further in Chapter 4.

Self reflection

How do you prepare yourself for the day ahead when you enter your work place or prepare yourself to work?

Think through your own mini-rituals. Consider how important they are. How do you feel when you are not able to engage in these rituals at the beginning of the day – for whatever reason – and you have to rush into a meeting or activity instead?

Finally ...

FOR BEN

Welcome   *Jake is smiling and says "Hiya Ben" encouraging Ben to respond to their special handshake. "Good to see you. Are you up for some breakfast or have you had some already?" Ben shakes his head. Jake says "Well, we'll see what they have for us in breakfast club eh? I thought I could smell bacon this morning, but that might just be wishful thinking!" They have some toast and hot chocolate together, and then head to Ben's classroom.*

Pre-scan *Jake sits alongside Ben on the comfy chairs at the back of the classroom. He joins Ben in having a good look around, mentioning what he sees as he does so.*

Engagement *Jake asks Ben about last night. He knew he was going to play at his football club and so he asks how the game was. Ben gets out a new wild animal book his adoptive dad got him. Jake shows interest by looking at it, and asking Ben which of the animals he is most interested in. Jake then says that the book could be kept safe in Ben's special treasure box.*

Preparation *Jake directs Ben to his individual timetable. Together they check out the class board and match up the appropriate laminated cards on Ben's individual card. Jake asks what Ben has after Literacy, and what's before break. He then goes on to ask Ben what he thinks about his lessons ahead today. He asks* *what his favourite might be and the one where he might need more help.*

Being kept in mind *Jake says he is going to go now, but that he will see Ben later when the film starts up in Literacy. "I'll be thinking of you, wondering how you are getting on. Shall we swap our pens so that you remember you're in my mind?" Jake then leaves and Ben settles into the day with his class teacher.*

FOR LENA

Welcome and engagement *Ann looks up as Lena enters the Inclusion Department. "Lena, how are you doing? Good to see you." Lena slumps in a desk with her head down. "Oh, are you not too great today? What's up?" Lena then proceeds to tell Ann that she's really tired and can't work today. "What were you up to, to make you so tired this morning, eh?" Lena says that she had a late night as it was her foster mum's birthday and that they had put on a special do for her. "Ah I see. So you are really tired today. Have you had breakfast?" Lena nods.*

Preparation *Ann says its week A and Tuesday, and puts Lena's tray on the table. "OK so what have we got today then?" Lena yawns and rocks on her chair. "You're letting me know you are really, really tired because of the birthday party. You're going to have to take it easy then. It's good that all your morning classes are seated eh?! You've got Maths first and* *then what's after break?" Lena looks across at her timetable: "History". Ann reminds her of the artwork she was working on for her history project. Lena looks up as Ann flicks through her history book, showing interest in everything she has done to date.*

Being kept in mind *Ann says that it's time for tutor group now, but that she will see Lena in period 1 for Maths. "Work hard. I want to hear that you tried your best even though you're tired today". On her way out, Lena turns back to Ann and says "Me and Darren are going to meet up after school!" Ann nods and smiles and says "Tell me later in our individual session!"*

On the lookout
Safety

A sense of safety comes from consistent, attentive, nurturing and sensitive attention to each child's needs. Safety is created by predictability and predictability is created by consistent behaviours. (Perry, B. 2009)

PRIMARY PHASE

Ben wanders around his classroom checking everything there and asking his teacher about each change he notices: "Why is that there?" "What's that?"

SECONDARY PHASE

Lena wanders along the corridors looking into rooms as she goes. She notices that the Deputy Head isn't where he usually is and goes off around the school looking for him.

In this chapter I'll be looking at why it's important to be explicit with pupils who have experienced relational trauma and loss about the fact that they are safe in school. I'll look at why this is an issue, and how we can manage it to help our pupils settle to learn.

I'll first explore how important it is for us to recognise how significant 'scanning' is, as an indicator that a pupil doesn't feel safe (even though we know he is, in class), and how essential it is to allow this. I will consider the aspects of safety many of us find helpful in our own lives, as these provide helpful clues as to what our pupils need; that is, for us to over-compensate in order for them to feel safe. I will then have a go at identifying similar safety features within our school systems. I'll describe how to be explicit in our communication about safety, by, for example, noticing examples of safety out loud: by taking pupils on safety tours around their schools: by creating 'anchors' of safety: and through setting up safe spaces that pupils can use, in addition to their usual secure bases – the primary classroom or the secondary Inclusion Department. Finally, I'll look at the implications for Ben and Lena, our two case pupils who we're following throughout this book.

Scanning

Hyper-vigilance and hyper-sensitivity are common amongst pupils who have experienced relational traumas and losses. These pupils are often observed scanning their environments or checking things out, as I noted in the previous chapter. So we really need to pay attention to the issue of safety, which is just so important to them. If we don't, then our pupils are likely to remain stuck in this lonely mode, spending their days at school anxious and unable to engage in learning – to their full capacity.

Safety is a key component of secure attachment. The presence or absence of safety (perceived or real) will influence the pupil's ability to be in a position to settle to learn and to make optimum use of their 'exploratory system' – our internal hormonal, neural and behavioural responses and processes, responsible for any of us being able to take the many risks required in learning.

In schools we often make too many assumptions about pupils realising that they are safe in the building and with us. It's true that most pupils entering our school gates are from 'good enough' backgrounds, and to them, the possibility of danger is extraordinary. For most of us, safety is ordinary and expected. However, the opposite is true for the pupils we are especially concerned about in this book. Safety is simply not anticipated by those who have experienced relational trauma and loss. They are wired to expect 'danger', and are constantly on the alert because of this possibility. They have learned to engage in their own ways of checking out their environments. They have also learned to defend against vulnerability by creating distance from others in many different and often very subtle ways. It's important to recognise that many of these pupils will consider other people's motives and agendas as potentially harmful – regardless of how charming and genuinely helpful we might be!

Survival is often the primary agenda for why they do what they do. If we don't keep this in mind, we can often be knocked off-track in our interventions, ambushed when a pupil suddenly reverts to survival-type behaviours. When we check out background information on pupil files concerning their early experiences, it's really not hard to understand why many engage in survival responses. And let's be mindful of the fact that what we read is never the complete story. Even those pupils with substantial files will have internalised so much more than is recorded; the files give us a mere snapshot of what he or she has lived through. Our pupils' bodies hold the totality of their experiences in the form of unconscious and conscious memories stored in both sensory and cognitive formats, whatever the age the pupil was when they experienced the relational traumas and losses. Whether it was pre-birth, at birth, at two months, three years, seven years … it matters, and it has an impact.

THE IMPORTANCE OF SCANNING

We'll need to allow our pupils some time for scanning the environment during their meet and greet time, and, in addition, some extra time to scan the environment of each different context as they arrive in it. Trying to move them on too quickly without attuning to their need to do this is likely to be counterproductive. Over time, these children and young people will need to scan less and less, as they become familiar with the consistent environment of the school, as I discussed in Chapter 1. The more attuned and responsive we can be – giving commentaries – the more likely the pupil is to make progress in this. Giving words to what seems to be going on is very powerful – reducing the intensity of hyper-vigilance. So for example, when a pupil is getting to know a new room, we might say, *"You are checking to see where everything is in this room"*. And further down the line, when their need to scan seems to have reduced, we might say, *"It's great that you are getting stronger at trusting that you are safe here. I've noticed that you don't need to check out the rooms so much now."*

Self reflection

What do you have in place, unconsciously and consciously, to keep yourself safe or to help you know you are safe as you go about your day? What assumptions have you made?
What are they based on? Remember that these pupils don't necessarily have the same kind of in-built mechanisms.

Often at conferences I ask delegates to reflect on what's in place for them, internally and externally, to keep them safe. There is always a sense of nervousness when I initially start this activity off. Why? Because we assume safety. It feels quite odd to even draw attention to matters concerned with safety. Carrying out a 'safety tour' on ourselves feels very unfamiliar, as so much of what we do and why we do it is carried out on an unconscious level. However, I believe it's a good starting point so that, based on our reflections, we can truly understand what might be worth over-compensating in the school context for our pupils. I will summarise commonalities shared and then link them up to how these could be translated into school in order to over-compensate safety for these particular pupils.

SAFETY FEATURES	WHAT HELPS?	
SECURITY		
	Adult	Closing windows and locking the front door
	In school	Attention given to security measures around the school's entrance. Safety tours of school *(see p.54)*
PROVISIONS		
	Adult	Food in the cupboard, petrol in the car …
	In school	Attention given to how large numbers are catered for, how resources are distributed in class/school, making connections
BEING KEPT IN MIND		
	Adult	Family and friends knowing whereabouts
	In school	Key adult knowing timetable of key pupil and making that known. Regular check-ins with their key adult, use of a check-in card to his safe base or space
EXIT PLAN		
	Adult	Knowing emergency numbers: police, fire, ambulance, car breakdown service, bank
	In school	The pupil being given an exit strategy. What can they do if there is a problem or if they feel uncomfortable? Knowing where can they go, who they can find? Helping hand: names of trusted others

PREPARATION

Adult   Making plans in advance: diary, map, checking routes, obtaining information

In school   Going through the timetable in advance, preparing for any changes to the routine, accessing information to look through, making preliminary visits

STRUCTURE

Adult   Knowing social norms, rules, expectations, boundaries in different contexts, knowing start and finish times

In school   Going through clear expectations and boundaries for different contexts and different relationships.
Ensuring understanding on an individual basis.
The use of social stories, checklists and individual, visual timetables. The use of calenders and timers

SAFE BASE

Adult   Having a home to return to

In school   Predictable, consistent space – class, Inclusion room, safe space explicitly used for this purpose.
Check-ins allowed with significant others, especially the key adult – use of *check-in* cards.**
Anchors of safety
(visual images pupils keep in their bags *(see p.55)*)

**These pupils will often get themselves put 'on report', because they need someone to keep them in mind or remember them, and to have a sense of a safe base. Let's not engage with this in a negative sense, but introduce these pupils to a check-in card so we are consistently responding, actively and kindly, to their basic developmental need, not doing so indirectly and inconsistently via punishment.

FAMILIARITY

Adult	Being around family and friends on a regular basis
In school	Doing everything we can to keep pupils in close proximity to a small team of familiar staff. Not moving pupils around in the name of 'fresh starts'

PREDICTABILITY

Adult	Knowing that when X happens, Y will happen … experience promotes a sense of safety
In school	Consistency, routines, repetition, close partnership with other staff and home. Making connections. We know that neural connections are reinforced by repetition

The absence of the sense of safety means that we will need to introduce our key pupils to another way of interpreting their environment, their peers and the education staff, and this is going to take time. There is no fast track possible.

In addition, I'd like to further explore two issues that I recommend as most significant for the work of enabling pupils to feel safe: staff stability and structure.

Staff stability

Staff stability is crucial. Effective leadership that recognises and celebrates areas of strength and expertise in each member of staff, enabling each member to feel they are contributing to the overall effectiveness of the school, is a must. In our schools we need to go further than we do in connecting staff up, in being relational in our approaches, remembering that we are involved in the core business of working together with humans, not technology!

In order to enable such children to improve access to learning, one has to pay particular attention to processes of relationship. (Greenhalgh 1994, pp.13-14)

As far as we can, we need to ensure that staff remain in post in our schools. Relational permanence will impact our pupils significantly. Ensuring staff have access to good stable support for themselves usually helps with this *(see Chapter 15, Staff Care, p.245)*.

We need to limit the number of education staff with whom our pupils have regular contact and can become familiarised – in fact, the fewer the better. A small team, who work well together with a consistency of approach, is the most effective way to support our pupils to settle into school. Such a team communicates safety. Where this isn't possible, say, in a large secondary, then let's limit the number of staff who are closely involved with the key pupil so that any successes or difficulties are dealt with by the same tight team of staff, rather than any number of teachers becoming involved. So, for example, we could have one lead senior manager (Deputy Head/Head of Year/SENCO/INCO) closely involved as well as a key adult. In both primary and secondary provision, it's good practice for staff to go to and through key staff, rather than simply intervening themselves. It's perfectly acceptable for us to explain to the pupil or to others involved that a discussion needs to be had first with their key staff, and that the outcome will then be passed on. So often in school we feel that immediacy is the best option, but it is much wiser to wait for familiar key staff to be involved with those they are supporting. Existing work can be unintentionally but all too easily undermined by others jumping in without knowing the bigger picture.

Pupils who have experienced relational trauma and loss need us to put on a strong front, even if we don't feel that way inside. What we know as adults, or need to remind ourselves that we know, is how and when to get support. These are two of the core elements of resilience. These pupils need to experience us as the strong ones – able to withstand difficult situations without falling apart, and able to contain our states, sensations and feelings without being overwhelmed or falling apart. As Glasser (2007) puts it:

> Intense children have an absolute need of adults in their lives who demonstrate an ability to handle them. Ironically, when a child finally perceives that the teacher is in charge, the challenges come to a halt.   (p.233)

Structure

The most basic thing we can do to support these pupils to feel safe is to ensure that their day is as structured and routine as possible, so that they have a sense of what to expect. The introduction of routines and rituals are so supportive for our key pupils. Whenever possible keep these pupils on timetable – their usual timetable. In schools we do sometimes come off timetable at different points, and if this really is inevitable, let's engage in sensitive care. Just because there is a rehearsal morning, a trip or an extraordinary day planned, there is no reason why this can't be broken down and documented in a visual format, to allow for some preparation and knowledge about the day ahead – a timetable. The more information we can give these pupils, the better *(more about handling change in Chapter 8, and about coming off timetable, Chapter 14)*.

Creating a sense of pace and rhythm is very important for our pupils. Predictability is essential. As far as possible, ensure consistency of approach in –

✔ The use of spaces
✔ The response of staff
✔ The structure of lessons
✔ The expectations of structured times
✔ The expectations of unstructured times
✔ The expectations of formal times
✔ The expectations of informal times

Be very aware of changes and differences – subtle and overt. At times of transition or difference, map out verbally why and how something might or will be different. For example, explain the difference between informal and formal interactions, smart and casual clothes, structured and unstructured times. Having a predictable day will engender safety. Protecting and honouring routines are therefore imperative. Some pointers to keep in mind when starting a day together:

Does the pupil:

have access to a means of monitoring the passing of time?	→ A sand timer, watch, mobile, clock, stopwatch, calendar ...
know how the day is going to pan out?	→ Timetable, pre-warning of any changes
know the expectations during lessons and free time?	→ Checklist, social story
know what to do at the beginning of a lesson?	→ Checklist, role-play
know what to do when a task is completed?	→ Checklist, role-play
know what to do at the end of a lesson?	→ Checklist, role-play
know which parts of the day require formal/informal responses?	→ Colour coding, role-play, signal
know which parts of the day are structured and unstructured?	→ Colour coding, role-play, signal
have all the equipment/kit he needs for his day?	→ Checklist, peer mentoring, co-modelling
know what to do if he experiences difficulties?	→ Checklist, exit strategy, safe space, check-ins, bubble time, thinking chair, role-play, social story

Explicit communication

Once we've established the need for staff stability and structure in our pupil's time at school, the concept of safety needs to be introduced explicitly, and referred to regularly as some of the safety features outlined on page 51 describe. The best starting point is to assume that our pupils don't trust that they will be safe or attended to well by the education staff around the school. They will need us to make the relevant connections to the evidence for safety for them – we cannot expect that they can do this for themselves.

So, how can we actually communicate safety to our pupils? In a number of ways. I will describe the tools of *noticing out loud, taking pupils on safety tours* and *creating anchors of safety*. Finally, we will think about the possibility of creating additional protected spaces within the school environment, in order to practice safety – safe spaces.

WHAT HELPS US ...
"People being nice to you"

NOTICING OUT LOUD

There are concrete examples of safety being provided on a daily basis somewhere around us in our schools. Let's draw attention to these, as they will begin to form an evidence-base for our pupils. These children and young people are going to learn about safety though what they witness, experience themselves or hear being identified out loud. For example,

> **Key adult**
>
> *"Did you notice that, Ben? Did you see Ms Evans looking after Sîan when she had her nose bleed? We take safety very seriously in our school".*

Let's not assume that our pupils will necessarily notice an instance of protection or safety themselves. They need us to highlight it and point it out. We don't need to make a big deal of it, but we do need to keep repeating the same message.

SAFETY TOURS

I often encourage the use of safety tours, whereby the pupil moves around the school together with their key adult; they take a clipboard with them noting anything that is in place which is designed to provide and maintain safety for all pupils. Some of these features will be more obvious than others. Examples of what could be noticed and discussed are as follows:

Physical safety

→   Voice and CCTV entry to reception area

→   Visitors signing-in book

→   Identity badges

→   Fire extinguishers

→   First Aid box/room

→   Enough food in the dining room

→   Access to water

Physiological safety

→   Rules and expectations

→   Predictability of routines

Mental safety

→   Professional staff

→   Staff supervision of pupils

Social safety

→   Staff supervision of pupils

→   Senior managers with walkie talkies

→   Rules and expectations

→   Anti-bullying policy

→   Anti-racism policy

→   Anti-homophobia policy

Emotional safety

→   Individual care/planning

→   Information sharing on a need-to-know basis

→   School counselling

→   Mentoring

→   Safe space *(see p.57)*

ANCHORS OF SAFETY

Let's also support these pupils to create visual, concrete reminders of safety. There are many different ways we can do this. Encourage the pupil to create an image that represents safety to them. For example, one pupil might make an image using toys, another makes an image in a sand tray. Create images using mixed media. Take photos of these images and laminate them so they last. Encourage the pupil to carry their anchor of safety around in their school bag. Once an image is created, let's remind the pupil that whenever he feels wobbly or anxious he can check out his image. Let's encourage him to explore the created image with his different senses. I recommend that the pupil imagines placing himself in the centre of his image (in his imagination) and asking himself four or five questions as follows:

- *What would he see there?*
- *What would he hear there?*
- *What would he smell there?*
- *What would he taste there?*
- *What would he feel there?*

The key adult can guide this imaginary journey, especially in the initial stages of work. The adult and pupil can talk about the states, sensations and feelings created and imagined. These can then be referred back to as and when necessary at differing points of the school day when we might want to support them back to a place of calm and safety.

For example, let's imagine that Lena has chosen a waterfall picture as an anchor of safety:

What would Lena ...

see?
beautiful rushing water, bubbling, spray, fishes jumping, brown shiny pebbles, splashes, circular movement in the overflow, mist, clear water

smell?
freshness, greenery

feel?
restful, calm, happy, cold, wet, icy, joy, light tickle, powerful touch

hear?
roar, dripping, gushing, filling

taste?
cold, pure water

Safe spaces

It's sometimes necessary and helpful to set up one or two specific areas in school in addition to the classroom or Inclusion room. I suggest considering this if your pupil engages in running off, hiding or leaving the school site. as often they are communicating through their behaviour that they need a safe space.

I once worked supporting a pupil who used to suddenly run out of class within the secondary phase and climb up the nearest tree! When I first got involved, I witnessed different senior managers trying their best to coerce him down with different strategies, but to no avail!

> WHAT WE NEED…
> *"Safe spaces where pupils can relax"*
> Key adult – primary school

The breakthrough came when his key adult looked up at him in the tree and stated, *"Ah, I've got it now. You're letting me know that you need a safe space. I'm so sorry for not getting it. I get it now. When you're ready to come down we'll go and find a place that you can use when you feel wobbly".* The frequency of tree climbing during lessons decreased dramatically.

Why? I believe it was because of three reasons. Someone bothered to take the time to think what this pupil was trying to communicate by heading up the tree: behaviour is communication. Secondly, this key adult took the pupil's needs seriously, cultivating mutual respect. Finally the pupil's needs were attended to. In this case two spaces were identified, a corner in the school library and the parent/visitors room. When one was already in use, the other was used.

We often overlook just how over-stimulated our pupils can be within our busy classrooms. Many will need this additional time in a safe space to simply 'down load' or to process everything that's been happening. Many pupils have processing difficulties, often meaning that it takes them a lot longer than other pupils to make sense of what is going on. So if we don't make provisions of this kind, we can simply be leaving them in a dysregulated state, overloading their senses.

Dependent on the size of the school, available space and finances, all kinds of creative options are possible! These spaces can be named safe spaces/safe zones/ calm areas. They will be most effective if they can be set up as multi-sensory rooms/areas that a pupil can retreat into from time to time on a 1:1 basis together with their key adult *(some ideas for resources can be found in Signposting p.279)*.

When a safe space is set up in school, ensure that there are only two/three expectations on the door. List expectations in a positive sense, in other words what a pupil *needs to do*, rather than what he *must not do*.

For example,

SAFE SPACE EXPECTATIONS

Respect the objects in the room

Respect each other in the room

Leave the room as you find it

The safe space can be used in three ways, depending on the needs of the specific pupil. He can either have regular slots timetabled in there as part of his daily routine, be directed to use the space as and when the key adult feels this is appropriate, or determine himself when he needs to go there. The latter example is useful if you are beginning work with a pupil who tends to be a runner or a hider! It's far better to encourage him to meet you within a designated area if things get too much rather than having to search for him all over the school. We all know that it really isn't appropriate to chase or attempt to corner pupils wherever they're lurking or concealing themselves. Let's pre-empt this possibility by ensuring we actually have a designated area/room or zone for this purpose to facilitate co- and self-regulation. The effectiveness of this strategy is summed up beautifully by this key adult:

Inclusion Mentor

"I reminded Paul at the beginning of each day that if anything became too much for him that I'd meet him in the safe space. This was the beginning of containing his anxieties and his unwanted behaviours calming down significantly. Until this was in place he'd have me on a wild goose chase around the school. Inevitably he'd be hiding somewhere. I reckon he was crying out for a 'safe space'. He just didn't know where to make it or how to tell me what he needed. I have seen a tangible difference in Paul. I never thought he would ever be able to relax but he does in the safe space!"

Some staff express concern that the pupil might over-use the safe space or manipulate its use in some way. However, this has not been our experience out in schools. Safety is a basic need of every human. Once a child's needs for safety is very obviously attended to disturbances reduce – sometimes considerably. In fact Paul's initial erratic and then regular usage of the safe space reduced over time, and we moved to daily, timetabled slots which he enjoyed.

Finally ...

FOR BEN

"You're letting me know that you are doing a scan right now. Take a seat over there by the wall so you can have a good look around and make a note on here of any changes you can spot. Then we can sit together for five minutes and talk about it".

FOR LENA

"The Deputy Head is here and is in a meeting at the moment, Lena. Go to your Maths class now. Ann will be waiting for you. You are safe here."

Chapter 3

Settling to learn
Taking on the curriculum

Optimal learning is driven by curiosity, which leads to exploration, discovery, practice and mastery. In turn, mastery leads to pleasure, satisfaction and confidence to once again explore ... The cycle of wonder, however can be stopped by fear. (Perry, B.D. *Creating an emotionally safe classroom**)

PRIMARY PHASE

The class teacher introduces the Literacy lesson to the class. The class watched the final part of the DVD, 'Good night Mr Tom' last week, and are now expected to complete a written task about the structure of the story.

SECONDARY PHASE

Week A. Period 1. Maths. Lena pulls a face when she sees the page of work she has to do and starts to make excuses, saying she can't do Maths.

We need to remember that children who have experienced relational trauma and loss need to be enabled to feel secure, so that they can 'settle to learn' (Geddes, 2006). Our first step must be to attend to their 'attachment systems' as a matter of priority.

Our attachment systems are concerned with safety, stability and security (Panksepp 1998). So the previous two chapters which deal with how to help settle our pupils are crucial to the process of creating the right context of safety for them. We need to attend to all these factors with our key pupils so that their attachment system switch off (because they are no longer feeling anxious) and their 'exploratory systems' engage and can be maximised. The exploratory system is the hormonal, neural and behavioural system we all share that is drawn to going off to pick things up, to touch, to look, check things out, to enquire … to explore and be open and receptive to the world around us.

In order to be free to do these things, we need to feel at ease within ourselves. We all need a fully functioning exploratory system in order to engage in the risks we come up against in the learning process. If someone trying to learn doesn't feel safe, stable and secure, their attachment system will always override the exploratory system; safety is our primary and most primitive need. Learning demands that we expose ourselves. Why would any of us expose ourselves if we didn't feel safe, stable and secure? So we need to pay utmost attention to facilitating this kind of environment for our pupils. As well as the preceding chapters, do check out Chapter 6 on stress, as it complements everything I'm writing about here. For example, a learning friend *(p.119)* will benefit pupils' learning by supporting regulation.

Assuming the pupil's attachment needs have been attended to in the school context, we can now turn to what we need to do in order to free our pupils up to be all that they can be; to reach their learning potential in school. Initially, I'll look at why we need to keep them close to us, and then reflect on the importance of creating pauses for thinking, reflecting and processing. Next, I'll look at how we can support our pupils to build on their achievements to date by creating a 'book (or folder) of success'. I will then move onto seven areas that we need to carefully consider in order to promote effective, individualised learning development plans for our pupils.

These are:

i)   Creating an appropriate learning environment

ii)   Differentiating to a pupil's learning style

iii) Acknowledging and working with the pupil's 'intelligences'

iv)   Supporting the pupil to initiate and organise

v)   Promoting Literacy

vi)   Being sensitive to lesson content

vii) Supporting abstract thinking

I'll conclude by considering how important it is to provide additional support when one of our pupils arrives late to a lesson. As we all know, this can happen for any number of reasons, and it's not something we often think about. But I'd like us to recognise that it does present specific challenges for a pupil who has experienced developmental trauma, and, what's more, I'd like us think of it as an opportunity to really get alongside the pupil and help them 'arrive' and integrate into the class smoothly, so that they can settle into a state ready for genuine learning.

We should never just be content with pupils looking busy. We need to be certain that they are engaging with learning and that they are making progress.

> All teachers should expect to teach children with special educational needs and all schools should play their part in educating children from their local community, *whatever their background or ability.*
>   (Removing Barriers To Achievement:
>   The Government's strategy for SEN (2004), *my emphasis*)

* teacher.scholastic.com/professional/bruceperry/safety_wonder.htm

Close proximity – keeping our pupils close

We can learn a great deal from Nurture Group principles and practice. This pedagogy lends itself perfectly to pupils who have experienced relational traumas and losses.

> Teaching children as individuals according to their developmental level rather than some arbitrary age-related level, is the way to healthy psychological growth and educational achievement. It is not about a set of learned behaviours but a two way process, a dynamic relationship between people.
>
> (Boxall 2010, p.25)

Learning is where the key adult will see the power of the relationship she is creating with her key pupil, in the effects and benefits it brings for that pupil. To create that safety initially, it's crucial that the key adult uses proximity to support the pupil in her care. Proximity with an attuned and responsive adult, who is bringing their mind, their body and their feelings to the work of co-regulating the pupil creates the neccesary safey. We need to reach a careful balance of separation and togetherness, dependent on the individual needs of the pupil we're working with. Getting this balance right requires attunement, really working hard to know what's going on with your pupil. If you're unsure, it's always a good idea to err on the side of more proximity rather than less; pupils will always let us know when they're safe enough to start exploring, just as a small child will wriggle and want to go and play when they've had enough cuddling. Remember to get alongside your key pupil at his height, rather than towering over him if he's physically smaller than you. Use touch too. This will be explored in detail in Chapter 6, page 117.

> Being in a relationship with a trusted and responsive adult allows a child to return to base, to emotionally refuel and recover before setting off again, curious and hopeful that the next new experience can be managed.
>
> (Read 2010, p.14)

Creating pauses

Read (2010) draws on Eliner Goldsmied's work, suggesting that it is important that we create pauses across the school day. She describes how these pauses are necessary to give our pupils time to gather themselves, and to experience periods of calm. These pauses are best initiated and facilitated by the key adult. Let's create windows for thinking, reflecting and processing during tasks. Let's deliberately name what we're doing *("Let's stop and think for a moment"),* and model how to do it by processing our thinking out loud in front of pupils; writing notes, drawing, breaking things down into simpler steps. Let's build in thinking time at the end of lessons as well, and at the end of the day, in order to reflect and integrate learning. For example, *"Let's take five minutes to think about what's been learned today".* This may seem obvious. But unless we make explicit what we do naturally, our key pupils won't necessarily integrate the new learning into their existing knowledge.

Holding on to success

Many of the pupils we are concerned about in this book have an extremely poor concept of themselves and their value. They're more likely to remember what they struggle with and their failures, rather than what they did well. This is where we intervene! We can become human memory banks for them. Let's also set up visual cues for them, to be able to hold onto successes, however small. We can use 'books/folders of success' in school. Let's catch any moments of success, achievement or progress in this book. Moments of success will be the evidence of our pupils engaging in healthy and appropriate tasks and activities. The key adult needs to look after this book, and determine how and when it is used or referred to. Incidentally, the book or folder must be protected, as pupils will sometimes seek to sabotage their success when they are feeling distressed or because praise is too unfamiliar (and therefore anxiety-provoking, *see below*) for them.

The book may contain:

- ✔ A specific compliment signed and dated by a member of staff
- ✔ A photo of the pupil 'in action'!
- ✔ A piece of completed work
- ✔ A comment by the pupil themselves, *"I felt proud when I ..."*
- ✔ Certificates
- ✔ Stickers
- ✔ Awards
- ✔ Newspaper cuttings

Everyone needs encouragement, but these pupils do even more so, because of their often very poor self-concept. We're basically collecting tangible 'evidence', to help them gradually build the belief that they are able to succeed. Then, whenever we hear them putting themselves down or entering into a phase in which they are regressing, sabotaging or becoming very self-critical, we can pull out the book or folder to draw attention to specific illustrations of success. For example,

PUPIL

"I'm totally crap at reading. I can't read!"

KEY ADULT

"You're letting me know you're feeling critical about yourself right now. I'm not sure what you're saying is completely accurate though. I've a picture of you here reading, and who received this certificate for having reached level 3?!"

Support the pupil to remember that they have parts. Integrate parts language *(see Chapter 6, pp.124-30)* into your conversations with them. So in this situation, for example, you could extend your commentary thus:

KEY ADULT

"You're letting me see your critical part right now. I know you also have a part of you that is proud of your success. I've got a picture of that proud part in your book – you getting level 3 in reading. You also have another part – your observer part that can see both of these parts and can help both parts learn from one another. The self-critical part needs to be encouraged by the proud part sometimes. The proud part needs to be helped to see if there is anything that could be even better".

It's important that we honour the self-critical part, accept it and treat it lovingly and hear its message too: it might have valuable information, for example, about what's hard today.

WHAT HELPS US ...
"Knowing what to do"

Please be aware that just as shame can be overwhelming *(as described in Chapter 6),* so can praise. This surprises many people! Remember that praise is often unfamiliar and so can provoke increased levels of anxiety. Many of the pupils we work with feel unworthy of praise because of the depth of shame they have internalised. So if we over-do praise, these pupils can feel flooded. The pupil will feel especially overwhelmed with praise if it is directed at *them*, rather than at tasks, (in other words at who they are, rather than *what they do*). Behaviour difficulties might then escalate. I know of one pupil who went into the cloakroom and covered herself under a stack of coats after receiving praise from three consecutive members of staff!

However, even if it's hard to receive, we do still need to give praise to these children and young people, as they really need it. The best advice is to give 'droplets of praise' – that is, little and often, and to link that praise to a specific task or activity. Give praise that is specific, for example, *"I liked the way you were kind to Ceri, sharing your game with her".* In this way we can subtly help them to digest the message that they need to hear, without triggering their defences!

Promoting effective, individualised, learning development plans

i   CREATING AN APPROPRIATE LEARNING ENVIRONMENT

Our environments have a tremendous impact on us, in terms of whether we feel under-stimulated or over-stimulated, tired or alert. Each pupil will respond uniquely to different features within their environments. This is true for all of us. If I'm at a conference or training session for example, I always prefer to have a lot of space around me, natural light and an open window so that fresh air can circulate. If there are strong odours I can easily become distracted. I prefer to have a desk or table rather than just a chair as this seems to help me to focus better and to write good notes! I prefer rooms to look personalised in some way. If they are neutral or too corporate they can seem clinical, and I find I don't relax into my learning as well. We're all different in our responses – what might work for me might not work for you, and vice versa. So we are going to need to test out a range of variables to check which type of environment this particular pupil responds best to, in order to settle to learn. In school we are obviously looking out for behaviours that would indicate optimal focus and concentration. Some questions that might help us in assessing this include:

- **Lighting**   does this pupil respond best in natural daylight or artificial lighting?

- **Air flow**   does this pupil respond best to a regular air flow, for example the window being left open, air conditioning, a fan, or just as it is?

- **Sound**   does this pupil respond best to silence, music, activity, background chat, interactions or noise?

- **Décor**   does this pupil respond best to light or darkly painted/decorated rooms?

- **Positioning**   does this pupil respond best when seated at the front, in the middle, to the side, at the back?

- **Seating** does this pupil respond best to being seated on the floor, on a chair, on a beanbag, on a stool, standing?
- **Smell** does this pupil respond best with natural smells or artificial smells, for example incense, room fresheners, room oils?
- **Surroundings** does this pupil respond best to minimalism or a room filled with mobiles and eye-catching displays?

Self reflection

What kind of environment do you respond best to when needing to focus or concentrate well?

I'm sure we all know of at least one great example of an environment that has been really thought about in terms of facilitating optimal learning.   From the toilets to the lecture rooms, great care will have been taken over décor and organisation of materials and furnishings. People using the venue will be heard commenting on their positive, nurturing experiences there. There will be an atmosphere of peace, tranquillity and freshness. Let's learn lessons from those who are already discovering that time taken to create and maintain such an environment increases learning potential, as anxiety subsides and calm prevails.

> WHAT HELPS US ...
> "More support in lessons to help us feel confident"

PLEASE NOTE: Because pupils who have experienced relational trauma are often hyper-vigilant and have a strong need to scan their environment, it's most helpful to place the child or young person to the side of the classroom, rather than at the front or in a central position. If possible, it's preferable that they can be near a wall they can lean against, as this can be grounding, particularly for those who become easily dysregulated. From this position a pupil need only scan 180 degrees rather than 360 degrees, so immediately the possibility for anxiety decreases.

Self reflection

How could your Inclusion Department or classroom be adapted to facilitate a more conducive environment for learning?

Once we know what our pupil needs, let's start adapting our classrooms accordingly. We can also make a note of what we have found out on the pupil's fact file *(see example p.273)*, so that others can continue with the most supportive strategies as the pupil moves through the school. Then, from the starting point of the pupil knowing what it's like to be working well, we can gradually help the child/young person to build up their capacity over time to work well even when the environment *doesn't* suit them.

ii   DIFFERENTIATING TO THE PUPIL'S LEARNING STYLE

Schools need to identify and support the preferred learning styles of our pupils. Presenting our teaching materials in a multi-sensory form usually works best for pupils who have experienced relational trauma and loss.

When we pay attention to the specific learning style of the pupil we're supporting, we can note, for example:

- **Feeling** (tactile) Does this pupil learn best when touch is incorporated?
- **Seeing** (visual)   Does this pupil learn best when supported by images?
- **Listening** (auditory)   Does this pupil learn best by listening to the human voice through fact-giving or verbal instructions?
- **Doing** (kinaesthetic)   Does this pupil learn best by being active – making and doing?

Self reflection

Think about the type of learner you are. Do you respond best to a particular approach when learning something new?

One school I've come across assesses each pupil in order to decipher the pupil's optimum learning style. Classrooms are then adapted accordingly at the beginning of the school year in preparation for the particular mix of styles the pupils in their care will respond to.

Interestingly, the specific pupils we are considering in this book often seem to respond best to visual, tactile and kinaesthetic approaches, rather than those focussing merely on communication through auditory processes – talking and listening. From my experience out in schools, I've found that pupils often seem to 'tune out' voices especially when they have lived in loud, chaotic, frightening contexts, such as those marked with physical abuse and domestic violence. This could be part of the primitive fight/flight/freeze response: after all, it's more relevant to watch for a hand curling into a fist than it is to listen to words that might be misleading. It might be because words have the power to induce shame, if the pupil doesn't quickly understand. It might also be because the capacity to use the symbolic significance of words isn't well developed in children and young people with traumatic backgrounds. It might be that without being able to engage their bodies, these pupils may dissociate if they feel anxious when having to listen for lengthy periods without chance of response. Further research would be necessary to look into these hunches, but in the meantime, let's really get to know the preferred style of each key pupil, and when we do have to use more auditory means then let's be mindful of modulating our voices to communicate calm and warmth.

iii   ACKNOWLEDGING AND WORKING WITH THE PUPIL'S INTELLIGENCES

Each pupil has multiple 'intelligences' which are different but equal in status. Pupils can sometimes access work they would otherwise find difficult by using their stronger intelligences, so it's important we take note of what these are and utilise them accordingly.

- BODY SMART   good motor co-ordination, as used in sport and dance
- WORD SMART   using language to express oneself, or to learn new languages
- MUSIC SMART   skills in performance, composition, and appreciation of music
- ART SMART   appreciation of art, and skill with colours, pattern and shapes
- THINK SMART   problem solving ability
- NUMBER SMART   mathematical and logical ability
- EYE SMART   building, designing, using maps and solving visual puzzles
- FEELINGS SMART understanding your own needs and feelings
- PEOPLE SMART   understanding and getting on well with others
- NATURE SMART   good at observing and understanding nature

from Pallett et al 2010, p.35

Let's encourage the pupils in our care to explore HOW they are clever. We need to think differently from being focussed on merely academic results. If we truly learn a pupil and what their communication style is, then they will be more likely to be able to access the curriculum we are offering in our schools.

Every teacher I know can tell stories about how sullen young people are magically transformed into intelligent and committed learners when something engages their interest and fires their passion.   Confusing disengagement with lack of ability is one of the most dangerous mistakes a teacher or a school can make.

(Claxton 2008, p.18)

Let's adapt tasks in response to what we know about our pupil. If we engage in this inclusive practice, we truly will be supporting pupils to reach their learning potential.   Failing to do this may put them at risk of becoming disaffected or disengaged. Claxton (2008) describes eight qualities necessary for effective learning:

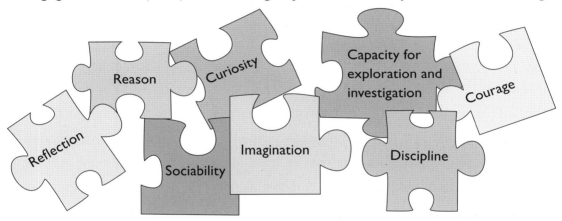

Let's keep these in mind in terms of how we measure progress within our schools. Let's see our roles as going well beyond the job of merely imparting knowledge or just helping our pupils to get through assessments, tests and exams. Let's engender the qualities needed for life-long learning.

iv   SUPPORTING THE PUPIL TO INITIATE AND ORGANISE

As described in the section earlier on developmental trauma *(p.17)*, many of our pupils will have difficulties in initiating tasks because of their vulnerabilities in executive functioning, and so we need to get alongside them to support them in starting tasks.   As Pearce (2009) states, we need to ensure we have appropriate

WHAT HELPS US ...
"Time"

developmental expectations as we plan tasks and activities for our pupils.

Many pupils will have organisational difficulties too – trouble organising both themselves and the tasks in hand. So it isn't appropriate to just set them open-ended tasks and leave them to get on with it. To start with, we need to check that they have the appropriate equipment in preparation for the task ahead. It may be that we carry a spare set of equipment with us or have a spare set to hand. Rather than getting into arguments about this, let's model checking out equipment and arranging it on the desk in such a way as to support learning. Allow proper time for this and let the pupil know what you are doing and why. This is such important learning. I really like Action For Children's logo as it sums up what's required in five simple words! It's relevant here – *"As long as it takes ..."*. We need to remember that our pupil is central to all our interventions. This isn't easy, as we've all got many other demands on us as education staff, but we do need to honour their pace and not rush them along because of our own agendas.

Our pupils will also need supportive scaffolding in order to tackle the task itself. They will need us to model how they can organise the task in hand, and an appropriate way to tackle it. These are strategies that will help these pupils in this area:

✔ Sequencing activities
✔ Check-lists that can be marked as the pupil completes each stage
✔ Simple numbered instructions
✔ Flow charts
✔ Colour coding
✔ Writing frames – starting pupils off, for example,
    "When I was at home I ....
    Then I .... *"*
✔ Cloze procedures: missing out words so that pupils complete the gaps rather

writing a full piece of text, for example,

"If you mix red and yellow it makes the colour ...."

In one primary school a whiteboard template is used as follows:

- *What equipment do you need?* ☐
- *List what you have to do.* ☐
- *How will you know you have finished?* ☐
- *What will you do once the task is complete?* ☐

Together with their key adults, pupils plan tasks at the beginning of each lesson. This is really good practice – modelling organisation for our pupils.

v   PROMOTING LITERACY

I believe it is important to draw attention to one curriculum area in particular – that of being able to read. This area is fundamental. If a pupil can't read, he will be immediately excluded from so much of what goes on in the school context, and beyond. So we must do all we can in order to support our pupils in this. Two pilot studies carried out by Catch Up working together with Compass Childrens' Services and then with Norfolk's Educational Psychologists and the specialist support service of Norfolk's Virtual School, amongst pupils in care, are worth noting in this context *(documented in Special Children, 2009, and in Literacy Today 2009)*. Catch Up is a charity that aims to help pupils who have literacy and/or numeracy difficulties. The Catch Up Literacy intervention is a structured one-to-one programme that teaches pupils how to read. Compass Childrens' Service is an independent fostering agency that supplies training and resources to carers of looked-after children in the Midlands. The pilot studies carried out between 2007-8 demonstrate the significant benefits of involving carers in supporting pupils' literacy levels by carrying out this intensive support 1:1 either together with their key adults at school or together with their carers at home.

The tool being used is obviously significant, but I would expect that the way this intervention uses the vehicle of a 1:1 relationship to be particularly significant.

vi   BEING SENSITIVE TO LESSON CONTENT

Work set by teachers must always be considered in terms of a pupil's:

- ✔ Developmental stage
- ✔ Educational level
- ✔ Gender
- ✔ Ethnicity
- ✔ Personal history (fact file) *(see p.273)*
- ✔ Current family configuration

Curriculum topics to be especially mindful about

Specific curriculum content is likely to bring up difficult and/or powerful feelings for a pupil with relational difficulties, for example

Death/Loss	Billie is grieving for his birth mum and dad: he doesn't live with them anymore
Mothers' Day	Kylie can't bear to think about her birth mum at the moment, as she hasn't had any contact with her for six months whilst she's been in rehab.
Christmas	Issac knows that dad won't be around this Christmas as he's in prison for GBH.
Sex education	Tom's older brother Marcus went into care after sexually abusing him and his little sister Lilly.
Baby pictures	Sonja is very sad as she has now had eight placements; life was too chaotic for her birth mum to take pictures. Sonja has never

seen any pictures of when she was a baby. She has pictures taken from when she was seven and in foster care, but that is all she has.

Autobiography Mika can't even start writing. He stares into the distance cut off from the task. His abuse was so horrific that he continues to dissociate; he's in care now, so hopefully over time his carers, social worker and therapist will be able to adequately prepare him for such emotive topics.

It is essential that we bring all our sensitivity to these areas. I am not advocating that pupils are excluded from those lessons or tasks which may

> **WHAT WE NEED …**
> *"To develop the curriculum to ensure that it is relevant and interesting to all"*
> Headteacher, secondary school

raise difficult feelings. I recommend that our pupils have prior warning and rehearsal time in the privacy of their homes, together with their parents/carers or adopters, so that they can express and explore whatever they need to. Otherwise we will have pupils engaging with something quite raw in public, and potentially experiencing powerful and overwhelming feelings. We need to think ahead and plan how to help them stay safe and feeling contained. If we don't, they may become overwhelmed and communicate their distress by behaving disruptively, and our quieter, more withdrawn pupils may be become even more closed down and depressed or anxious. Additionally, unprocessed revelations may upset or offend other class members and even staff. Let's protect both the vulnerable pupil and the class.

PRIMARY PHASE AND KS3

We need to make sure that parents/carers have access to curriculum forecasts, so that we can give them notice. Together with their families, some pupils may need privacy to reflect on their experiences and some time to gather their thoughts before deciding upon specific scripts that they can use in the context of this planned lesson or activity.

SECONDARY PHASE

Pupils will need prior warning from a trusted key adult so that they can prepare themselves emotionally and mentally to deal with the proposed content. They too may need support rehearsing scripts they could use in order to protect themselves from revealing too much personal information. Pupils will also need support with knowing that it is OK to maintain personal boundaries around what they disclose and share, in order to feel comfortable.

A note for parents/carers: For schools to be in a position to be sensitive to these areas they really need to know about the pupil's background. I heard of an example where a pupil in secondary was asked to answer questions about her parents' height, as her class were studying genetics. The pupil didn't answer, and just stared into the distance. The teacher thought she was being insolent and so became quite cross with her, having no idea whatsoever that she was adopted and that her personal history had been quite traumatic. The pupil then engaged in disruptive behaviour, because of her distress. It will always be important to work in partnership with the school as there is so much opportunity for misunderstanding and misinterpretation if we don't.

In this context, I really like the **WISE UP** programme created by Marilyn Schoettle in the States (adoptionissues.org/wiseup.html). Originally intended for families adopting children from overseas, I think it's a very useful tool for all those who have experienced relational trauma and loss. Pupils are taught to consider their different options for responding to questions and comments about their personal life stories. We need to encourage our pupils to realise that they do have options. Remember many of our pupils have been intruded upon, and so it's vital they have means of self-protection. The main components of **WISE UP** include the following choices:

W to *walk* away and ignore

I *it's private*: to remember their choice to keep things private. No-one has to share personal information with anyone, not even adults.

S to *share* something, part of the story, but not all of it. Decide which part feels comfortable.

E see yourself as the *expert*. Use the opportunity to *educate* others. Ensure you communicate clearly and well as there are lots of mis-assumptions made about being in care, adopted or having experienced relational trauma and loss.

Obviously this tool is not only helpful in class contexts but in social contexts too, out in the corridors, in the playground, on the field, in the dining room and after school. Let's ensure our pupils know how to manage different situations.

vii   SUPPORTING ABSTRACT THINKING

Pupils with a background of relational trauma and loss are likely to need to use concrete tools for much longer than most pupils. Let's access resources from younger classes or partner schools to facilitate this possibility. Allow pupils to use whichever tool they need, as there can often be a developmental delay in their capacity for abstract thinking.

Pupils with attachment difficulties find the concept of time especially difficult.

They will need visual and concrete reminders. In primary school I encourage the wearing of analogue watches. In secondary school, I encourage mobile phone timers. It's important that key adults refer regularly to the pupil's position in time and the duration of time. Connectors such as *'before', 'after', 'next'* and so on are particularly significant for these pupils, as described in Chapter 1, *Meet and greet*.

Arriving late

Finally, some pupils may be either late to lessons or only access part of a lesson, sometimes because of the additional discrete support provisions they have as part of their support package, for example therapy or 1:1 time with their key adult. If the pupil does enter the classroom after the lesson has started, we need to ensure that we provide support to settle him in. We also need to be welcoming of him as he enters. If we respond negatively as soon as the pupil enters the room, we are opening up the possibility of this pupil experiencing toxic shame *(see p.124)*. We often fail to connect with pupils who come in late; but however engaged we are in what we're doing, it's really important that we pause for a moment and briefly but sincerely greet the pupil, with warmth. Relationship is crucial for these particular pupils.

Sometimes we also forget to inform our pupils of the context they are walking into. We assume they'll use what are actually higher level social cues and work out their place and activity within the classroom. But the reality is that pupils who have experienced developmental trauma don't have the skills to do this. Let's approach the child or young person on a personal basis, and be explicit about the task in hand.

In general, we need to support the pupils in our care with getting from lesson to lesson on time, by providing the supportive scaffolding they need in both individualised timetable preparation and organisation – as discussed earlier. Discrete provisions should be kept to an absolute minimum, so that the pupil is *in* class, more than out of it. This will support them to develop more of an integrated sense of self.

Self reflection

How do you feel if someone takes the time to include when you walk in late to an appointment, meeting, activity or course?

Finally ...

FOR BEN

Thankfully, Ben's teacher had taken some time to prepare Ben's adoptive mum and dad for this curriculum focus, as she realised that the topic would be emotive for Ben. The family had all watched the film together at home and had talked through the relevant themes. Jake, Ben's key adult, had been in class to provide him with additional support and to reassure him if he appeared anxious when the film was shown. Ben works best sitting by the window on the side of the classroom, towards the back. Jake now sits with him, showing him how to collect the right equipment for the task and to go through the questions to ensure comprehension. Jake knows that Ben works best doing things and that he is art smart. He decides to ask Ben to draw out the story in cartoon form, by structuring it for him first. He then asks Ben to stick in some captions alongside his cartoon frames, from a list he has written up after discussion with Ben.

FOR LENA

As Maths is a class Lena struggles with, Ann is there by her side. Ann refers Lena to her portfolio of success, reminding her of what she has managed to date. She suggests they break up the overall task into smaller chunks of ten minutes focus time with pauses in between. Ann divides up the work expectations. Ann is very aware that the internalisation of number is still so difficult for Lena due to her developmental vulnerability, and that she also needs to make the lesson quite active in its style as Lena is a kinaesthetic learner. She gives Lena a clipboard and says that they are going to go out for a few minutes to practise counting. Around the school, Ann finds objects for Lena to estimate numbers and then to count. She asks Lena to record their findings on her clipboard. They then go back into class to use a software package that is very visual, allowing her to move objects around in order to count. The results are printed out and collated with her hard copy results from earlier.

Chapter 4

Who's in charge?
Practising dependency

Nurturance means teaching the child hundreds of times how to ask for help, how to live with the consequences of one's choices, how to learn to trust someone who has the power to abuse but will never do so, and how to begin to feel intensely the range of emotions that occur within a healthy family (school).

(Hughes, 1997, p.199)

PRIMARY PHASE

Even though Ben is really hot he doesn't want to leave his jumper and coat on the pegs. He wants to carry them about with him.

SECONDARY PHASE

Whilst Lena is in Maths, she notices a fight emerging between some year 10s she doesn't know, in the corridor. She rushes out to try and sort it out on her own.

To negotiate the school system, pupils need to know how to follow the lead of an adult. Yet so many pupils who have experienced relational trauma and loss are accustomed to taking the lead themselves. This is because of the way in which they had to adapt their behaviour in order to survive the very difficult circumstances in which they grew up. So we are going to have to over-compensate for this tendency to want to take charge, by engaging in a particular kind of nurturance to support them to learn what I and others think of as 'relative dependency'. First, I'll address why it's important to address this area of difficulty in the school context. I will then explore why practising relative dependency could well be the hardest task of all for some of the pupils we work with. Next, I'll outline six possible ways to support this task:

i   Using the vehicle of relationship
ii   Returning to base
iii   Engaging in interpretation and translation
iv   Using random acts of kindness
v   Using the game 'Follow the leader'
vi   Using memory cards

Finally, I'll look at the implications of these strategies for Ben and Lena, the two case pupils who we are following throughout this book.

The presenting difficulty

Many pupils continue to relate to the outside world in the survival mode which served them well as they struggled with relational trauma and loss in their home context. However, as we've seen, these ways of managing and behaving don't serve them well within the school environment. At a profoundly primitive level of their psyches, these pupils have learned that staying in control is a means of survival.   It is this level of control that has, in effect, kept many of them alive. For others, staying in control has helped them be somewhat safer psychologically, by keeping overwhelmingly painful feelings at bay.

By the time we meet them, our pupils have often become totally familiar with taking matters into their own hands. Ben is probably working his way through the school day absorbed in his own world, meeting his own needs in the way he thinks best. Lena is probably assuming she needs to deal with all her problems alone. For Ben and Lena, this is simply life as they know it.

Since this behaviour developed as a survival strategy, it's not hard to appreciate how demanding it will be for pupils like Ben and Lena to relinquish control to someone else – especially to a grown-up. Many adults find letting someone else take charge problematic, so our pupils are not alone in having this difficulty! But to be able to survive, manage and really get the most from the school system, pupils have to be able to follow the lead of the adults on their way to developing interdependence. As I mentioned, my sense is that this is probably one of the hardest lessons these pupils will ever have to learn, so we need to prepare ourselves for the long haul.

The task before us is clear. We are going to need to introduce these pupils to a relatively secure system (school), where they *can* assume safety, security and stability. Whatever we think about the setting we work in, no matter how much we know about what contributes to making sure pupils are safe there, we can't assume these particular pupils realise this as things stand at the moment. They will need us to map out *how* the school is made safe for them by being explicit about what is happening, as I described in Chapter 2. And we will need to facilitate opportunities to support these particular pupils to practice relative dependency in school through the vehicle of a close, genuine relationship with an adult.

Once again, this is going to challenge our usual way of 'doing school'. Most pupils coming into school will have experienced 'good enough' care, and are ready for the next stage of development, that of gradually moving towards the independence our schools are prepared and set up for. However, we will need to take pupils who have experienced relational trauma and loss back to an *earlier* developmental stage, as many have become 'pseudo adults' before their time. We cannot afford to leave them there. For healthy development, pupils need to be able to learn how to move between following the lead of another and leading themselves, between dependency and independence: and to know which contexts are appropriate for what. These are the essential ingredients for healthy *interdependence*. Pupils who have early experience of relational trauma, and who manage by being controlling, are unlikely to have experienced a healthy dependency; so we need to introduce them to this possibility.

As working in this way is presently unchartered territory, some schools may experience an initial hesitancy about the possibility of 'creating dependencies'. However, if we are serious about wanting to help our pupils move forward from a secure base, this is what we do need to be encouraging sooner rather than later. It is crucial that we see this aim as a key part of attachment support work. Ideally, we need the parents/carers to be or become the primary attachment figures at home and the key adult in school to become an additional attachment figure. We can't control what happens within the home, but we do need to ensure that we make the most of the vehicle of a healthy, secure relationship in school.

A healthy dependency is the stepping stone towards healthy interdependence. When I hear that pupils are actually forming meaningful, genuine relationships with the support staff caring for them, I know we are going to see progress. Naturally, we will need to gradually introduce boundaries or gentle challenges to move them on step by step. But this will be far easier to work with over a period of several years, as opposed to trying to manage a year 10 who has never had any experience/practice of following the lead of any adult in their life to date, and is now on the edge of permanent exclusion due to their significant controlling behaviours.

If we don't address dependency as a very necessary stage of development, we are leaving many of these pupils at risk of disengagement and of exclusion at a later stage. If we allow this, society as a whole will later incur the costs, at so many different levels.

I know that it's possible for pupils to learn how to follow: I've seen many making progress in this very area over the years, and I hope you have too. As I mentioned in the introduction, and as I'll reiterate throughout the book, relationships are both powerful and pivotal within adaptation and recovery type support.

> Attachment is not a static personal trait, but an adaptive, relational quality.
>
> (Taylor, 2010, p.35)

The biggest ask?

Many pupils who have experienced relational trauma and loss have engaged in pseudo-independent behaviours for a considerable time. These pupils need to know that we realise this adaptation, that of giving up control at school, will be hard, and that we know it is a really big ask. This understanding needs to be communicated quite early on. Empathy speaks volumes, especially for pupils such as these. We understand: not because we have necessarily lived through similar experiences ourselves, but because we have taken the time to truly learn the pupil. We know something of what they might have experienced and we take it seriously, knowing there are considerable social, mental, emotional, and physiological consequences resulting from relational trauma and loss. Of course adapting is not going to be easy. How could it be? We are challenging something fundamental about their beliefs about adults. We are trying to introduce the idea that maybe some adults can be trusted. That maybe these pupils don't always need to be in charge. That maybe, just maybe, the motives of these particular grown-ups might be to bring them good this time around, rather than harm?

What the work will involve

i   THE VEHICLE OF RELATIONSHIP

> If adults wish to influence children directly, their influence flows through their relationship with them, through any trust they begin to inspire. It may seem trite, but it is still true; adults will get close to children, to the extent that they earn their trust. If adults invest the time and attention, they may earn the dividend of trust from their investment. Then they may begin to glimpse what drives behaviour or motivates learning.   (Gilligan 2007, p.58)

WHAT WE NEED ...

"Understanding that inclusion is determined by the strong relationships we build"
Headteacher, secondary school

Relationships are powerful vehicles. One of my key motivations for writing *Inside I'm Hurting* and this current book has been my deep sense that we really do need to be using the power of relationship far more than we currently do in our schools. For far too long we have reduced the time that grown-ups and pupils actually spend simply talking together; for example, in many schools, form time/tutor group time has been reduced significantly. We have also moved too many pupils on in the name of 'fresh starts', away from the adults who had started to become very significant to them, with no clear explanation, considered ending rituals, or goodbyes. We have the capacity to introduce these pupils to the world of secure attachment at school, through genuine relationship with an adult based there – over time. But we have to make this a priority, not 'assume' that healthy relationships can simply grow by themselves

Let's ensure we allocate the most appropriate support staff to the pupils with the greatest needs. One or at most two (key adult and back-up adult) supportive staff are required. Individual teaching assistants or mentors are best placed for this role, not senior management, teachers or general class teaching assistants, who all have responsibility for a large group of pupils at any one time.

Do not allocate a key adult who:

    ✗ Takes things personally

    ✗ Loses their temper easily

    ✗ Is impatient

    ✗ Takes themselves too seriously

    ✗ Has *unresolved* issues of trauma and loss in their own family

    ✗ Doesn't work as a team player

    ✗ Is planning on leaving

    ✗ Doesn't like the pupil!

You get the idea! *(for more information on the* positive *character traits needed in a key adult, see Bombèr 2007, p.67).*

Over time we will see the pupil's attachment style adapting to the new experiences. Attachment is not static, as the quote earlier observed. Every relationship has the capacity to either confirm or challenge all that's gone before. This means that many pupils will start forming different views of themselves, others and the contexts they find themselves in, just because someone took the time to get alongside them.

How long for?

This is an area where persistence and patience are going to be necessary. We are going to have to find creative ways to support these pupils to start lowering their defences – to trust those around them to bring good, not harm. I'm afraid there are no fast tracking alternatives, despite our desire for this – for them and for us! So if anyone suggests a term's support, this is really unlikely to be sufficient. These pupils need access to individual relationships that *remain in place* over time, in order to work on this area of development. Pupils who have experienced relational trauma are not going to learn dependency through many people coming and going, or through a text book. In fact, in a 2011 lecture, Dr. Bruce Perry stated that relational permanence is essential for resilience and that relational *impermanence* can cause real damage. Relationships that last over time are the most effective ways to bring about adaptation and recovery, with those who carry wounds from their earlier relationships.

ii   RETURNING TO BASE

The key adult who is present, attentive, attuned and responsive to the pupil becomes a *secure base* for that child or young person *(see Chapter 1 p.32)*. We need to honour this, and allow our pupils to check in with their key adult from time to time, so that they can –

> … become a surrogate 'secure base' which can contain the inevitable anxiety engendered by the challenges of learning.   (Geddes 2006, p.141)

iii   ENGAGING IN INTERPRETATION AND TRANSLATION

The way we communicate within our relationships in the school context is so different to what these pupils have experienced. They will need interpretation and translation. We will have experienced countless times when our pupils have misinterpreted our motives; yet we probably won't have realised that this is what was happening. This isn't necessarily because we were bad communicators (though we may have been!) but rather because these pupils are used to 'expecting the worst', viewing the world this way because of what they have lived through previously. Contrary to cynical belief, these pupils are not 'out to get us' or consciously setting out to manipulate us (though it may seem this way), but merely attempting to survive in a world they have interpreted as neglectful, frightening, hostile, intrusive and dangerous, because their early world was precisely like that. Their responses are not always personal to us. We need to remember that many responses *aren't meant for us.* Our pupils have learned from an early age that you look after number one, and/or you look after each other (in a group of siblings). Their internal working model of how the world works (*see p.27*) may well read, *"The grown-ups don't know what they are doing. The grown-ups can't be trusted"*. These pupils interpret the way others interact and relate through their filter of insecure attachment. There really is no other agenda.

In view of this, we are going to have to step in and provide some necessary translation. Let's introduce them to the meaning of our interactions and why we are maintaining our close proximity to them in this specific school context. We will need to notice out loud any evidence that would suggest that the grown-ups in this school can be trusted with the needs of the pupils in their care. One example of doing this would be to point out interactions which demonstrate pupils' basic needs are being attended to by adults, as they occur during the school day. By basic needs, I mean food, safety (physical and mental), warmth and shelter. For example,

KEY ADULT

"Did you see that? Darius got really upset when he fell. Did you see Miss Fairns looking out for him just then? As soon as he fell over, she rushed over and attended to him immediately. She took him inside and treated him from the first aid box. The grown-ups/adults in this school attend to pupils' needs, we take health and safety seriously".

'Good enough' care and getting it wrong

Obviously there will be times when we grown-ups will get it wrong, and wish we'd taken alternative action. We need to remember that as long as we are providing 'good enough' care most of the time, this will be sufficient for the pupil to learn dependency in this area of need or interaction. If we do make a mistake, it's always best to own up by apologising, and maybe even extending this by saying what we would have liked to have done differently. This engenders respect and prevents the pupil from getting stuck in the cycle of distrust, as they will notice everything – believe me!

iv   RANDOM ACTS OF KINDNESS

A subtle way to introduce a pupil to being cared about by someone else, and to encourage relative dependency or bonding is by going the extra mile and facilitating opportunities for expressing kindness. As you spend time together, you will start to learn what is important to them. For example, it might be that one day you bring in their favourite game from home to play with them; or at the end of term you share a favourite treat, for example a particular type of biscuit or cake. It may be that you give them some extra quality time – not when they demand it, but because you want to. I know of one key adult who took their pupil for a game of squash. Another went with her pupil to a café for hot chocolate at the end of an academic year. What we want to communicate loud and clear is that we can pre-empt their attempts to meet their own needs by getting in there first, being imaginative and attending to their needs ourselves.

> **WHAT WE NEED …**
> *"Commitment and passion of staff to work beyond the remit of their job description in the interests of children"*
> Inclusion Manager,
> primary school

Let's:

- ✔ express care in a tangible way
- ✔ demonstrate understanding
- ✔ respond to needs before they are expressed
- ✔ respond to wishes that have been shared

Many of these pupils will not have had nearly enough experience of spontaneous warmth; initially, they may rubbish or reject what we offer with suspicion. But let's keep persevering. Let's get alongside and bowl them over with our small acts of kindness!

v FOLLOWING THE LEADER

I use a game called 'Follow the leader' as a starter for 'translation' work. Our pupils need support in practising following since they will be more familiar with leading or taking control. It basically involves a writing utensil and paper, but it can be extended in many ways to engage the pupil. The key adult introduces the game and states that there are two parts to the game. The first half involves the pupil 'taking the pencil on a walk' around the paper, creating intricate designs. The key adult follows with their own pencil on the paper at a parallel distance, in tune with the pupil, trying to exactly copy what the pupil does, commentating as she does so.

WHAT WE NEED …
"Time allocated to enrichment activities that don't have a purely academic focus"
Assistant Head – Special school/ Outreach

The second half of the game involves the key adult taking the lead and the pupil following in the same way as the key adult did in the first half. The key adult commentates throughout both parts of the game.

The activity and language used in this game is designed to encourage a dialogue about following and leading. The pupils need to know that there are always at least two possible parts that they can choose to adopt in their relating – their leading or their following part. These two parts and their usage can be developed through practice.

The dialogue used in the game can then be transferred into other settings within school. For example, we can notice out loud when a pupil demonstrates evidence of using their leading or following part appropriately and well. From the most basic to the more complex interactions, we can notice out loud what we see. The possibilities are endless!

KEY ADULT

"Fantastic following, Ross. I noticed the way you lined up for assembly first time of asking":

KEY ADULT

"Great leading, Maxine. You helped Rita with that task by showing her what to do next in a sensitive and respectful way".

As well as giving feedback in this way, the key adult also encourages self-reflection. From time to time, we can ask the pupil we are working with how strong he feels he is becoming with the skill of learning to trust. We encourage him towards having accurate self-awareness of how he's getting on, as we know that self-awareness is a major stepping stone towards self-control.

vi   MEMORY CARDS

Since these pupils find it very difficult to trust adults, they also find it very difficult to trust that what is important to them will be remembered or respected. They seem to respond best to visual cues, so this is when memory cards can come in. If an activity has to be interrupted or delayed, two cards are used to represent whatever has been happening. A quick symbol or picture is drawn on the cards, or a short phrase representing whatever needs to be attended to at a later time. One of the cards is given to the pupil, and one is kept by the key adult, who says, for example:

KEY ADULT

"These cards are to help us so that we can both remember that we need to carry on with this task on Tuesday".

This strategy not only supports the relationship with empathy and respect, but builds healthy dependency. The pupil is enabled to gradually learn to rely on the adult's commitment to continuity, and at the same time, is learning a simple technique for the development of their memory capacity. In effect, the key adult is modelling how to 'do memory', how to keep things in mind and how something or somebody can be kept in someone else's mind *(this latter point will be discussed more fully in Chapter 14).*

Self reflection

How do you behave when there's suspicion or mistrust in the atmosphere around someone else? What helps you relax and trust?

Finally ...

So now, thinking specifically about what was happening for Ben and Lena at the beginning of this chapter, the following might be appropriate in the context of the genuine relationships they are building with their respective key adults.

FOR BEN

Jake lets Ben know that he realises it's a big ask for Ben to let go of his personal things, that he is still learning to trust the grown-up to look after things for him "Ben, I can see you want to keep hold of your stuff. You don't quite trust the grown-ups to take care of it for you. Would you be able to have a go at practising letting me look after your things for you today?".

FOR LENA

Lena's key worker Ann says "Lena, I've just realised that you thought you'd have to deal with this as the adults might not know what to do. Since we started together,

I've been pointing out examples of the adults being trustworthy in this kind of thing. Do you remember the other day, when we saw Mr Stott sorting out that big argument in the corridor? Shall we give the adults a go, and see what happens? Remember we're trying to help you to practise using your following part a bit more so that it gets really strong: as you're very used to using your taking the 'lead' part, aren't you? OK, let's see what happens. Then we can talk about it together".

Chapter 5

What's next?
Moving from one activity to the next

Whilst some children cope remarkably well with change, for others change, even on a relatively small scale, can be a difficult and ultimately stressful experience.

(Plummer 2010, p.16)

PRIMARY PHASE

The class teacher tells everyone to line up quickly for their visit to the garden project or they will be late. Ben continues with what he's doing, and then becomes very agitated when the teacher hurries him along. He drops his books and then squares up with Billy who he says is looking at him strangely.

SECONDARY PHASE

The History lesson is now over. Time for period 2 which is in F block, room number 323. It's French with Mrs Peters. Mr Tomlinson tells everyone to move quickly to their next lesson. Everyone has their bags packed ready to go, apart from Lena, who is left staring into the distance.

In schools we aim to pack so much into one school day. We have become facilitators of efficiency. There are countless changes that need to be negotiated throughout each school day, each term and each year by both the pupils and the staff. Most manage this negotiation well, the majority of the time. However, we need to be aware that many pupils who have experienced relational trauma and loss find change very difficult, and are not able to move at the fast pace required during transitions. The kinds of transition I'll be looking at in this chapter include:

from one task → to another

from one person → to another

from one space → to another

from one teaching style → to another

from routine → to a change of plan

from familiarity → to the unknown

Many of these pupils have significant difficulties in the area of executive functioning *(as described in the Introduction, 'Developmental Trauma', p.19)*. Here I will mainly focus on two of these areas of difficulty, those of shift and of organisation, both relevant to transition. Pupils with these kinds of difficulty are going to need preparation in order to manage change well.

Preparation is one way to help mitigate unsettling effects of transitions.

(Taylor 2010, p.64)

I'll consider what happens if we don't pay attention to transition support for these pupils. I will then highlight the importance of allowing additional time. I'll consider the use of transition rituals and visual prompts, including the use of checklists and the kind of memory cards I've mentioned. Finally, I'll look at the implications for Ben and Lena, our two case pupils who we're following throughout this book.

When we carry on regardless ...

SHIFT

The school context demands a number of transitions in the daily school context on a moment by moment basis. In particular, the secondary phase context is a minefield of changes. Imagine Lena walking down the corridor in between lessons. There are so many opportunities for difficulty for her. For example, she may:

- Become distracted due to having other priorities, such as needing to check her environment out for safety
- Become disorientated by her own startle response *(see p.109)* triggered here by a loud yell down the corridor
- Get picked on, because she presents as immature, fragile, vulnerable or just different
- Get into conflict, because she misinterprets an interaction with a peer or a member of staff, potentially resulting in an argument or fight
- Get encouraged into risk-taking behaviour by other pupils – for example, skipping a lesson, leaving the school site, taking drugs or alcohol. There is an increased likelihood of risk-taking behaviour with pupils with the kind of background I've described, as often, especially at adolescence, they don't have a strong sense of themselves, nor a sense of their limits, healthy boundaries, or a firm and positive sense of 'belonging'

- Lena may flirt with someone, needing close connection with someone else and not knowing how to manage this growing need, mixed up with all the intense feelings generated by hormones
- Become very dysregulated because of something out of the ordinary that just happened, leaving her experiencing sensory overload

At the same time, Lena may be feeling anxious and stressed because:

- She doesn't feel the next teacher likes her
- She knows results are being given back today that will prove again how poor she is academically
- Last week she was late and the class teacher told her off, and now she assumes their relationship is completely severed
- She may be put on the spot again for something and it may tip her into toxic shame
- She may not have all the resources and equipment she needs for the lesson, and sir will probably have a go again
- She just got yelled at for wearing her hoody indoors

These experiences and feelings are a combination for disaster! Lena may end up either not making it to the next class, not settling in the next class, or causing a disruption of some kind to other peers' learning or the 'whole class' learning. It's essential that as education staff, we consider how we can attune to and attempt to provide supportive scaffolding for all the Lenas and Bens in our schools as they try to make transitions.

What about the pupil who moves from an informal lesson to a formal lesson, or the other way round? Where will he have learnt how to change how he behaves? Maybe no-one has ever shown him. Because he doesn't have the necessary understanding of different social contexts and how to be in them, the pupil might be seen as behaving inappropriately *(and see Foreword).* So the pupil may be being put at risk in terms of being tipped into toxic shame and/or exclusion from the lesson.

We may well see challenging behaviour arising in response to the anxiety inherent in shift, if we merely insist on moving all our pupils along at the pace we often demand in classrooms. Pupils who have experienced developmental trauma can have huge difficulty 'changing gear', so will need additional processing time built in at times of transitions to support them in this area of vulnerability.

Self reflection

... how do you feel if you are being rushed on from one experience to another?

What do you appreciate at times of transition?

Building in extra time

Let's take the pressure off both ourselves and the children and adolescents we are working with by simply allowing more time! Let's not get into control battles about this. At present we seem to pay particular attention to the need for more time only when the pupil is about to sit SATs or GCSEs. What about extra time needed during the ordinary school day? Why not consider this as an option then as well? We know that shift is a proven difficulty for these pupils, so let's prepare for it. Some patient moments spent with a pupil 'processing' a transition in advance is an investment into his or her capacity to optimise the next learning opportunity. As such, it will help the teacher and the rest of the class as well.

In this context, 'processing' might mean supporting a pupil to finish something earlier than others to provide some necessary transition time. Or it might mean preparing a pupil earlier to start the next activity, so that she is ready when the others are. Let's differentiate our expectations and tasks so that these pupils are fully included. We need to be very wary of disciplining pupils for developmental difficulties they are known to have in this area; to genuinely honour anti-discriminatory practice, we need to anticipate difficulties and provide support.

Thinking/reflective time

Let's also build reflective time into the end of

- Lessons
- Days
- Weeks
- Half terms
- Academic years

Reflective time involves space to think through what has been achieved and learned along the way. This reflective time is invaluable in terms of processing everything that's happening at school, rather than letting it pass by unnoticed. For example, dependent on the context and age of the pupil, a combination of simple words and pictures might be used to explore a specific transition journey, with the following prompts:

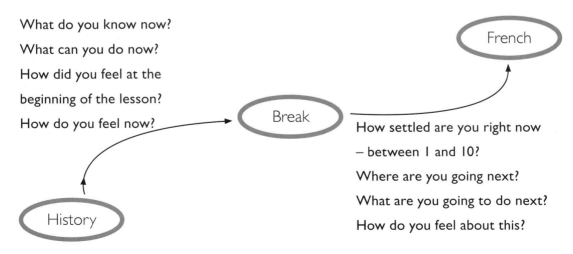

What do you know now?
What can you do now?
How did you feel at the beginning of the lesson?
How do you feel now?

How settled are you right now – between 1 and 10?
Where are you going next?
What are you going to do next?
How do you feel about this?

Transition rituals

Our pupils need us to create transition rituals for them. These will allow a window, a breathing space to emerge in between changes, providing time for the pupil to process and prepare for that change. If we don't create such spaces, then the pupil may become increasingly dysregulated. This may be especially true when something emotionally upsetting is already happening, for example if the pupil's class teacher is about to leave. The pupils are less likely to be able to settle to learn. There may be battles of will. They will not have space to make sense of their feelings and then the feelings may build up to a pressure cooker effect, the explosive reactions resulting in the possibility of disturbed behaviours.

> WHAT WE NEED ...
> *"Better attitudes on differentiation"*
> Key adult, secondary school

Some of these pupils may not have a sense of *their place in relation to time*; they can become disorientated. This is not surprising when we consider that for much of the time in their early lives, events felt completely beyond their control. Imagine how it would feel if we as adults felt this sense of helplessness as we went about our day; it would be immensely disempowering. To a pupil who has experienced huge losses, it can feel terrifying.

So we really do need to intervene to reduce the *duration* of any increased anxiety in response to imminent change. We can do this by providing visual cues to support our pupils in developing a sense of their place in time, so that they can know about the process of change that's coming up. They will then feel a greater sense of control as they have the feeling of being more prepared for the imminent transition – whatever it might be.

Visual cues

There are a variety of visual timers we can use in schools, such as:

GEL TIMERS sand timers
INDIVIDUAL VISUAL PLANNERS/
DIARIES **water   timers**
STOPWATCHES
day-by-day/

w e e k -

by-week

calendars
INDIVIDUAL
VISUAL TIMETABLES
mobile phone timers
OUTLOOK   DIARY/PLANNER

Mere words won't hit the spot with our pupils. The developmental needs of these particular pupils suggest that visual and tangible cues are much more relevant for them, just as we would use with much younger children. They are far more likely to tune into a visual cue than to us telling them that something is five minutes or five days away. Many of these pupils have no concept of time. They need someone to set up an opportunity to 'feel' what five minutes feels like, or five days.

We need to introduce the visual cue that is most appropriate to the task in hand; for example, offering a small visual cue for an extra five or ten minutes to prepare for activity transitions, whereas a variety of tools and planners might be needed to help the pupil cope with significant transitions of longer duration. Such transitions might necessitate weeks/half terms to prepare for *(such as those described in Chapter 13, Moving on ...)*

CHECKLISTS

Checklists can also be created to help prepare for transition. Checklists break down complex tasks that involve many expectations into simpler chunks that are clear and straightforward to follow. A simple list can mean that the pupil is less likely to feel overwhelmed. Checklists can make even the most difficult task bearable. Checklists teach the brain how organisation works so that transitions can be made successfully. We need to provide our pupils as many opportunities that generate success as possible.

WHAT HELPS US ...
"Kindness"

So for example, in ending an activity/lesson, the checklist might look like this:

Put your pens and pencils away in your pencil case

Put your pencil case and books in your school bag

Find your timetable/planner

Check what lesson or activity you have next

Check which room this is in

Make your way there as quickly as possible

Or in starting an activity/lesson:

Find yourself a seat and sit down

Put your pencil case on the desk

Find the books you need from your bag. Put these on the desk

Write the date in your book

Sit up ready to listen to your teacher

MEMORY CARDS

As mentioned in the previous chapter, *'Practising dependency'*, memory cards are very helpful in terms of supporting pupils to 'hold on' or 'wait', so that they can temporarily come away from something that they might be in the middle of. Many pupils will find it extremely hard to stop mid-flow. Not all lesson timings will allow for completion of work in one sitting. So we need to prepare for this possibility with some supportive scaffolding.

WHAT HELPS US ...
"More time to
do work"

Finally ...

Reflecting back on how we might support Ben and Lena with transitions, the following ideas might be helpful for key adults and/or teachers:

FOR BEN

→ *Go through his individual timetable at the beginning of the lesson, preparing him for the possibility that assembly will happen after forty minutes of Literacy.*

→ *Leave the timetable on his desk or very close by, so he can refer to this as a visual cue.*

→ *Plan to stop Ben ten minutes before everyone else is asked to line up.*

→ *About twenty minutes into the lesson, use a sand timer of ten minutes to prepare him to stop.*

→ *Once the sand timer is through, let Ben know he needs to stop now.*

→ *If he is finding it hard to stop, then give him a memory card so that he can cope better with waiting to finish his current activity another time.*

→ *Use the ending checklist to prepare him.*

→ *Line him up ready. It may be that the rest of the class is now ready to line up as well, but if there are still a few minutes spare, let him know that you would like him to show the rest of the class how to line up.*

FOR LENA

→ *At the beginning of the History lesson, the teacher can ask Lena what she is doing next by directing her to her planner if she doesn't know.*

→ *The teacher can support Lena to set her stopwatch to ten minutes before the end of the lesson.*

→ *When her stopwatch alerts her to the imminent end of the lesson, the teacher can support Lena to engage in the activities outlined in her ending checklist.*

→ *If Lena finds it hard to stop, the teacher can give her a memory card.*

Please note that though Lena is that much older, she may still have the developmental need of a younger child to check in with her safe space before moving on to the next lesson, which is, in this case, in the Inclusion Department (*see p.32*). This should be allowed. She can use her check-in card to gain entry. If, knowing Lena, her key worker expects she'll want to do this, then allow her to leave class a little earlier, as soon as she has addressed her ending checklist. This supportive care will not only mean smoother transitions but will teach these pupils how to organise themselves. It is good practice to allow an extra five or ten minutes to engage in endings and beginnings during school lessons throughout the day. This practice can then be later transferred onto individual study, and on out into the work place.

Chapter 6

The temperature's rising!
Stress

How we individually manage stress is influenced by the way we interpret or perceive the situation. Interpret things one way, and we feel stressed, interpret them differently and we feel fine.   (Taylor, 2010, p.35)

PRIMARY PHASE
Ben starts rocking on his chair and sucking his jumper sleeve after the teacher asks him a question.

SECONDARY PHASE
Lena has asked to go to the toilet three times during her French lesson.

Pupils who have experienced high levels of stress in their early years will often present with sensory integration difficulties. We can observe these difficulties in school in their hypersensitivity and dysregulated responses. For example, we might notice:

- A pupil fidgeting with objects on their table and regularly turning around to check out what's going on around them.
- A pupil startled by and asking questions about background sounds, for

example, a water pipe expanding as hot water passes through it:
"What's that?"

There may be times in school when we will observe over-reactive responses to what we'd consider very low-level stressors. Pupils may also engage in sensory-seeking behaviours, for example holding and touching nearby objects, chewing and rocking in order to release anxiety and to restore a sense of stability. There will also be times when the pupils' heightened stress levels might be masked by physical ailments – aches and pains. Sometimes we might not even be aware of the level of stress the pupil is experiencing, because he or she may be keeping it very well hidden.

Whether we notice or not, and however they manage their experience, this high level of stress is a serious consequence of the traumatic history the pupil has lived through. These pupils arrive in our schools on a regular basis tense, anxious, and on full alert, ready to defend themselves and their innate sense of vulnerability. Obviously we can't remove the after-effects of what's been happening before they come into school or what happened in their early lives. We can, however, identify and minimise the range of potential stressors they may experience in school, so as to ensure that anxiety levels are kept to a minimum and their pre-existing stress levels are not exacerbated but are brought down where possible. They then may have a chance to settle into learning. We need to be mindful of responding to the pupil's needs, as well as their behaviours.

Straightforward verbalisation can help in this. This might include wondering aloud about the possible states, sensations, thoughts and feelings the pupil might be having. Also, don't forget the benefits of doing something as basic as asking them if anything is bothering them. I was shocked recently to hear of a young person who had been involved with many professionals, but who said that she had never been directly asked how she was doing and what was bothering her. Some pupils are desperate for us to notice and to ask that simple question. We can use wondering aloud *(see below)* to support them to tell their story.

In this chapter I'll consider how aware these pupils are of what's going on for them internally. We will think through the importance of teaching them how to become self-aware and how to help them use a range of tools to self-soothe, using the vehicle of relationship with their key adult. I'll describe how *reflective dialoguing* can be used by key adults to support this learning, and go into a range of settling techniques that can be used to soothe or regulate their dysregulated states, such as touch, multi-sensory tools, choice language, parts language and scaling.

WHAT WE NEED …
"Clearer strategies for EBD children to help them remain in the classroom learning alongside their peers"
Teacher, primary school

Becoming aware

Pupils who have experienced relational trauma are probably not even consciously aware that their behaviour is fuelled by stress, just as it can take any of us a while to notice when pressure starts driving how we act. Claxton (2008) helpfully describes stress as when the demands made on someone far outweigh the resources they have to meet those demands. Many of our pupils with these kinds of difficulties have been through terrifying experiences which they did not have the emotional or developmental capacity to deal with or manage. The high levels of stress in their early childhoods frequently leaves the individual pupil feeling inadequate, anxious and out-of-control.

In addition, many of these pupils haven't had the opportunity to develop the basic building blocks of self-awareness. They are unconscious of their sensations, states and feelings, and often can't locate an accurate sense of themselves. It may be hard for the individual pupil to even know what makes him who he is – where does he begin and end? Is he hot, cold, thirsty, hungry, full, tired, wobbly, or what? He may not know even if you ask him. Pupils from these kinds of background are also likely to have poor muscle tone, and so will not be receiving the necessary signals and feedback they need from their bodies in order to function well and work out what's going on.

But more than that: many of our most vulnerable pupils will have not had anyone to give them the words to help them describe their sensations, states and feelings in such a way as to make sense of what is going on within their bodies, no-one who paid sufficient attention to get to know them this way. So why would they know a) what is going on inside them or how to talk about it, or b) how to meet their sensory needs appropriately? If there has been such a significant lack of empathic attention, then no wonder appropriate and healthy self-soothing and self-control are rarely evident.

Our pupils are not going to be able to make change happen on their own. Perhaps we have forgotten that our self-awareness only grows within the context of close relationship with another person. If we really want to help, then it is essential that we provide opportunities in school for our pupils to get to know themselves better.

So our starting point is to guide them into a better self-awareness. We can then give them tools to self-soothe. We can introduce the tools by engaging in their use together - by modelling how to find and maintain a calm state. If we do this repeatedly, our pupil will gradually move to a position in which he will be able to exercise self-control over his senses, states, sensations and feelings, by knowing when it is necessary to self-soothe.

In school, we often demand self-control from our pupils who have no idea what is even going on in their bodies! As I mentioned in Chapter 4, self-awareness is a major stepping-stone towards self-control.

Self reflection

How self-aware are you?

In what situations do you need to exercise self-control?

How do you know when to do this?

What do you do?

Are there situations you'd like to be able to manage better?

What would be the first step towards doing this?

What support might you need?

Co-regulation

We all learn about our emotions, and how to regulate our emotions by soothing ourselves, through the process of co-regulation within the context of relationship *(see below)*.

> None of us is born with the capacity to regulate our own emotional reactions. A dyadic regulatory system evolves where the infant's signals of moment by moment changes in his state are understood and responded to by the caregiver, thereby achieving regulation. The infant learns that the arousal in the presence of the caregiver will not lead to disorganisation beyond his coping capabilities. The caregiver will be there to establish equilibrium.
>
> (Fonagy et al 2002, p.37)

Many of the pupils that we are concerned about within this book have either not had this experience before or have had poor or intermittent experiences of regulation, leaving them prone to becoming very dysresgulated at times of heightened tension or stress *(see p.22 for effects of dysregulation)*.

Consequently, a significant role we can play in the life of our key pupil is to help him to find ways to self-soothe when times get tough, supporting him by actively joining in with what we suggest he does. Pupils like Ben and Lena need someone who can get alongside them to model regulation. So clearly it's crucial that key adults know how to calm/soothe themselves at times of dysregulation, in order to be a good role model for this important function.

We need to also be mindful of not allowing these pupils to suddenly experience too much external stimulation, for example when there's a special themed day. These pupils need staff who will keep an eye on the level of sensory input the pupil is receiving, and recognise that he or she will need extra time to calm down from stimulating situations, however pleasurable. Let's pace the extraordinary so that our pupils don't experience sensory overload! When extraordinary events are planned, we'll need to carefully manage the pupil's exposure to settings and situations which might increase their stress levels, providing pauses at regular intervals for processing and settling.

Obviously we don't want these particular pupils to be excluded from the fun or excitement of the extraordinary events that come up within school life, but we do need to think ahead and notice how they are managing – as we would quite naturally with a much younger child.

So our aim needs to be to provide tools within the context of relationship:

✔   to decrease inappropriate or unhealthy sensory-seeking behaviours which the pupil may be using in an unconscious attempt to decrease or dissipate stress
✔   to improve body awareness
✔   to facilitate experiences of calm
✔   to improve attention and focus

We can address these four aims in many different ways, including the use of:

i   Reflective dialoguing

ii   Touch

iii   Multi sensory tools

iv   Choice language

v   'Parts' language

vi   Scaling

Reflective dialoguing

Reflective dialoguing involves the tasks of making observations, commentating and wondering aloud. These pupils need us to support them to make connections; in other words, to provide a possible *translation* of the states, sensations and feelings arising from the dysregulation they experience when their bodies are unable to manage sensory overload, as a means of helping them move into a state of regulation. We need to bring out into the open that which is usually left unsaid.

Obviously we may not always be 100% accurate about what might be going on internally for a pupil when they are experiencing stress or becoming agitated, but if we truly invest time into 'learning the pupil' we will get increasingly better at this skill – as a 'good enough' parent or carer does. Let's keep in mind that what we're trying to achieve is a *good enough sense* of what makes this pupil who he is and what makes him do the things he does.

In order to be able to do this well we must first engage in the first, essential stage of *observation*, then the second stage of *commentary*, and lastly the final stage of *wondering aloud*.

OBSERVATION

Take time out to observe these specific pupils in a non-intrusive way. Let's wait, watch and wonder about them. Do this internally, in your own mind, in the first instance. Such basic thinking time is vital and yet we will probably have to make special arrangements to protect space for this, as all the busyness within the current context of our schools doesn't usually encourage this type of reflection.

COMMENTARIES

Once you've spent some time making your own observations (which will subsequently help inform your practice), you can then begin making gentle statements out loud that describe what you can see, in a respectful manner. For example,

KEY ADULT

"You blushed when the teacher asked you a question":

KEY ADULT

"I notice you are rocking on your chair".

Feedback that is made gently will start raising the pupil's awareness.

WONDERING ALOUD

As you 'learn the pupil', you will begin to realise why he does what he does. We won't always get it right. What is most important is that we have a go at making connections for him. This is only what would have happened in a 'good enough' care environment in a pupil's early years and is therefore not intrusive. It is OK if the pupil disagrees. Acknowledge what he says and reply, *"Oh, OK, I was just having a go at trying to understand what happened then. I guess I got it wrong that time. I'll continue thinking as I so want to get to know you well; then I can help you understand yourself and why you do what you do".*

If, however, you think you might have got too close to what might be really going on, do back off for a short while and try again at a much slower pace as you give your feedback. Acknowledge out loud in front of the pupil that you realise what's happened and what you will do about that. For example, *"You're letting me know that you want a bit of space and I'll respect that right now".* Continue at another time. Remain sensitive to their feelings. We want to respect them but also support them to move on so that they don't become stuck. We have a responsibility to attempt to strike a balance here, but remember, we only have to be 'good enough', not perfect!

Firm touch

I am a strong believer in the use of touch to support and reassure pupils who have dysregulatory difficulties. Touch can be very powerful, bringing a state of calm. When dysregulated, pupils like Ben and Lena can lose connection with their own bodies. This can then mean that the pupil is and will behave in a way that reflects being 'out-of-control'. Touch can put them back in connection with themselves by enabling them to feel 'grounded', a state we can all recognise as stabilising.

In late 2010, the UK Secretary of State for Education Michael Gove made a public statement declaring that it should be permissible to use touch in our schools (Guardian 1/10/10). I am hopeful that we will no longer hear comments in school that scare staff away from using this valuable, affirming and very relational 'tool'. Naturally we need to be sensitively attuned to the individual's background, needs and responses. I am not advocating that we force this, if the pupil is resistant. However, we do need to keep in mind that the aim for any pupil is to be able to have a healthy response to appropriate, healthy touch and the reassurance it can express.

Firm touch can be supportively used by the key adult in an integrative way throughout the school day, as and when they feel it is appropriate; for example whilst in class working on a task or as the pupil is moving about the classroom. It can be included in a range of helpful options written or drawn on cards in what I have described elsewhere as an individual's personalised 'calm box' (*see below and* Bombèr, 2007 pp.206-11 *for more information on making and using calm boxes*).

I advocate using an open palm and firm or medium pressure on the pupil's top mid-back, top shoulder or forearm. Pressing down slowly on both shoulders at the same time is particularly effective when we can see that the pupil is starting to become increasingly dysregulated. The aim is to bring the pupil back 'down', to give them a soothing experience, in order to settle the pupil so that he can make the most of everything on offer to him at school. Alternatively, if he can handle sustained or intermittent eye contact, sit in front of the pupil and ask him to hold his arms out. Hold his upper arms firmly and gently engage in a rowing action. This is very soothing and has the effect of bringing calm (try it yourself first with a friend!). There are also many types of hand/back/head massage to try out, using a variety of activities and tools.

A couple of activities that I recommend are Jungle Fun, the pizza game and the Weather Report. Jungle Fun is a great game in which the adult imprints 'animal footprints' on the pupil's back using different movements of fingers and hand, and the pupil has to guess the animal. There is also pizza-making, (*see* Bombèr 2007, p.207) and the Weather Report which many schools might be familiar with; an impression of different weather conditions is created by touch on the pupil's back and he has to guess what each is. So for example, outlining fluffy clouds with brisk finger movements, making warm, repetitive circular movements for the sun using your index finger, using a whole palm for giving gentle thunder-claps; a quick whizzing finger for lightning …

> WHAT WE NEED …
> *"Resources such as calm boxes, games, visual cues, individual timetables etc"*
> Key adult, secondary school

Multi-sensory tools

There are many multi-sensory tools out there that can really support these pupils to settle to learn *(see 'Signposting' for stockists)*. I'd like to draw specific attention to a few of them.

TANGLES

My most used tool. Since I first wrote about them in 2007, many different varieties have become available! Twisty tangles, metallic tangles, fuzzy tangles, textured tangles and even 'tangle therapy', to name just a few.

I suggest that tangles are used from year 6 (10/11 years of age) onwards. Learning friends – small 'beanie' animals – can be used until then. It's important that we boundary the use of different tools for differing age groups or else, as pupils are entering adolescence, they may feel we are patronising them. I suggest changing the type and texture of the tangle as the pupil enters each academic year so that there is some variety as well, to reflect the fact that you are honouring the pupil changing – growing up – and that you are not 'babying' them.

Tangles are especially helpful for fiddling with. We need to be mindful that it is not physiologically possible for pupils who have experienced developmental trauma to sit completely still if they have experienced high levels of stress or are experiencing high levels of stress right now. Fiddling usually happens when they are starting to become dysregulated. Maybe the work is challenging and they start to experience stress. The pupil is attempting to relieve the uncomfortable feelings that stress can bring, and fiddling soothes stress. Us giving the pupil something to fiddle *with* brings both the need and a support tool into their awareness, meaning that the pupil will be empowered to practice self-control *consciously* – making healthier choices during the school day.

And we have a choice here. We could allow them to fiddle with whatever they wish, but in doing that, we need to be aware that it might:

✗   result in the pupil choosing inappropriate things to fiddle with

✗   result in the pupil being reprimanded for fiddling because of what they
     have chosen, or the effects of choosing something on themselves or
     another person

✗   interfere with other pupils' sense of comfort and ease of learning

✗   over-stimulate the pupil

✗   end up distracting the pupil or other pupils around them

Or, we can step in and provide them with something that is boundaried, for the purpose of focussing and concentrating. I believe this is more advisable because:

✔   it gives the message that the teacher understands the pupil's need and is proactive about supporting it. This intervention will support relative dependency, as the pupil starts to learn that the adults can meet their needs; so they can develop the sense that they don't have to 'go it alone' or be in 'survival' mode anymore

✔   it means that the pupil is prevented from engaging in behaviour that might be reprimanded, for example, making their legs bleed by constantly picking at scabs, or damaging or destroying something – thus bringing shame. We want to generate success, not shame

✔   having one object contains anxiety for the pupil. If the pupil just uses whatever, whenever, the action can start off by being soothing but can quickly end up over-stimulating the pupil, resulting in inappropriate or disturbed behaviours.

✔   it means that we can monitor the duration of using the tool/s to support regulation over dysregulation, since it's far more practical to observe the usage of just one tool.

CHEWIES

If the pupil chews things, for example, their pens, pencils, or jumper sleeves you may want to try using a gel ring, chewy tube or 'chewlry' in the first instance. These sensory tools provide an alternative means of self-soothing and at the same time, protect the pupil from engaging in behaviour that may then lead to shame as their things and others' possessions become damaged or destroyed by chewing.

WOBBLE SEAT/BEANIE CHAIR/GYM BALL

Because these three types of seating allow a level of movement, these chairs not only provide self-soothing at times of stress, but through the additional sensory input they provide, can also help support the pupil to sit up and be more alert physically by increasing his self-awareness; so that he can settle to learn. As mentioned earlier, many of our pupils have poor muscle tone, so increasing sensory input can be helpful. The contained movement the chairs allow enable pupils to feel more in touch with their bodies; they become more aware of themselves, which means they are in more of a position to make appropriate and healthy choices.

For example, one pupil I observed during carpet time had been given a chair to sit on, as he used to wiggle about all over the carpet without one. However, on observations he swung back and forth on this chair with his feet off the ground most of the time. I felt as if he needed someone to sit behind him and hold him to help him settle, but obviously, this wouldn't be practical! However, we found that as soon as we gave him a beanie chair, not only was he at a more similar height level to the others in his class group, promoting inclusion, but he seemed more grounded; his feet were firmly on the floor and his body was supported by the firm material and bean contents surrounding him. It was as if someone was holding him! This type of strategy makes such a significant difference to a pupil who has survived high levels of stress.

THINKING DOODLES

You can create these yourselves by purchasing a couple of small jotters for the key adult and pupil to use. The pupil is permitted to draw/scribble/graffiti whilst listening, and the key adult can do the same. These jotters are especially helpful for focussing and concentrating. Sometimes allowing a pupil to engage in a task like this, this whilst being expected to listen, frees up another part of their brain to listen well. It's often the really simple tools such as this that can be so, so helpful in working with pupils who've experienced developmental trauma. We don't necessarily need complicated strategies.

WEIGHTED BLANKETS OR AROMA CUSHIONS

'Weighted blankets' provide sensory feedback to pupils with sensory issues, helping them to feel safe, relaxed and calm. A weighted blanket is a safe and effective way to apply weight and deep pressure, both of which have been found to be calming and comforting. They are more usually used with pupils on the autistic continuum, but have been found to support pupils with experience of relational trauma and loss as well. Aroma cushions are more readily available, and are long bags filled with wheat; they are often scented. Aroma cushions can also be warmed (in a microwave), which makes them more effective and provides pupils with a calming scent, usually lavender, which can help to settle them. The blankets or cushions can be draped around a pupil's shoulders, supporting the pupil to feel grounded or calm.

The weighted blanket or aroma cushion is essentially providing the firm touch that can also be applied by someone resting their two hands on the pupil's shoulders. Obviously it's not practical to stand doing this for long periods of time. That's when these tools come in! They are especially helpful to have available in the school's safe space area, but can also be applied when a pupil might need to be seated for long periods of time, for example during assembly or when topics are introduced. Even better if the key adult uses the tool as well to engage in modelling and co-regulation.

CALM BOX

A calm box is a decorated, personalised box full of cards on which short, multi-sensory type activities are written that each last a few minutes *(see Bombèr 2007, p.206-11).* They can be used to engage the pupil in opportunities to practice calm/ self regulation. All the activities need to be structured to include a range of sensory stimuli, especially at the beginning of doing this type of work, because pupils will need opportunity to try out different ideas in order to determine which of them are most supportive in self-regulation. Each pupil is different in their responses. After a period of work with the pupil, the box becomes more and more individualised, so only a few activities will remain. Those activities that don't interest the pupil or dysregulate the pupil further will be put to one side.

Choices

Choices can help these pupils to settle in school, since, if they experience feeling 'cornered' by a rigid approach, their stress can be exacerbated. We don't want to give them too many choices or else they may feel overwhelmed, but just two or three presented positively will suffice.

There are many matters over which pupils can be given choice, since the issue is often of little or no consequence to the teacher; for example, which pen to use or which chair to sit in to complete a task. Let's not create unnecessary stress by being stubborn or fixed about how we want something achieved. Flexibility is imperative. If we engage in offering positive choices, then we will end up meeting the pupil's legitimate needs to retain a degree of control, whilst, at the same time, reinforcing the teacher's authority.

However, if you find yourself really struggling in this area of working more flexibly than usual, it could well be that you may have unresolved issues of power and control from experiences in your own background. It's really important to seek professional input for this, for your own sake as well as for the sake of your teaching. The regrettable fact is that if power struggle dynamics are allowed to be played out in the school context, the intensity involved in these interactions can increase to dangerous proportions; the pupil can easily end up being scapegoated by exclusion. This is not an option for a school that is centring its provision around a pupil's needs, rather than the adults'. We all have an ethical responsibility to contain our own issues, and we all need support to continue our own development. So there is no shame in seeking support *(and see Chapter 15 on 'Staff care' for more information on this)*.

'Parts' language

These pupils need us to start off the process of helping them figure themselves out. Pupils with significant attachment difficulties often have low self-esteem, and are struggling with what is known as 'toxic shame'. Toxic shame describes a false, pathological shame that debilitates a person's sense of self. Bradshaw (2005) states that toxic shame is induced by child abuse. He also explains how this type of shame can induce dissociative effects, whereby the pupil is not even aware of what he might be thinking or doing. The pupil is therefore at risk of losing touch with reality.

Because of the effects of toxic shame, our pupils often have very polarised views of themselves, seeing themselves at different times as *all good* or *all bad*. We sometimes collude with this in school through our own language: we imply there are good and bad days: good and bad lessons. We need to be aware that many pupils believe that *they* are the reason why trauma and loss happened in their lives, that they are 'the mistake'. This is why we need to be so careful in school with our discipline. We want to teach all our pupils the difference between right and wrong, and to experience a degree of guilt for misbehaviour. However, these particular pupils can easily tip into toxic shame, which is a long way away from guilt.

Guilt implies,   "I have made a mistake".
Shame implies,   "I am the mistake".

Therapy is obviously very helpful for understanding the roots of toxic shame and for learning the truths about ourselves *(for more on how unaddressed shame contributes to potentially negative outcomes after conflict, see Chapter 11, p.193).*

WHAT HELPS US
"Encourage teachers to be more supportive"

However, there is also a lot we can do in school to support these pupils develop their self-understanding, without necessarily engaging the pupil in therapy. We need to communicate to them that we are all a combination of parts. Parts that we like and are proud of. Parts that we'd rather no-one saw or noticed. The healthy way forward is to learn to view ourselves as integrated brings – a mixture, rather than as being 'all good' or 'all bad'. When we realise that we are in fact a sum of parts, we can then start to take control over the influence of these differing parts. We can explain this to our pupils, and discuss the fact that whilst we might not be able to get rid of certain parts completely, we can definitely choose how much significance a specific part can have in our lives, as well as seeing if we can put it to more constructive use. We can also explain how we can choose which parts we allow to come into the foreground, in the 'here and now', for others to see, and which parts we might want to leave hidden in the background *(and see Bombèr 2007, pp.178-80).*

Creating 'parts pictures'

To introduce this concept to pupils, their key adult can initiate work on 'parts pictures' over a number of months in private 1:1 time.

PRIMARY PHASE

- Find a large roll of paper
- Draw around the pupil
- Paint in his skin tone, hair and clothes … to match his true colours
- Find his flags of origin and paint these on the top of the paper
- Use Post-it notes to describe the parts that make him who he is *(see below)*
- Spread these Post-it notes out all over the body picture

SECONDARY PHASE

- Find a big sheet of paper – the bigger the better
- Draw a jigsaw design all over it
- Write in descriptors to describe the parts that make the pupil who she is *(see below)*

To identify parts

For both the primary and secondary phase:

a)   Always start with the positives, strengths and 'likes': come up with these parts together (key adult and pupil), giving examples as you do so. You'll need some clear evidence of what you're describing, otherwise these pupils will just think you are talking nonsense. They aren't stupid and will see through any fake or sugar-coated compliments! These pupils are very alert to how they feel about themselves and this is usually quite negative; so we're going to have to work especially hard to make the connections for them so that they believe the positives we identify.

Be real. Be also wary not to flood them with too much 'good stuff', as this may overwhelm them if they are not used to being appreciated (as so many aren't). If they do feel overwhelmed, they may reject what you are attempting to do or may become disturbed in their behaviour. Try and engage in this talk sensitively and at a slow pace, so that they can take it all in. Try two or three parts at a time. Remember that this work is intended to be ongoing over several months and even years!

Ben   patient part, smiley part, sense of humour part, playful part
Lena   kind part, intelligent part, friendly part, having-a-go part

b) Move on to the parts that the pupil would rather hide, is embarrassed about or finds difficult to discuss. To do this, start with your own ideas about you, so that it doesn't feel too threatening and the task can be normalised; we all experience uncomfortable feelings about these parts. Be wary not to share anything too personal about yourself that might burden the pupil. With this in mind, I suggest that we stick to parts that we can describe that are true about ourselves in the school environment.

For example, *"I've got a forgetful part. The other day I had a meeting written down in my diary to attend at lunchtime, and I completely forgot about it! I just went and moved my car and sat down to have my lunch. I was so embarrassed when I realised what I'd done!"*

Try and use real life examples from the pupil's context to introduce discussion at a more personal level about the pupils harder-to-name part.

For example, *"I know you probably would rather forget about the other day as I know you probably feel really embarrassed about it now, but remember when you kicked Martin when you got really cross, when you used your kicking part?"*

Ben   snatching part, unkind part, eating lots part, sad part
Lena   selfish part, critical part, bitchy part, raging part, stealing part

c) Use arrows to indicate which parts the pupil wants to increase
d) Use arrows to indicate which parts the pupil wants to decrease
e) After doing this exercise, which can be added to over time, the key adult can start to use the language of parts in all her interactions with the pupil.

Jake to Ben

"I can see you're using your snatching part right now. Where's your patient part?"

Ann to Lena

"I can see you're using your bitchy part right now.   Where's your kind part?"

This will start up a dialogue with the pupil, and serves the purpose of helping them keep in mind everything that makes them who they are, rather than allowing the pupil to think that they are 'all bad': in other words as I've outlined above, 'the mistake'. If we persist in doing this, we will be supporting the pupil to continue thinking – using the reflective part of their higher brain – in stressful situations, rather than allowing them to tip into toxic shame which would then mean they might retreat into their habitual fight/flight/freeze responses originating from the brain stem, where there is no reflective capacity.

We will be supporting these pupils to realise that there are many parts that make them who they are. So the pupil will become increasingly aware that he does have choices, when before he is likely to have believed that this was *"Just what I'm like"* – confirmed by the many negative messages they've heard or interpreted from the punitive actions of other significant people in their lives, who devalued them. So many times we have spoken about choices to pupils in our schools, but haven't realised the way that these particular pupils might have viewed themelves in the first place. It is so, so important that we remind ourselves of pupils' starting points before making interventions.

The longer we can support these pupils to continue thinking or reflecting, the more capacity we are building for the possibility of change. These pupils are then freed up to make wiser, healthier and more appropriate choices.

f)   The class teacher/form tutor starts to use the language of parts in all of his/their interactions with this pupil. Being explicit about what we can see is helpful and builds self-awareness.

Jake to Ben

"Ben, I can see you are using your 'playful part' right now. You could have chosen to sit on your own, but you are joining in having lots of fun with Sarah and Simon".

Ann to Lena

"Lena, I can see you are using your 'having a go' part. This experiment is tricky, but you're really putting some effort into getting it working".

We can all think through the above process for ourselves. The more self-aware we are, the more helpful we can be to the pupils with whom we work.

Self reflection

What parts make you who you are?

Create a parts picture for yourself privately in a journal.

Scaling

As these pupils often have very over-the-top responses to low level stressors, it's important to start introducing them to the fact that their alarm systems might well be going off inappropriately within the school context. Let's notice how often our pupils present with behaviours that are fuelled by their fear and panic. We need to acknowledge with them that their alarm system served them well in their home context, enabling them to survive often very challenging and painful circumstances; but that different responses can be used at school because the circumstances of school are different. The school is operating as a relatively secure system. We need to be explicit about this, otherwise our pupils will continue to react with exaggerated responses, *as if* they need to defend themselves again in the school context as well.

In the first instance, we need to talk about what's happening in a matter-of-fact way: for example, to Ben: *"You are probably feeling all wobbly inside because you are thinking something terrible might happen. You are safe and secure here, Ben"*, or to Lena: *"You are probably feeling really stressed right now because you are thinking something terrible might happen. I can assure you that you are safe and secure here"*. Our next step will be to suggest that people sometimes misinterpret each other or what is going on, that there are lots of opportunities for miscommunication in school, and that our job is to help interpret other people's motives and intentions so that Ben and Lena can gradually relax and be open to safe, new experiences.

> WHAT HELPS US ...
> "Extra-curricular activities help me find my talents and what I enjoy doing"

It is very helpful to set up what we can call 'stressometers' with these pupils, so that we can scale their responses in relation to different contexts *(see Chapter 11, p.187)*.

We need to engage our pupils in a dialogue about how they might have interpreted a particular event. More often than not they will make wrong assumptions about another person's intentions towards them. They will therefore need us to provide translation as soon as possible, as in the following examples. Suggest that together, you can start to think up some *other* possibilities of what might be going on when their stress is triggered. I always think it's helpful to think up at least five possibilities, and using the fingers on your hand can be a visual reminder of these *(see the 'hand of options', Chaper 11, p.186)*. For example:

PRIMARY PHASE

Someone brushed past Ben in the corridor outside his classroom. He threw his bag down and laid into the culprit. This was a stress response of 10, as rated by Ben. Really it only necessitated a stress response of 2-3. A 10 suggests panic – that serious danger is imminent. Ask Ben what he thinks the motive of the other pupil might have been, or suggest what you imagine it might have been. Feel free to over-exaggerate! (for example, "Oh I get it – you reckon that person was probably walking down the corridor scheming how to ruin your day!"). A little humour can diffuse anxiety.

A 2-3 suggests the following possibilities – that maybe the other pupil was just not looking where he was going as he was busy chatting; that maybe the other pupil has spatial difficulties; that maybe the other pupil was distracted looking at his friend's book ... and so on.

SECONDARY PHASE

In the corridor, someone looked directly at Lena and then smiled. She started yelling at him saying, "What are you looking at?" She said she was livid and gave a stress response of 8. Really this only required a stress response of 1-2. An 8 suggests panic – that serious danger is imminent.

Ask Lena what she thinks the motive of the other person might have been or suggest what you reckon. Feel free to over-exaggerate! (for example, "Oh, I get it, you thought that he was out to get you, that maybe he was even planning on attacking you!"). A little humour can diffuse anxiety. A 1-2 suggests the following possibilities – that maybe the other pupil wasn't focussing on her at all but someone behind her: that maybe the other pupil thought he recognised her from somewhere: that maybe he thought she was good looking and he wanted to acknowledge this: that maybe he had seen her around, thought she looked friendly and wanted to be her friend, that maybe he has his own social difficulties ... and so on.

Self reflection ...

What type of interactions/events would require a panic response?
How do you respond emotionally, mentally and physically in a panic situation?
What would help you develop your own capacity to handle genuine panic situations?

When a pupil remains dysregulated

If you think that the pupil is too dysregulated to engage in any of the above activities at a particular moment, you might want to consider using the following suggestions. They have proved helpful for supporting the pupil back into the right state to re-engage their reflective capacity.

✔ *Safe space*

Spend time together (or in close proximity) in another boundaried space that has been set aside for longer periods of calm time than the classroom can provide. Set up an area in a corner, a tent or a small room allocated for this purpose. Fill it with multi-sensory items that facilitate calm. Think through appropriate lighting, colours, temperature and smell. Spend some time in here. Ten to twenty minutes can usually be sufficient to bring a pupil back to a place of calm or of being regulated.

✔ *Energy*

Notice which part of the pupil's body seems to be expressing their dysregulated state. Think up something else the pupil can do instead with that same part of the body, within clear, set boundaries. For example:

kicking	instead, go for a short sprint
*spitting/talking lo*ts	instead, blow some bubbles
fidgety	instead, pound some clay

Stress responses don't need to interfere with life at school. Pupils can learn to manage their stress well. However, this isn't something that they can learn alone. Getting alongside pupils like this will support them for life.

In fact, if pupils learn these skills in the presence of their key adult, the benefits are considerable. The lessons learned in this area of development are a real gift. How rewarding for the key adult to know that perseverance with these skills will benefit the pupil not only in school but will set them up for the rest of their lives, as *life is stressful*. What greater gift could we possibly pass on to a pupil than what to do to manage stress?

Finally ...

FOR BEN

Jake notices Ben is becoming wobbly. Jake uses commentary to feed this back to him. He suggests that Ben could use his chewelry bracelet to chew on, and sends him over to collect the gym ball to sit on at his desk.

FOR LENA

Ann notices Lena's responses and can see she's becoming dysregulated. "Lena, I can see you're feeling a bit stressed at the moment, as you've asked to go to the toilet a few times. Let's pick one of your calm box activities. How about we put some lavender oil on our hankies and breathe in the scent together for a few minutes".

Chapter 7

Out and about
Playtimes and break times

There are three key areas of social intelligence: the art of relating: the capacity to negotiate, resolve, and be a greater team player: the capacity for compassion and concern.

(Sunderland 2006, p.219)

PRIMARY PHASE

The class teacher tells everyone it's playtime. Everyone rushes outside, running onto the playground and field. Ben darts about madly, unsure of what to do. Within ten minutes he's being escorted to a chair outside the Headteacher's office where he's told to sit until lessons begin. He kicks the leg of the chair and groans.

SECONDARY PHASE

Time for break. Lena goes off to the canteen to buy a snack and then wanders over to the Inclusion Department area to see what's going on there. The door is shut with a notice on it saying 'Closed'. She hovers about in the corridors and gets picked up by a senior manager, who shouts at her for being indoors.

She sulks off outside, gets irritated by some girls staring
at her and slaps one of them in the face.

Pupils who have experienced relational trauma and loss are usually at a very different developmental stage to that of their peers.

> It is not unusual for children living in substitute care to be emotionally and socially much less mature than their peer group. This can be hidden behind pseudo-maturity as the children try and manage by themselves.
>
> (*in* Golding et al, 2006, p.339)

In this chapter, we are going to consider what we need to have in place to support our pupils at break times. Firstly, I will explore why there might be a need for a special kind of support. Then we will unpack a range of strategies that have proved helpful, and I will look at varying the levels of supervision and structure which may be appropriate for many of these pupils. Finally, we will consider the implications for Ben and Lena, our two case pupils who we're following throughout this book.

Break times are key times for vulnerable pupils, because they are usually unstructured times demanding a high level of skill in both organisation and relating. As we saw in the previous chapter, many of our pupils are already dysregulated, and so can present with exaggerated responses to low level stressors or input, becoming –

● too excited   ● too rough   ● too angry   ● too stressed

So why is it that in many of our schools at the moment, these times seem to be such a low priority? We often under-staff break times, and frequently employ people who may not have much interest and very rarely any specialist training in working with the pupils whose level of emotional development presents additional needs. In addition, many staff supervise standing at a distance, observing, perhaps believing that their only role is to ensure that health and safety expectations are being adhered to. Human CCTV doesn't really provide sufficient care; if staff simply record incidents in log books, we are missing the opportunity to engage creatively in an educative task that could be so meaningful for these pupils.

Let's intervene in a way that is constructive and purposeful. We need staff who are keen and willing to actively engage in the task of relationship - as a matter of urgency. We really can't afford to settle for less than this.

Unfortunately though, as things stand in many schools at the moment, the pupils who engage in immature, silly or risky behaviours are viewed as a nuisance. Situations can quickly escalate, and the pupils are all too frequently excluded from break times. What should be happening is that the pupil is noticed by staff, attended and responded to in a way that meets their developmental needs – for their sensory input to be regulated, and for support to be given to raise their self-awareness and awareness of others. This is necessary so that

> WHAT HELPS US ...
> "People to have people to play with. Shorter lunchtimes"

these pupils can be in a position to make choices that are both healthy and appropriate for specific purposes and contexts. We all learn how to do this through the eyes and mind of someone else. It really isn't a solitary task, despite many education staff relinquishing the responsibility in the past, believing it would be OK to leave it to the vulnerable pupils to work out themselves – alone. Neuroscience has shown us this work needs to be done in the context of relationship.

Pupils like Ben and Lena haven't developed the social intelligence necessary for negotiating how to relate with their peers during break times, and often end up excluded from break times because of the kind of challenging behaviour that ensues from their developmental vulnerability. This hardly seems fair. We have already identified that these vulnerabilities come about as a result of their traumatic early childhood experiences. So it makes perfect sense to view them as pupils with additional needs in this area – needing support – not exclusion!

Just as academic expectations and tasks are differentiated, we must differentiate social expectations and tasks as well. For example, a white stick is necessary to support a pupil who is blind, so that she has increased mobility. Similarly, a pupil with developmental vulnerability needs a relationship with a key adult to support her to have increased *sociability*. Break times could actually offer these pupils educative opportunities for developing social intelligence, but instead they are often simply used to communicate loud and clear that the adults are 'in control'. Differentiation is needed both inside and outside the classroom. This is fair.

WHAT WE NEED …
"Playground buddy activities"
Assistant Head, Primary school

As you can no doubt see, I really want us to challenge our existing ways of 'doing school'. We don't have to continue relating to our pupils like this. I'm sure you'll agree that maintaining an authoritarian approach or exclusion (rather than using supportive practices) often leads to further disturbance and lower self-esteem. If what we were doing already worked effectively, there would be no reason for us to challenge our existing practice; but the exclusion statistics clearly indicate that it doesn't.

I strongly recommend that all schools view break times as as important as literacy, numeracy and science lessons. Why shouldn't break times be viewed as an essential part of the curriculum? Let's get involved! Let's reach out to touch and not stand around as mere onlookers. Let's facilitate meaningful relationships. Let's initiate dialogue, activities, games and clubs.

Staff may be concerned that working differently may compromise their own need for a break. This doesn't need to be the case. Why can't we stagger our breaks? In fact, why does the whole school have to have the same break times? It doesn't have to stay like this. Let's engage in a different way of being in school together.

Supervision

Let's release appropriate staff to be fully present and fully engaged in break times, just as we'd expect to do at any other point of the school day. Let's get our break and lunchtime staff trained up to fully engage with these pupils, as some pioneering schools are already doing. We could even consider employing those with early years experience and youth work training to undertake this very important task. Some schools have senior management on duty at these times in regular, familiar spaces. These schools are clearly thinking about who is going to be around and the skill-mix they will bring.

Let's provide the increased level of structure and supervision that is so essential when working with pupils who come from traumatic backgrounds, rather than waiting for them to create negative situations in which we then have to involve ourselves in what can become a rapidly worsening cycle. We will often need to relate to these pupils as much younger than they actually are chronologically, providing activities that are appropriate for their developmental stage. The best practice I've observed in both primary and secondary settings is when support staff engage in differentiated practice, employing varying degrees of structure and supervision as deemed necessary.

Obviously some pupils might initially resist our new ways of engaging with them, not understanding that they are not ready yet for certain tasks or experiences. This is a natural response, of course, as the pupil may feel a sense of shame or an initial loss of control. They

> **WHAT WE NEED …**
> *"All staff in schools trained to have a better understanding of pupil's needs"*
> Outreach teacher

may not always understand our motives and intentions. Pupils like Ben and Lena may think we are just trying to cause them harm like other adults might have done in the past. So sensitive engagement needs to be employed, whereby we attempt to do all we can to support the pupil to continue to feel included. We must press on, using both explicit communication and empathy, constantly communicating that we are rooting for them and want them to practise the skills necessary so that they can be strong in this area, helping them to generate a sense of success.

> When you need to provide the external control, it is important that you do this with a high level of empathy. The additional supervision and structure is not a punishment because of bad behaviour. Rather it is a support, because the child is not yet ready to manage successfully without the structure and supervision you are providing.   (Golding 2008, p.183)

I have known of Inclusion Departments closing at break times. This seems absurd! Break and lunchtimes are the *key times of day* that Inclusion Departments should be at their busiest. These safe bases/safe havens need to welcome unconditional access: this is the key function that they serve.

To continue the example of the comparison between physical disability and developmental vulnerability further, if a pupil who was blind started to misuse her stick, we wouldn't remove it from her but get alongside to support her to use it differently. Likewise, we can't remove relational support, structure and supervision because of inappropriate behaviours from pupils with developmental vulnerability, but rather, we need to *increase* our support at these times. If any difficulties or conflicts are encountered during these times, they need to be worked with, and used as educative opportunities: certainly not avoided.

Vulnerable pupils can learn some of the most important and valuable skills necessary to relationship through their interactions with attuned and empathic key adults during their break times. So let's not overlook this significant window of opportunity that occurs each and every school day.

Structured activities

Let's be open-minded as to how we structure and facilitate break times. We don't have to restrict our contribution to this time to merely leaving out hoops and balls in the hope that pupils will know what to do with them! How about a key adult and a pupil –

BUILDING A DEN TOGETHER **playing a board game together at a picnic table** GARDENING TOGETHER **painting together** **MAKING A NEWSPAPER TOWER TOGETHER** making a bridge together MAKING A BUG'S HOME TOGETHER acting out a play together **talking together** setting up a chess club together PLAYING BADMINTON TOGETHER SETTING UP AN OBSTACLE COURSE TOGETHER **playing parachute games together** facilitating skateboard tricks together SETTING UP A PHILOSOPHY CLUB TOGETHER going for a run together **PLAYING FOOTBALL TOGETHER**

Please note that in all these examples the fact that we are 'together' is the most significant element. These pupils need to practice relationship and to learn what to do in their 'free time'. So it really isn't helpful for the pupil to only engage in solitary activities at these times such as playing on their play station, being on a computer or watching a video. Yes, these activities might well keep them quiet - but this shouldn't be the aim of a break time! I'd like to strongly recommend that break times become the time for relationships to be facilitated and for healthy relating to be learned 'on the job'.

WHAT HELPS US ...
"Help to run our own
cool clubs"

These structured activities must first be engaged with in the context of a relationship between the key adult and pupil and then extended out to include other pupils – not the other way round! Let's mirror the natural order of development, which starts with a child having close proximity with one adult first, followed by siblings/peers joining that adult and pupil. Start small, gradually increasing the numbers of others, as appropriate.

Let's look out for examples of good role models for this kind of relating, and learn from them. One I've come across is a primary Headteacher who goes out every lunch time to play football with his pupils. His presence and availability has a powerful, positive impact on both the children and staff in the school, which has a high proportion of vulnerable pupils. Other staff took the initiative of setting up a well-structured football training programme using two of their mentors for each small group of vulnerable pupils.

Ideally, we all need to be creating opportunities for our vulnerable pupils to develop meaningful relationships with adults in which dependency can be practiced *(as discussed in Chapter 4, Practising Dependency)*. There is really no reason why any pupil should be isolated or bombing around aimlessly, engaging in anti-social behaviour. Let's not waste a moment to get involved.

Playground buddies, detached play/youth workers, time to talk

Good practice also includes identifying sensible peers or older pupils to get alongside vulnerable students, looking out for the isolated, the fragile, and the anti-social ones especially. These are often known as playground buddies or their 'circle of friends' (circle-time.co.uk, inclusive-solutions.com/circleoffriends.asp). Peers can provide ideas, guidance and support through talking and facilitating different activities. They can also signpost pupils to key adults and structured clubs within the school premises. Detached play and youth workers can also be used creatively to get alongside vulnerable pupils in a non-threatening way, having a bank of games and interventions at their disposal. There are some schools which have been very creative in their responses to difficulties by actually providing trained school counsellors and therapists at break times for drop-in sessions, for example, Place2Be – 'Place To Talk'. These sessions provide pupils with the opportunity to learn ways to manage both difference and conflict out and about within the school community.

> WHAT WE NEED …
> *"Gardening clubs/chicken keeping to give children incentives and an interest"*
> Headteacher, primary school

Finally …

So in view of the examples given at the beginning of this chapter and my recommendations, I'm going to outline a couple of alternatives for both Ben and Lena for the difficulties described on p.135.

IDEA (1) FOR BEN

When the lesson finishes, Ben's key adult Jake goes to collect him to escort him out to the playground. He lets Ben know that he has set up some games for them to play on the picnic table near the field. He can see that Ben's got loads of energy today, and so he challenges him to run as fast as he can to meet him there! Other pupils are interested too as Sir has some great games ready. He plays one of the games with Ben first, and then, when he thinks Ben is ready, Jake invites Ben to invite another pupil in to play too. Over the weeks the sequence stays the same, gradually building up to games which involve 4-6 others.

IDEA (2) FOR BEN

When the lesson finishes, Ben leaves the classroom and heads straight to the wild area to meet his key adult Jake, who is running a gardening club for four vulnerable pupils. Jake is there waiting for him and smiling. "Hi there Ben, today we've got some planting to do. Do you want to get a bucket and trowel from over there?"

IDEA (1) FOR LENA

After Lena has been to the canteen she goes along to the Inclusion Department. There are staff around available and smiling, ready to welcome pupils as they arrive. Lena's key adult Ann welcomes her and asks her how her day has been so far. She then makes Lena a hot chocolate and listens whilst Lena talks about her weekend. A couple of other girls are nearby, and so Miss draws them into the conversation. Knowing they love fashion, she collects some magazines and encourages them to pick their favourite clothes. "Imagine you had £100. What would you girls buy from this lot then?"

IDEA (2) FOR LENA

As soon as Lena has been to the canteen she goes to meet her key adult Ann on the field, as they are running a hockey club together. Ann has spent quality time with Lena getting to know her and knows that Lena loves hockey. Ann has wanted to encourage this interest and Lena's strength in this area by facilitating additional time for the game. "Hi there Lena! Right, we've got five members present today, so let's get our hockey skills practice underway".

These are just some quick ideas. If you let your imagination flow, the possibilities are endless! Let's invest quality time into these key times during the school day. Yes, these pupils need attention. If they receive it in healthy, constructive ways (rather than negatively), the benefits both to them individually and to the wider school community are immeasurable.

Chapter 8

Where am I?
Out of the ordinary

Change has deep rooted meanings. This may be related to feelings of being out of control, and extreme insecurity.

(Peake. A (2006) in Golding (Ed) et al, p.116)

PRIMARY PHASE

Ben discovers that now there won't be any time today to finish making his Lego model, the Deputy Head wants to come and talk to the class about the class' behaviour on the school trip. Ben kicks the table and sulks.

SECONDARY PHASE

Lena arrives in the studio to discover that her favourite art teacher is off sick and a supply teacher is taking her place.

As I discussed in Chapter 5, 'shift' is difficult for pupils like Ben and Lena. Shift is involved when a transition of some kind is required – either on a minor scale such as moving from a classroom to assembly, or on a more significant level, such as moving schools. There are transitions that are known and can be prepared for in some way, and there are transitions that come as a surprise, where preparation would not have been possible. Shift is usually more difficult and anxiety-provoking if the changes aren't expected or prepared for; in other words, they are 'out of the ordinary' events, such as those described in the above examples for Ben and Lena.

Other examples might include:

In primary:
- indoor play as its raining
- not going swimming because the bus broke down
- best friend is off school sick
- another room needs to be used as the heating is not working properly
- assembly has been moved to an earlier time

In secondary:
- key adult needs to go to an emergency meeting
- the plumbers are in today due to problems with the toilets
- there is a professionals meeting on today in the Inclusion Department as no other rooms were available
- the school nurse has arrived and has space to see our pupil today
- the pupils are split into groups for performing arts today when usually they all stay together

Some of these transitions might not seem of much importance to us as education staff; but for pupils like Ben and Lena, they might represent another experience of heightened anxiety or even panic in some cases.

Why? Because 'out of the ordinary' events trigger alarm for these pupils, because of what has happened to them and around them in the past. What we then see is them engaging in responses adapted to survival (fight/flight/freeze) which they might have used in the past, or are still using in other contexts right now. These responses may include the pupil attempting to regain control in some way. So it's essential that we intervene as soon as we are able *to pre-empt* this response kicking into action to its fullest extent. We will need to provide co-regulation, so that these pupils' responses are regulated and can subside to be replaced by the capacity for calm and reflection. As I pointed out in Chapter 6, we need to remember that in the school context, we need to be doing all we can to keep anxiety levels to a minimum so that pupils can be in a position to settle – to settle to learn.

In this chapter I will look at what we need to do so that we can manage situations when things happen that are out of our control, those times when we just don't have the opportunity to prepare our pupil as well as we might want to. I'll discuss the importance of creating what I call 'disappointment rituals' for our pupils. And finally, I'll consider the implications for Ben and Lena, the two case pupils who we're following throughout this book.

WHAT WE NEED …

"Greater understanding by all staff regarding pupils and their attachment styles and needs"

Head of Year, secondary school

Managing disappointment

Whenever we can, let's give a warning about a forthcoming change, so that we can prepare our pupils as early as possible. Ideally, let them know when you know. Pupils who have had early experiences of the need to be hyper-vigilant will need some time to deal with whatever is 'out of the ordinary', so let's help them learn to regulate their responses through adult support.

So, rather than casually mentioning the change in passing, give the pupil your full attention. Expect the pupil to be disappointed; this is very likely response, even if the change seems positive, exciting or interesting. It's the fact that it wasn't expected that is disappointing. This disappointment may manifest itself in all manner of ways, for example:

- slumping in their chair
- having a full-blown tantrum
- crying
- pulling out their hair
- feeling sick
- withdrawal

This is what we need to work with and address, rather than attempting to deflect the pupil away from difficult feelings by changing the topic or jollying them along, which is often a natural instinct when we observe a pupil upset or distressed. Instead we need to engage in a response that conveys that we are joining with the pupil in acknowledging their disappointment. This is far more helpful.

We may be able to foresee when 'the familiar' is likely to be back in place again. For example, we may know from checking the board in the staffroom that this is just for a brief time (for the pupil disappointed about having to move rooms) or maybe we heard the weather forecast on the way to school predicting sun later! (for the pupil disappointed by wet play). If we do have a sense of when things will return to normal, then let the pupil know the relevant time-scale. If we don't have an idea of what's going to happen, then let's share our wonderings about what might be happening with our pupils. It's the 'wondering aloud' that will help these pupils process and adapt to change.

Don't under-estimate how much pupils who have experienced relational trauma will learn by joining in with us as we do our own processing of change. In their short lives to date, these pupils may not have had anyone before who has engaged them in this type of process. They may not have had anyone who has helped them make sense of change. Maybe they haven't had any experience of having an adult alongside them who has *themselves* managed to tolerate the anxiety inherent in any change; these adults will have communicated to our pupils that anxiety is the only option possible. These pupils desperately need role models – those who will be explicit and will help them in this very necessary relational capacity. Tolerating uncertainty is often unbearable for many of these pupils, so what better gift could we give them than a human bridge at these times, to show that uncertainty can in fact be borne, and borne well.

> WHAT WE NEED …
> *"To stay in frequent communication with one another about specific students/situations"*
> Key adult, secondary school

I will now outline some possibilities for handling disappointment.

DISAPPOINTMENT RITUALS

We forget that we have developed our own ways of managing disappointment. It might be worth spending a moment reflecting on how you cope yourself and how you learnt to do this. One of my key ways is to breathe and to remind myself that it will all be OK in the end, that I have managed disappointments before and I have always survived! I say to myself, *"Why wouldn't I survive this time?"* This kind of self-talk is helpful to me. I'm sure we all have different ways of coping with disappointments large and small, and they are all valuable.

Why do we assume that these pupils will know how to manage disappointment? They often don't know what to do with their powerful feelings, so they are really going to need our support at these times. There are four steps to providing support which I recommend following in the same order each time, so that the pupil's brain becomes familiar with the process. Repetition supports these pupils to adapt (Perry 2011).

STEP 1 ▶ ACKNOWLEDGE WITH THE PUPIL
THAT HE IS DISAPPOINTED

Let your voice convey this in an empathic manner. *"You are really disappointed that we can't go outside as usual for playtime"*. If the pupil is engaging in a behaviour that might communicate their disappointment rather than verbalising it (for example, flouncing about, pouting their lips, withdrawing …), let them know you've noticed. *"You are letting me know you are* so *disappointed"*. You may notice that the more you do this, when you or someone else notices and makes a connection in this way, inappropriate behaviours usually decrease. This is because the pupil then feels 'heard', and so it becomes less important for him to communicate his feelings again through his behaviour.

STEP 2 ▶ STATE WHAT IS HAPPENING NOW INSTEAD

"We have to stay indoors for break time today", said with a neutral tone, an empathic look and friendly eyes.

STEP 3 ▶ 'TRANSLATE' THE POSSIBLE MOTIVES/REASONS
BEHIND WHY SOMETHING HAS CHANGED

If we don't know exactly what's going on, let's have a go at wondering why. *"I know you're probably thinking the grown-ups are just being mean and spoiling your fun, but the only reason we can't let everyone outside right now is because rain makes everything very slippery and cold. So we're more likely to have some accidents and pupils may get ill. Our job in school is to keep pupils safe. We take safety very seriously"*.

Ensure you pay attention to the pupil's *own* interpretations of the underlying motives/reasons. As we've seen, pupils who have experienced relational trauma often make wrong assumptions, and these need to be both acknowledged and then gently challenged by offering another alternative. Most of the time, they genuinely do not understand why something has been stopped or changed or not allowed. Most of the time, they will assume that our intentions are to cause them harm/discomfort. Given their backgrounds, why should they assume otherwise? If we don't pay attention to how they may be mis-reading the situation there is lot of opportunity for conflict. The key adult needs to work very hard to hold onto the fact that there is probably a significant misunderstanding going on: bearing this in mind, we can recognise that any rejecting behaviours must not be taken personally.

STEP 4 ▶ FINALLY, EXPLORE THE POSITIVES

Sometimes change can be a good thing. The key adult can now have a go at thinking up some possible positives about the situation in hand. *"Do you know it might be quite fun staying indoors today, as I know there are some new board games that have just arrived. Let's play one and test it out. They look like a lot of fun. Let's go and take a look".* Please notice that looking for positives in the situation should never come before you have spent some time acknowledging the pupil's feelings, especially disappointment. Incidentally, this might be a good moment to use memory cards, as discussed in Chapter 4 *(p.94).*

So in the example with Ben we might:

> **Acknowledge** *"Ben, I can see you are really disappointed, as you were hoping to finish your Lego tower today".*
> **State** *"The Deputy Head wants to come in and talk to everyone about the class trip".*
> **Translate** *"I don't think he had any other time free but now. He has to fit us in round a very busy schedule".*
> **Positives** *"He won't talk for long as he is a very busy man. Let's just hear what he has to say. It might mean*

that we can go on another trip if we let him know that people are really sorry for being silly on the last trip. Showing that we are sorry goes a long way. We can then continue with your Lego tower later. Here is a memory card so that you can hold on. We won't forget your Lego tower".

In the example with Lena, we might:

Acknowledge *"I can see you are so disappointed Lena, that Ms Shields is not here for art. That must have come as a shock".*

State *"Miss Burns is going to now take the lesson at very short notice"*

Translate *'I know you probably think Ms Shields has let you down. I can assure you that she would have rather been here, but she had a fall earlier today and needed to go home to take a rest. I don't know how long she will be before she comes back but she is coming back".*

Positives *"It might be really interesting with Miss Burns as I know she has some amazing drawing activities she's been using with other classes. Let's give it a go and we can then tell Ms Shields about our lesson as soon as she's back, OK?"*

Sensitive care

What is described above is basic sensitive care. Not many of these pupils will have experienced much or any of this in their short lives to date. Not only will this kind of input calm possible outbursts, but we will also communicate empathy, and we know that empathy breeds empathy. So this extra-ordinary event could actually be a fantastic learning opportunity on so many different levels.

Increasing familiarity when the unexpected occurs

In some situations, just having a familiar adult around and available can alleviate our pupils' anxiety or prevent it from escalating. So it might be extremely helpful if the key adult can be freed up to support their key pupil at this unexpected time. Just having a known person nearby is so, so reassuring; that's precisely what we mean when we talk about having a 'secure base' (that is, the person around

WHAT HELPS US …
"My teaching assistant"

whom our anxiety fades). So for example, in the case of the sudden appearance of a supply teacher, the key adult who is familiar with the pupil can reduce the child or young person's anxiety simply by being around more. This is when the provision of flexi-support in our schools is ideal, as I mentioned in my introduction. An alternative might be to direct the pupil back to the person they are most familiar with, as this can also be beneficial. So here this particular pupil could be directed to take their class with their previous class teacher, or to take their work to the special needs room or Inclusion Department where there are familiar staff around.

Increasing familiarity and predictability for these pupils is key to attachment support work in schools. In effect, we are ensuring these pupils experience the safety, security and stability of a 'secure base' – a fundamental requisite in attachment terms. The more these pupils have opportunity to experience this, the more secure they will become. They will then have the opportunity to adapt and recover from previously learned *insecure* ways of relating. What we are working towards is building them up internally, so that our pupils can become more robust in the different contexts they find themselves in, over time.

We want them to eventually internalise their 'secure base' so that they can be freed up to be all that they can be and not preoccupied with matters that hinder their engagement or progress in the learning process. To be able to internalise this, these pupils will need plenty of opportunity to experience the 'secure base' first hand, in tangible real-world ways.

Chapter 9

I'm starving!
Lunchtime

A 'maltreated' digestive system may carry as many traumatic memory patterns as the developing brain: little wonder that many maltreated children express their feelings through their stomachs, one way or another!

(Archer et al 2006, p.116)

PRIMARY PHASE

Ben rushes to the front of the dinner queue, pushing others out of the way. Once he's gobbled his lunch he lines up again for seconds of pudding.

SECONDARY PHASE

Lena wanders about out on the field hanging out with her friends. Before she realises it's time for afternoon lessons again. She has forgotten to eat.

Many pupils who have experienced relationship trauma and loss, especially neglect, may have difficulties of some kind in their relationship to food. Food is a primary, basic need for each one of us. We need food to live. If this basic need hasn't been attended to appropriately in the pupil's early home life, then all kinds of distorted associations and meanings can become attached to food.

This can then get acted out in a wide variety of ways.

It is worth pointing out that even when a pupil is now experiencing 'good enough' care in their homes, for example having moved into foster care or adoption, he or she may continue acting 'as if' certain neglectful environments are still in place, even when they're not. It takes the body a long time to process the change of circumstances and for the brain to re-wire in its interpretation of what's now going on. With this in mind we cannot afford to sit back and just hope they 'work it out' for themselves. We are going to have to get actively involved to support them to make sense of food in the 'here and now' of the school context.

So a pupil may:

- Not eat much
- Rush their food
- Be hyper-alert to what's going on around them in the background
- Forget to eat
- Gorge food
- Hoard food
- Steal food
- Hide food
- Push to the front to get food first
- Be very fussy about food
- Seem addicted to carbohydrates and sugary foods

This list is not exhaustive but you get the idea! Many of these strategies may have served our pupils well in the past or serve them well in another context, but they are not helpful in the school context. Or these may be strategies that have started up recently as a response to now being 'in the land of plenty' – just in case there isn't any food around again later.

Secondly, there is also symbolic meaning associated to food for these pupils, about being nourished (or not).   It therefore makes sense that some might want to fill themselves up, because of the 'emptiness' or 'ache' that they may feel inside both emotionally and physically.

WHAT HELPS US ...
"I go to breakfast club"

Thirdly, it is important to remember that many of our pupils may not have had much or any experience of sitting around a table together with their family, enjoying the experience of eating in a safe, relaxed context. So many will find the intimacy of sitting together at tables quite unfamiliar and possibly anxiety-provoking.   Many will not have experienced the *routine* of eating meals in a regulated manner – both in terms of food content (what they were given) and timings.   So it's not surprising that they aren't familiar with or drawn to the colourful variety of foods from different food groups, but maybe fixated on foods full of carbohydrates and sugars.   Nor should we be surprised that many pupils can go for hours without eating or even forgetting to eat, either through not having experienced eating routines, or having blocked out their hunger (another adaptive strategy).

In the school context we need to be prepared that we may be shocked occasionally by some of what we observe; for example, coming across the pupil who is gorging themselves or hoarding food away.   However, we must be careful not to merely view them as the 'greedy pupil', and tell them off which we might be tempted to do.   Use the 'lens' of insecure attachment to interpret what this behaviour might be communicating – (as I've done above) and see what you think may be happening in the context of that pupil's life.   As a final note, we also need to keep an eye out for the pupils who may not eat much or forget to eat, as they can easily get lost in the midst of a busy school context.

With this in mind, it's so important not to restrict food as a consequence for misbehaviour, to use food as a reward of any kind, or to impose long delays before

WHAT HELPS US ...
"... not feeling judged
by students and
teachers"

being able to eat. Food should always be given to vulnerable pupils with no strings attached. Meals should be given at regular intervals, so that the pupil can have opportunity to relax into allowing this basic need to be met, without having to resort to maladaptive responses.

It is also important that we provide additional support around anything to do with food and mealtimes. Often key staff are not even aware of what goes on at lunchtime. We need to encourage staff to be present from time to time, carrying out observations, so that we know how our key pupils relate to food. Let's notice the specific patterns that emerge and intervene accordingly. Let's remember the real range of difficulties that we might observe as we support vulnerable pupils in the school context. We will also need to work closely in partnership with home on this important area. These discussions need to be sensitively handled. Let's encourage parents/carers and social workers to give as much background history as possible in regards to food matters. Then we can attempt to make sense of what is going on in the 'here and now' of school.

In this chapter we will think through how we can best support these pupils in this area. We can start by coming alongside them to teach them two facts and two skills.

Fact 1	That it is important to eat
Fact 2	That there is enough food to go round in school
Skill 1	How to know what enough means?
Skill 2	How to eat?

Finally, we will consider the implications of this work for our two case pupils Ben and Lena, who we're following throughout this book.

Being alongside

It is not appropriate to just leave these pupils to try and figure all the issues associated with food, eating, mealtimes or eating with other people on their own. In fact, some of our pupils who have experienced developmental trauma, loss and unmet needs with regard to being nourished may actually draw a lot of attention to the difficulties they have in this area, by engaging in maladaptive responses when food is around. Regrettably, left unaddressed, the pupil's behaviour can lead to misunderstandings in the school context, even disciplinary action. Leaving these pupils unsupported around food and eating issues could also leave them at risk of other eating-related mental health difficulties, such as anorexia, bulimia and so on.

So a straightforward way to actively become involved might be to actually go into lunch with the pupil you are supporting. It is not enough to merely explain the facts above. We will need to support our pupils by facilitating opportunities for them to make the necessary connections by checking out the evidence of what we are trying to communicate. For example, don't just tell the pupil that there is enough food to go round. Why should he believe you? Where's the evidence? How do you know? In all of this work, remember to keep bringing that which is usually left unsaid out into the open. Be explicit.

One mentor, for example got alongside a pupil who kept pushing to the front of the dinner queue by going into dinner with him. She let him know that she was aware it was a big ask to expect him to trust there would be enough food to go round. She went to the front too at the beginning of this particular support phase. Then, she gently suggested having a go at being second, then fifth, then tenth ... you get the idea! By the end of the term they were both testing out whether there was in fact enough food to go round by standing last in the queue. We cannot assume anything! Many of our pupils will need us to get alongside to explore these issues together:

FACT 1 ▸   THAT IT IS IMPORTANT TO EAT AT REGULAR INTERVALS

Many of our pupils may have learned to tune out their need to eat, because of repeatedly experiencing the pain and discomfort of living somewhere where there wasn't anything to eat, or they were prevented from eating. So we need to stress that they need to eat in order to function well at school and have the energy they need for all the activities during the school day. This needs to be communicated quite early on in the work together with their key adult. If a pupil is not eating much or forgetting to eat, let's arrange to eat with them together for a time. Co-modelling is so, so powerful. We need to support these pupils to get into a routine.

FACT 2 ▸   THAT THERE IS ENOUGH FOOD TO GO ROUND IN SCHOOL

Many deprived children will have had to scrounge, binge or hoard in order to survive. Why would a child with this kind of background trust us when we say there will be more food later, or tomorrow? He is merely re-living what he has lived. Using consistent scripts such as the following can be helpful:

KEY ADULT

"Isn't it good to know that there is enough food?"

"We will always ensure you have dinner before expecting you to go into class in the afternoon".

"Meal times are important to this school".

SKILL 1 ▸   HOW TO KNOW WHAT ENOUGH MEANS?

The majority of pupils with a background of developmental trauma and deprivation have not, by definition, had anyone helping them to self-regulate in general, and specifically around food. We learn self-regulation through relationships with another person, primarily through the process of co-regulation. When we observe how our key pupil is behaving, it's helpful to remind ourselves that he is merely taking whatever he wants rather than being aware of what he needs. Why would he think about what he needs? No-one has thought about him in that way, so why would he do this for himself, or how?

We will need to provide firm guidance and supervision over the quantity and type of food eaten. Be prepared to educate the pupil you are supporting on what a healthy diet looks like. Be aware that many vulnerable pupils will attempt to overload on carbohydrates and sweet foods; this may be because:

*   they were given these foods as their staple diet
*   these foods were used to soothe/quieten the pupil when they were stressed
*   they were left to their own devices to feed themselves with whatever they found or wanted

Now it as if they have become 'addicted' to the buzz they feel after eating carbohydrates and sweet things. However, as we all know, there are considerable health risks with this way of eating, and their behaviour is also affected adversely by this sugar rush. This isn't good news for a pupil trying to get into or maintain a state ready to settle in school.

They will need our support to re-train their bodies so that they can experience more regulated blood sugar levels by eating GI foods which are much healthier alternatives - releasing sugars at a slower rate into the bloodstream and providing energy for longer periods of time. Where there are assessed imbalances, some pupils will actually need to be given regular, healthy snacks throughout the school day in order to support them to settle to learn. Dinner staff will also need guidance and training in not giving out second or thirds, despite pupils saying they are starving! Let's ask them to do this kindly, and to reduce and phase out any additional helpings gradually. Let's be supportive, as the pupil may need to learn how to manage the feelings that may be stirred up by denial.

As an extra note, it may also be important at special times like class parties to boundary how much is enough, especially important when there is already the likelihood of the disruption of a 'special time' causing over-excitement and anxiety. Over the years, I'm sure we have all witnessed pupils filling their plate to overflowing and then being sick! One idea is to prepare your identified pupil before special events. Go through how much would be appropriate. Use a paper plate and mark out quantities together to rehearse this, so they are prepared and have something visual to help them. As I've already mentioned, these pupils will need us to support them to self-regulate, as many won't have had this necessary guidance: nor may they have sufficient body awareness to know when to stop, especially when they are feeling excited.

SKILL 2 ▶ HOW TO EAT?

Many of these pupils don't use culturally appropriate table manners. For example, your key pupil may use other ways of taking in the food other than using a knife and fork. He may rush his food. He may leave his food. How would he know how to 'eat properly' if no-one has taken the time to get alongside and teach him? A key adult needs to model what is appropriate – setting realistic and achievable expectations. Sometimes it will be necessary to have a visual timer available to support pupils to have a sense of the time it takes to eat and allow food to digest. For example, whilst sitting eating your lunch with your identified pupil, you could use a 20/30 minute watertimer to help show him or her how much time they have to eat, to encourage them to slow down. Even if your pupil finishes early, ensure that he waits until the timer is through in order to learn how to engage with meal times, to fully savour his food and to allow for digestion before running about again. This may well be difficult to begin with as it may feel very unfamiliar for him. If it is, it may be helpful to have some ideas up your sleeve of how you could structure the meal time together.

For example:

- ✔ describe the different colours, textures and smells of the foods
- ✔ describe the nutritional value of the foods
- ✔ guess the different food groups
- ✔ chat about the day so far
- ✔ chat about what's happening next
- ✔ play a quiz whilst eating
- ✔ play a word memory game, for example,

  "When I went shopping I brought ..."
- ✔ guess how to cook a particular food
- ✔ think up another way of serving up what you had, for example, all the different ways potatoes can be cooked

It is invaluable to sit with vulnerable pupils and eat together. Set up supported lunches, by protecting a table or two where the Inclusion team can sit with their identified pupils to eat together. Occasionally, rather than having school dinner or packed lunch, prepare food together in the Nurture room, special needs room or Inclusion Department; set the table, make it look attractive and inviting, and enjoy eating and chatting together. This process can teach our pupils a huge range of key skills in a small protected environment.

The Nurture group model of support (nurturegroups.org) is also invaluable for these specific pupils. Nurture is a highly effective form of intervention as evidenced in numerous Ofsted, Estyn and HMIE reports. As quoted on the Nurture Group website,

> It (nurture provision) has been proved to reduce the number of permanent exclusions at both primary and secondary school and can raise both the attainment and aspirations of those most at risk of social exclusion in adult life.
> If all schools were to run on nurturing principles, the long term benefits to children and to society would be immense.   (Marion Bennathan OBE, Life President)

For those who don't eat much or forget to eat, it may be helpful to set them an activity later, such as filling up a paper plate with drawings/colourings/cut out pictures of food showing what they ate. Set them a challenge to see if they can fill up their plate each day! For the older ones, we can also create a food diary.

WHAT WE NEED
"Social/nurture groups"
Headteacher, primary school

Finally ...

WITH BEN

There is a supported lunch table available in the school canteen where Ben can be given some nurturing words and supportive guidance. Pupils such as Ben need to know that there is enough food to go round and that there is no way that you would expect him to go into afternoon lessons without having eaten. Your school treats eating seriously, because you treat safety and well-being seriously.

Ben needs Jake, his key adult, to talk to him about trusting that he can work out how much is enough, and that Jake will help him to practise trusting this, so that Ben doesn't feel he has to keep going up for seconds all the time. Jake can explain that Ben's system (in his body), isn't always giving him the right signals. Jake can be explicit about the way they will work together to re-train it! Ben will need support in limiting his portions and in learning about how to balance his dietary needs.

WITH LENA

There is a lunch club or lunch table set up within the Inclusion Department where Lena can have the experience of being invited to share food straight after her lessons, eating with others in a smaller, more nurturing environment. In addition, Lena can actually take part in the creation of meals together with Ann, her key adult, from time to time, including the planning, preparation, arranging food and clearing up. The key adults encourage pupils to join in with setting the table and so on. Ann talks with Lena about what might make the table more attractive, for example, using a colourful cloth or some fresh flowers. She is mindful of creating an enjoyable and fun experience together so that food and eating start to have some positive associations for Lena.

WHAT HELPS US ...
"To feel safe and relaxed"

As I've been stressing throughout the chapter, it's important in working with our Bens and Lenas that we adults join in at meal times, rather than merely observing. Modelling is so, so powerful. Many of our pupils will have missed out on the whole experience of sharing food and healthy modelling around eating in their early years: let's give them opportunities for second chance learning, so that they can move onwards into greater wholeness.

Chapter 10

Don't look at me like that ...
Body matters – PE and beyond

> When an individual suffers trauma, particularly sexual trauma, their sense of their value, function and dangerousness of his or her body often shifts.
>
> (Ashby, 2011, *"What is trauma?"* nourishing-the-soul.com)

PRIMARY PHASE

Ben draws a lot of attention to himself when getting undressed for swimming by using every kind of material he can to hide himself.

SECONDARY PHASE

Lena has said she doesn't like the way some people check her out when she is changing for PE. She has been found crying in the changing rooms.

The impact of developmental trauma and loss on the body is significant. Bodies have many sensitive receptors and store up memories in both a sensory and cognitive format. In this chapter, we will consider together some of the possible consequences which may be encountered in the school context. Finding it difficult to get changed in front of others is one of these consequences. There can be a number of reasons for this. The pupil may:

- have been put down for the way he looks
- have been laughed at or humiliated in some way about his body
- be or feel different to their peers
- want to fade into the background and not be noticed
- have experience of others not respecting his boundaries in the past.

A further reason could be because the child or young person has experienced some type of sexual abuse. Please note though, that the following behaviours *don't necessarily connect to abuse*, as other contributory factors can affect or stimulate these behaviours as well. However, the strategies for supporting pupils presenting with these behaviours remain the same as they are good practice; so you don't need to be concerned that you may cause harm in some way, by engaging in sensitive care. I will outline some basic principles that should be attended to.

As with other support strategies discussed in this book, we can expect to only need to use them for a time; in other words, they are temporary, flexible measures provided as a reflection of the pupil's developmental need at a given point, rather than permanent fixtures. It's important to note that if difficulties continue for long periods, or if difficulties worsen, that specialist advice should be sought which go beyond the remit of this book. *Please be aware that some pupils may be communicating through their behaviours that they are experiencing harm right now and so this needs to be taken seriously and investigated by professionals outside of the school context.*

In this chapter, we will think through the specifics about why changing might be difficult for some of our pupils. I will then move onto some educative work that we will need to provide for some of the pupils we are working with. I will differentiate between the needs of primary and secondary pupils here. Then, we will move on briefly to other associated areas of difficulty, such as the sex education curriculum, organisational difficulties, motor skills and stability difficulties, and sensory integration difficulties. Finally, we will consider the implications for Ben and Lena, our two case pupils who we are following throughout this book.

Avoiding PE

Some pupils may create delay in changing because they want to avoid PE itself. They may fear it will expose them in terms of their poor sense of self, their negative body image, their physical lack of strength, balance or flexibility, their low self-esteem, their fear of getting hurt. They may go to extraordinary lengths in order to not participate.

PE is in fact one of the riskiest subjects in terms of vulnerability - not just in a cognitive sense, but also physically. However, it's important that we remember that it can also provide some very powerful, therapeutic opportunities for adaptation and recovery as well. Being involved in any kind of activity that requires use of your body – dance, yoga, massage, swimming, running, trampolining, football – can bring a greater sense of self-awareness and awareness of others: can help regulate the pupil, attending to very primal systems that are disorganised lower down in the brain (Perry, 2011): can enhance self-esteem: can build relationship capacity and bring much needed stress relief, as well as all the benefits specific to individual physical activities. But it may take a long time for our pupils to acquire experience of these benefits, so we must be patient.

Why can getting changed be a problem?

The changing rooms can be a difficult context for many pupils. Comparisons, teasing and even bullying are often commonplace. It is not unusual for pupils to be self-conscious, especially when negotiating the adolescent developmental phase. However, there will be some for whom getting changed will be mortifying, beyond ordinary embarrassment. Some pupils may be very self-conscious about their bodies and/or especially aware of another's proximity to their bodies. This can be because of what was listed earlier, as well as –

- weight issues
- disfigurement
- bruises

- lack of confidence
- scars
- low self-esteem

WHAT HELPS US ...
"...having close friends
I trust"

This list is by no means exhaustive. Others may do everything they can to hide themselves, as they simply don't feel at all comfortable getting changed in front of others. There are also the pupils who will do the opposite: strip off, flaunt their bodies, pose and flirt – seeming to have no awareness of the appropriate boundaries that need to be maintained in public. This could be related to the lack of boundaries they have experienced in their early lives, and should not be seen as simply over-confidence. Pupils who have experienced developmental trauma are more vulnerable to putting themselves at risk. Given the increase in social media, for example, if someone takes a photo of their body and circulates it, there can be serious repercussions.*

In all the examples that follow, please note that we need only intervene with additional supportive strategies if and when difficulties arise. For example, just

---

*'Sexting' is a term given to the communication of indecent images of a pupil. Despite the images having probably been solely intended for friends, the pictures can end up anywhere once they have been sent. Once images are sent through texting or social communication sites, they can easily become 'public property'. This obviously puts this pupil at risk. So we need to be educating our pupils about these issues. A very good website that can be used to explore more specific strategies and resources in this area is ceop.police.uk. There are also cyber mentors available for pupils to talk to online at cybermentors.org.uk. The sites advise that pupils should not send any images to anyone which reveal their name or school. They should also be advised to only send images that they wouldn't mind their parents/carers or the whole school seeing.

because the tight education team around this pupil might be aware that the pupil has been abused, it is not necessarily appropriate to engage him or her in the strategies that follow *unless* the young person is actually presenting with difficulties. Please note that this advice is contrary to the rest of the book, whereby I am advocating preventative practice. If we jump in unnecessarily or in an insensitive manner with issues concerning body matters, we may cause unintentional distress. If you are unsure about whether to actively get involved, always check out your intentions with a senior manager at school or with an outside specialist agency associated with the school.

On this specific issue it is best to be aware of and to take the lead from the pupil, because this is an area whereby the pupil really does need to feel in control in order to keep themselves safe physically; within the school context, we are not involved in such intimate matters. In many chapters in this book we are encouraging these pupils to relinquish control, to start practising trusting the adults rather than being in control. In this context however, we need to be skilling our pupils up to be able to be boundaried and to take control themselves.

So we are going to need to be attuned to the individual pupil we are working with, so that we can notice any changes in their behaviour which might indicate their particular need for support. In all the support work advocated within this book, I hope you're noticing that there is one key element – the need to be flexible. My sense is that if we insist on rigidity or 'one size fitting all', we are setting up both ourselves and our pupils for further difficulty.

We need to support the first group of pupils I described earlier (those who are more introverted in their responses) to find discrete, creative ways of changing. It may be that additional garments are allowed under their clothes, so that increased privacy can be honoured. We can, for example, allow pupils to change into shorts at break or lunchtimes, so that they are protected from revealing more than they wish during public changing times. We can think about providing circular towels or robes

WHAT WE NEED …

"Better understanding of pupils'
needs and a willingness to adapt"
Assistant Head, Special school

to support their changing (in other words, clothes can be removed and replaced under the towel or robe). We can also ask the pupil's parents or carers and other key adults to teach the pupil how to change discretely. This is a temporary measure, a stepping stone to support these pupils through a period of difficulty. Over time, it's to be hoped that they will feel increasingly comfortable getting changed alongside their peers.

We are going to have to support the other group of pupils (the ones who are exhibitionist and apparently boundary-less about bodily exposure) more overtly, by introducing them to the idea of self-pride, self-care and developing appropriate boundaries. This will involve educative work, as follows.

EDUCATING

As soon as difficulties are encountered, it will be important to address a few specific areas within boundary education. Both primary and secondary aged pupils need to be able to identify:

a)   *The difference between 'private' and 'public' parts of people's bodies*
One good way of doing this is use body templates to map out visually what is OK to reveal in public and what needs to be kept private – using swim wear as a guide.

b)   *Who can access the private parts of another?*
We need to be very clear to all pupils that nobody has the right to access another's private parts. Explain that even at the GP surgery, a pupil under 16 should not be examined without the presence of an accompanying adult. Presentation of this information should include discussion about the risks involved in sharing dialogue and images through texting and online, as described earlier.

Secondary aged pupils also need to be able to identify:

c)   *Safe touch.*

Any intimate touch needs to be both legally allowed and consented to.   Both parties involved need to also have the capacity to understand what 'consent' means.

d)   *How to respect their own body*

Pupils need to be encouraged to use their own warning signals in their body and to respect those signals.   For example, a pupil should not over-ride their uncomfortable feelings for the pleasure of another.   The young person needs to be able to say assertively – *"No"* or *"Stop"* – to another person.   We may need to checkout they can do this by working through different scenarios together.

e)   *How to respect another person's body*

Pupils need to be encouraged to understand how to check out that someone else is comfortable with their behaviour, to always regard the other's feelings.   If the other person says *"No"* or *"Stop"* or looks as if they are uncomfortable (in their face or body language) the young person must take this seriously and honour the boundary that is being set.   Awareness of others is crucial.   In order to learn this, it may be necessary to engage in some role-play about body language.   The pupil may need very clear indicators as to what to look for in someone else in order to know that the other person is feeling uncomfortable.

For example the other person may have:

   ✗ said *"Stop"*, or that they don't like something

    ✗ moved away physically

    ✗ a sad expression

    ✗ a hostile expression

✗ slumped body posture

✗ a whiny voice

✗ started using aggressive/insulting language

✗ developed nervous habits such as nail-biting, hair-pulling

✗ become withdrawn or shut down

✗ tense body posture

✗ started to hide parts of their body

We will have to teach some of our pupils that when they observe these signals, they need to stop what they are doing. For example, *"Charlie is feeling uncomfortable because he is trying to move away, he isn't smiling and he said that he didn't want to join in ... so you need to back off"*.

Please note that once again, we need to be so explicit about encouraging observation. Our pupils will only be able to do this well if they have had facilitated opportunities to practice this skill in a small, safe context. We also need to be explicit about what to do when they get into these situations, for example, having scripts prepared like, *"I'm so sorry that I've made you feel uncomfortable. I will respect your boundaries and move away or go"*.

PSHE lessons will obviously be very helpful in all of this, but I would recommend that many of our pupils will also need 1:1 support as well, to ensure the understanding necessary for their developmental stage. We need to place additional emphasis on helping pupils to build their emotional resources so that they can become assertive in this area. We also need to support them to build their emotional capacity to manage the possibility of sexual relationships post 16, rather than merely describing the mechanics and science of sex. As an extra note, a pupil who has experienced sexual intimacy before the age of consent of 16 may well need access to specialist counselling or therapy, in order to be able to handle the big task of adolescence.

It is worth saying here that concern should be raised if there is a wide age gap

between those pupils involved intimately with one another in school or with those outside the school context.

Sex education lessons

Sex education lessons start in the primary phase. We need to be mindful that some pupils may well be traumatised by the content in these lessons, not only because of trauma they have experienced but because of the powerful and painful area of identity that it also raises. It is therefore essential that parents/carers are given warning of subjects coming up, so that they can have opportunity at home to think and prepare the pupil together in privacy. It is not ethically responsible to expect a pupil with a difficult early start to merely just get on with it. Many of the pupils we are concerned with in this book will need opportunity to watch video/DVD material in advance or to rehearse language that will be used to respond to the kinds of questions that may be asked *(perhaps using the* **WISE UP** *strategy, see p.79)*. Many will need scripts and support in order to keep themselves emotionally and physically safe and boundaried. They are at risk of being vulnerable again in the public context of class without adequate support to manage this.

Please note that we shouldn't be excluding these pupils from these lessons, but rather, giving them the time and the space that they need in order to prepare for and/or rehearse scripts that can be used at home with their parent/carer and social worker/therapist.

Organisational difficulties

Pupils like Ben and Lena will often have organisational difficulties as described in *'The effects of developmental trauma'* (p.17) at the beginning of this book. We will find that they are the ones who forget their sports or dance kit or the ones who lose their clothes. They'll be the ones who put things on back to front, or find that they've mislaid individual bits of clothing in the 40 minutes they were outside playing sport.

So, many of these pupils will need our support in modelling how to be organised. We are already familiar with the fact that these pupils will have difficulties in *shift* as described in earlier chapters, so here we need to recognise that we'll need to allow extra time for the transition involved in getting dressed. Visual checklists will also be particularly helpful at both home and school for ensuring our pupils have the right kit in their bags ready for PE. Create these visual checklists together. Go through them together. Then when they have the hang of this they will be able to do it on their own. For example,

TUESDAY:
☐ Check PE kit
☐ Gym top
☐ Gym skirt
☐ Sports socks
☐ Trainers
☐ Shorts

One key adult I've met in a primary school came up with the imaginative idea of creating a special clothes template for the boy she is supporting. There are many children and adolescents who will need visual cues and co-modelling in order to learn these tasks. Some pupils get easily distracted whilst they are getting changed, and end up taking far longer than anyone else. A clothes template and a visual timer may both help them organise themselves to stay focussed on dressing.

Motor skills and stability difficulties

These pupils can also have poor fine and gross motor skills. Research seems to suggest that this is especially common in cases of neglect:

> Neglect has very profound and long lasting consequences on all aspects of child development – poor attachment formation, under-stimulation, developmental delay, poor physical development and anti-social behaviour.
>
> (Pediatrics Vol 106, no.5, Nov 2000
> aapoliy.aapublications.org/cgi/content)

We are likely to notice these difficulties in a number of areas, from fastening or unfastening buttons to catching a ball. I am often asked what can be done to support these pupils in schools. I believe we need to build opportunity into the timetable to enable our pupils to develop and practice both fine and gross motor skills. Occupational therapists offer effective strategies for this type of work. Other vulnerable pupils will have difficulties around their core stability and balance. Again, they will need us to build practice time into the timetable for them.

Sensory integration difficulties

As discussed in the chapter on developmental trauma, these pupils are most likely to have sensory integration difficulties (this is when a pupil's central nervous system is ineffective in processing sensory information, in other words the sensations of touch, movement, sight and sound coming from their bodies and the world around them). So we are going to have to be mindful of this when expecting them to vary their use of their gentleness and strength within physical activity. They will need our feedback so that they become more self- and other- aware.

Finally, we do need to ensure that these pupils experience *fun* whilst engaging with their bodies. We must be wary of only making them aware of their limitations and inhibitions. We want them to have an opportunity to value and enjoy themselves and all that they can do with their bodies in a healthy, fun way. Remember we don't want them to be turned off touch, sport or sex for life! There is a balance as always. Let's engage these pupils in playfulness and encourage laughter so that they can begin to like themselves and all that they can contribute and experience. We want to be encouraging increased playfulness and humour whenever possible – at the level they feel comfortable with, whilst respecting their limits. Laughter is so good for them physiologically, as it counteracts the hormones involved in stress. Laughter also supports joining and building strong attachments. We could even consider using Theraplay principles and practice within our schools, as one school is doing in Corby, England (Adoption Today, Oct 2010)

WHAT HELPS US ...
"... when people make me laugh"

Finally ...

Let's look at supporting Ben and Lena:

FOR BEN

In his 1:1 time, Ben's key adult Jake lets him know that he's noticed Ben covering himself up. Jake explains that Ben is drawing attention to himself in the way he is currently getting changed. Jake lets him know that he realises that's probably the last thing Ben wants. He wonders together with Ben whether there is another way he could get changed discretely. He encourages him to see if he can find the quickest way to do this. They talk through some possible options by problem-solving together, and Jake challenges him to test out a couple of ideas at home.

FOR LENA

Lena's key adult Ann raises Lena's difficulties in PE during their 1:1 time together. She acknowledges that Lena is finding getting changed very hard: Lena tells her that she thinks some people are checking her out. Ann is not sure whether this is Lena's perception or the reality. She therefore decides to use the hand of options (see p.186) with Lena and then explore some different possible solutions.

Firstly, they think through together how she can get changed more discretely, so that she feels more comfortable. Lena likes Ann's idea about putting her shorts and t-shirt on underneath her uniform at lunchtime. Ann says she will clear this with the PE teacher so that no questions are asked. Secondly, Ann suggests they do a role-play together. She asks Lena to behave as the other girls do whilst Lena is changing: Ann takes on Lena's persona. Ann has a go at being assertive in front of Lena. She models being clear and confident: "Please don't stare at me whilst I'm changing. It makes me feel uncomfortable". She then encourages Lena to have a go. Lena asks Ann what she should do if they continue. Ann suggests she says, "I asked you to stop. You are now being disrespectful so I will need to take this further". Ann advises Lena that if she has tried these two steps, then she should come and tell Ann, and then the people involved would be dealt with by the Head of Year.

Empathy is a quality in which one person understands the perspective of another, accepts this perspective as belonging to the other person and conveys this understanding and acceptance back to the person ... sometimes empathic communication can pave the way for some joint problem solving.

(Golding 2006, p.102-3)

Chapter 11

It's all over!
Reparation

Emotional development is, in part, the ability to dare to feel the pain of what has happened to you, acknowledge it, and reflect on it, instead of cutting off from it. A child cannot do this without your help.   (Sunderland 2006, p. 205)

PRIMARY PHASE

Ben tells Mel, the girl next to him, that she is an idiot and that he doesn't want her in his team.

SECONDARY PHASE

Lena tells her key adult Ann to go away and then, when Ann remains at her side, says, "Fuck off and leave me alone".

In this chapter, I'll be looking at how stress and shame can impact on a pupil's behaviour. There is a real risk of misinterpretation of behaviour provoked by stress and shame in the aftermath of conflict, as it can often be viewed by education staff as wilful misconduct, attention-seeking, stubbornness and manipulation, rather than as a pupil communicating that they are stuck, in pain and needing support. Whatever the precipitating incident, pupils who have experienced developmental trauma find it very difficult to re-engage with normality once the heat of a difficult moment has passed.

Conflict can confirm to the Bens and Lenas in our classrooms that they are, in fact, 'a mistake'. They may experience self-loathing, believing that the other person involved may not want to continue in relationship with them any longer. They can't imagine things returning to how they were. They can't see a way back. They have no idea what to do. They can remain stuck, unless we come alongside. The strong and powerful feelings evoked by conflict can leave the pupil overwhelmed and disempowered. It is interesting that we often view them as 'powerful' at these times, and yet their experience of themselves is often the opposite.

I will be describing a range of ways in which those of us working with these pupils can support them back into relationship and into the present. The key adult's advocacy and action is critical at moments like this. Next, I'll look at why reparation is so important for vulnerable pupils, and I'll outline some effective actions we can take to create opportunities for reparation after disruptive incidents in schools. Then, I'll provide some additional strategies that can be used for specific instances of:

i   disrespect to an adult
ii   breaking/damaging property
iii injuring a pupil (physically or emotionally)
iv   lying
v   stealing

I will also outline some ways of building the pupil up in their sense of self, so that they can manage reparation better from a position of increased resilience, initially with support, and eventually by themselves. Finally, we will consider the implications for Ben and Lena, our two case pupils who we're following throughout this book.

The stress factor

As I discussed in Chapter 6, pupils with experience of relational trauma and loss are more likely to have difficulties in managing their stress than their peers. This is mainly due to the pre-existing levels of internal stress that they bring with them into school from another context, at another time. We need to be doing all we can in our schools to keep stress to a minimum, but we also need to be mindful that no-one is immune to stress. Life is stressful, and school can help pupils learn to deal with this.

In the early stages of our work with a vulnerable pupil, we'll notice that he or she may present unhealthy stress responses because of their:

- 'mistranslation' of motives and intentions
- faulty panic and fear alarm systems, leading to over-reactive responses
- lack of capacity to judge and make sense of situations
- lack of capacity to know how to handle themselves and situations in a healthy manner
- lack of capacity to give assertive responses

These difficulties will obviously take time to address. Let's incorporate appropriate activities (especially role-play) into our work together with these pupils, to address these areas. Here are examples, some of which we've already seen use of in earlier chapters:

- The 'hand of options'
- Stressometers
- Working through examples of social scenarios through role-play
- The calm box
- Assertive skills

The 'hand of options' *(see Chapters 6 and 10 for application)*

Talk through five possible motives and intentions that might have been behind whatever has caused the pupil you are working with stress or shame. The pupil is likely to have assumed immediately that the other pupil or adult was 'out to get them', to harm them in some way. This is a possibility, but usually is not the reality. We can help our key pupil to have more of a realistic view as to what might be going on behind the scenes. Talking it through together expands options.

Using the example in Chapter 6, for Ben *(p.131)*, the hand of options might look like this:

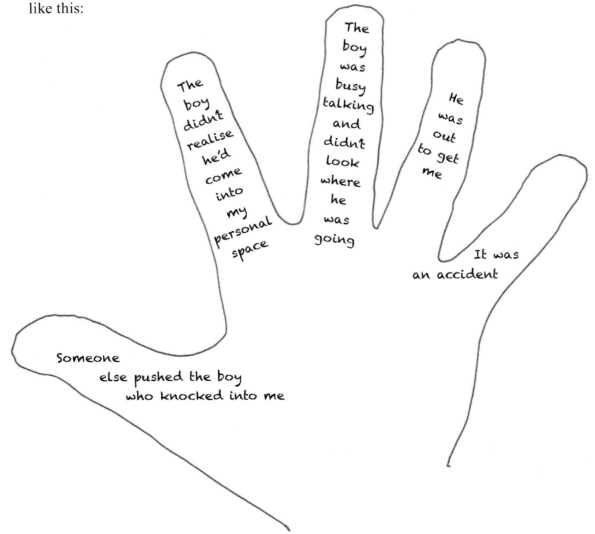

Stressometers

Yesterday, for example, Lena got really upset when the teacher said she was late to the lesson. Lena over-reacted and said she was never going to go back to that class.

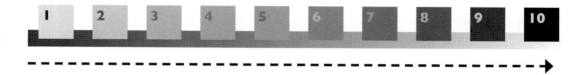

The stressometer above illustrates Lena's first stress response, where she went from what she thinks of as a 1, to a 10, very rapidly. Her key adult, Ann, can explain that this is the type of response we would be more likely to see in a situation of genuine threat – giving an example of what might realistically trigger this kind of powerful response, such as a plane suddenly dipping mid-flight. The key adult can then talk about a more regulated, realistic response to the classroom incident, where the stress level might rise to a 3 *(as illustrated below)*.

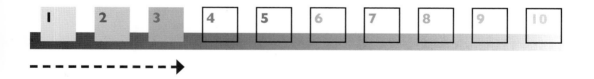

This visual representation will help pupil work out their differing stress responses, and be able to communicate about them, building their self-awareness so that they will be in more of a position to express more regulated, healthier responses at times of stress. Drawing your pupil's attention to the by-now familiar image of a stressometer after another incident has occurred, and asking them to mark her stress level on it, can be regulating in itself, in that it asks the pupil to move into the reflective, cognitive processing part of her brain *(see Chapter 6 for further examples with Ben and Lena)*.

Role-play

As incidents occur, role-plays can be used to explore a range of potential responses. A pupil may have been teased by their peers for not understanding something. The key adult would act out the scene again, this time taking the role of the pupil, offering different suggested scripts for use. The pupil would pick their favourite and then have a go practising the script within the role-play context (with the key adult playing the teaser). The key adult would then encourage the pupil to test the script out in reality when teasing happens again, and to feedback how she felt doing so and what happened *(and see Chapter 10 for an example with Lena).*

Calming

The key adult might notice increased fidgeting as an indicator of increased stress/anxiety and decide to direct the pupil to a calm box activity, as described in Chapter 6, page 134 (*and* Bombèr, 2007, pp.206-11).

Assertive skills

Many of our pupils will need specific support to identify and understand different responses that can be used at times of difficulty or conflict, for example, the passive, aggressive or assertive response. Role-play and other activities can be used to explore differences between these styles. Once the pupil knows and is more self-aware of their particular stress response, they can then be freed up to realise that they have a choice of how to respond. Together with the key adult, they can learn assertive skills to enable them to engage in healthier responses at these important times.

Also, let's remember that our pupils will respond best to directions and *outcomes* rather than directions and punishments (Pearce, 2009): for example: *"Complete your work and then you can take your break"* rather than *"Complete your work or you will have a detention".* Directions and outcomes must be presented calmly and with empathy, not with anger. All of us have a choice about the kind of language we use, and can learn to be assertive and non-violent in our communictions with pupils as well as each other.

The shame factor

Small doses of shame are actually helpful for our socialisation as humans. Experiencing a degree of shame is largely how we learn the difference between right and wrong. Most pupils entering school who have received 'good enough' care from their families will have experienced this. These pupils will therefore be able to cope with the usual behavioural approaches used in schools for managing and shaping their behaviour, if and when there are difficulties.

However, the pupils we are especially concerned about here have often endured being left in shame for long periods. They have often been punished and humiliated for very natural and developmentally appropriate activities and tasks, without any opportunity being created for disruption between them and their caregiver to be repaired. For example, they may have been yelled at and sworn at for wanting to go to the toilet, for expressing hunger, for not being able to pick up tiny things. Even worse treatment may follow if they did something viewed as 'wrong' or 'bad', like spilling or dropping something. When this happens, shame can tip over into 'toxic shame' very quickly *(see p.124, Chapter 6, for definition).*

> Shame as a healthy human emotion can be transformed into shame as *a state of being.* As a *state of being,* shame takes over one's whole identity. To have shame as an identity is to believe that one is flawed, that one is defective as a human being. Once shame is transformed into an identity, it becomes toxic and dehumanizing.
>
> (Bradshaw, 2005, p.xvii)

This type of shame is debilitating.   It is from this premise that the pupil will experience a strong sense of *him* being the problem, not what he has done. He will frequently assume that because of this, there is no hope of the relationship continuing, so the possibility of a way out is not even considered. Remember his internal working model from the Introduction *(p.27)*, which is likely to contain the following beliefs:

> I am not OK
>
> Adults are not OK
>
> The world is not safe
>
> It's all about survival

It is important to realise that shame de-activates positive attachment-seeking behaviour.

> Lacking primary experiences of re-integrative shame, the child falls easily into a black hole of pervasive shame, with no hope of relationship repair or attunement.   (Taylor 2010, p.83)

We need to know that these pupils will often experience a deep sense of shame in association with the usual kinds of discipline we use in school. Unaddressed, this shame promotes very difficult feelings which are counterproductive for building relationship. The overwhelming feelings that accompany toxic shame will mean that this pupil could then be at risk of escalating their inappropriate behaviours, in an attempt to dispel the intolerable feelings.

WHAT WE NEED …
"A greater understanding of how pupils' needs can be met, reducing the 'fear factor' of working with them"
Headteacher, seconday school

The presenting difficulty

These pupils will often get themselves into tricky situations and then don't have the means to get themselves out again. In fact, despite seeming provocative and as if wanting to initiate further conflict, they will very quickly collapse in the midst of it, overwhelmed with shame. Many of their behaviours are fuelled by fear and panic, but to those of us involved, it doesn't always seem this way. We may just view them as 'difficult', and, often, as 'manipulative'. However, in this kind of work we need to remind ourselves that things are not always the way they seem. These pupils often don't even know how they reached this point. In school, we attempt to ask questions at these times of heightened tension, but this is counter-productive: the pupil often can't answer. The pupil is often acting out very primal responses such as the fight/flight/freeze reflex triggered in their brain stem when threat is perceived and anxiety is provoked. *There is no reflective capacity present in this part of the brain.* We will have to facilitate the reflection necessary, on their behalf, at a later time: but at this precise moment, our main focus must be to defuse the tension and stress of the situation, not escalate it.

Pupils with significant attachment difficulties will need considerable support through times when they engage in unhelpful, inappropriate or harmful behaviours. We cannot merely discipline then as we do with the majority. These pupils will need an alternative approach which includes the possibility of reparation.

Meaningful relationship

This is the time when the relationship with their key adult will be most helpful. The key adult can play a significant role in the task of reparation. However difficult, it is important that we do all we can to hold onto our thinking and reflective capacity at these times *(and see Chapter 15 on Staff Care for further thoughts on this).*

Those most disintegrated children need the most integrated thinking ...

(Golding et al 2006, p.362)

We also need to be mindful that as a relationship between an adult develops into something meaningful, the possibility for experiencing *increased shame* is likely. We may notice a withdrawal of some kind. This withdrawal is a defence against experiencing shame whilst more open and vulnerable within the growing relationship. At these times we will have to work extra hard to reassure the pupil of our continued connection – that we want to still remain in relationship with him. A flash of shame often goes unnoticed in schools and can easily lead to all kinds of inaccurate interpretations (by the pupil as well as the adults). This may result in staff using punitive approaches, resulting in further shaming for the pupil. The most immediate antidote to this potential spiral of negativity is reassurance: it offers a way back to a more relaxed way of relating by providing a human bridge.

Opportunities for reparation

The key to moving these pupils on into more healthy ways of relating is in the attention we can give to the 'repair' of these incidents. This is what these pupils have not had much/any experience of. So this needs to be our focus, rather than focussing on 'changing their behaviour' through discipline. More and more of us are having the experience of watching pupils' behaviour change once they experience genuinely 'being attended to'. We need to engage in interactive repair as soon as possible, so that the pupil we are working with knows he will not be rejected because of his behaviour.

Beyond the point of no return

These pupils genuinely don't believe that there is a way back. They will feel as if they've reached the point of no return. They move very quickly to a position of despair. Be aware that in this work, we may sometimes experience this level of distress ourselves, as our pupils can sometimes push us to our emotional and mental limits during 'shame cycles'. Be kind to yourself and tell someone how you are left feeling after working with your pupil. Then do something that brings you joy, reminding you of 'who' you are, as we can sometimes lose our sense of ourselves in the very powerful feelings that arise in this work. I go for a long swim. This supports me in this emotionally draining work! *(and see Chapter 15, Staff Care)*

Once our pupil is in this state of despair, which will present itself in many different guises, we are going to have to find a way to facilitate a human bridge for him to find his way back into relationship. Although *we* may be clear that it is his behaviour that is the problem – not him – this is likely to be the opposite of what he is experiencing at this point. If we think back to his early history, we may recall that his experience has taught him to believe that he is not OK as a person, that he is fundamentally flawed with no hope of relationship. This is why so many of these vulnerable pupils expect and even unconsciously set up scenarios that facilitate rejection. It's as if they are merely proving an internal belief to themselves. We need to be so mindful of this, and stay careful not to collude with the unconscious projections that are likely to be going on.

Many pupils who have experienced developmental trauma will be surprised that we even offer them an opportunity to be re-united, especially to their key adult, who will either have observed, heard about or been the focus of their outburst. Surprisingly to some, these pupils can later experience deep remorse. Pupils who have experienced relational trauma and loss always need explicit permission and opportunity to repair things. It is essential that we allow this reparation cycle, and not leave the pupil in the midst of damaging toxic shame.

… overwhelmed, fearful and miserable, colouring our thoughts, feeling and perceptions with a sense of threat or dread as if everything we need to do is far too hard.   (Sunderland 2006, p.87)

In school we must work very hard at not allowing these pupils to remain in this place for very long, remembering they end up there very quickly. We must intervene to provide a way back as soon as possible. The following is a useful sequence of responses at these times:

a)   Be explicit about the fact that something has happened. Describe the
      events neutrally and with empathy

      *"I noticed that you were trying really hard in your Maths work this
      morning. You started getting frustrated around question 5. It was as
      if you felt you just couldn't cope with any more. It got too much. You
      threw your book and then before you knew it you were in a real state".*

b)   Gently let the pupil know that you realise the pupil is probably feeling all
      shaken up/disturbed now.

      "You are probably still feeling quite shaken up and need a bit of space".

c)   Be explicit about that fact that something needs to happen to 'repair'
      what's gone wrong. Give them an idea of how that could be done.

      *"When you are ready, let's go and pick up your Maths book and repair it
      with some Sellotape, as it is ripped. We can then make a small apology
      card for Sir, as it wasn't his fault that your patient, persevering part*

disappeared for a few moments".

d)   Let the pupil know that we now know that he is not as strong as we
      thought, and that we will help him practise in the area that he had
      difficulty in – so that he can cope.

      *"I'm sorry because I thought the work was the right level. It wasn't. I
      will make sure that tomorrow the work is more suitable for you. Let's get
      your confidence back before moving onto more challenges".*

e)   Supervision, structure and support are also necessary to varying degrees
      in order to facilitate the reparative stage. This is most familiar for us
      in the 'good enough' care of toddlers but needs to be replicated here
      whatever the age of the vulnerable pupil.

      "Let's go get the book and neaten it up together".

f)   Once pupil has engaged in reparative activity, we must also be very
      explicit about the fact that his relationship with his key adult remains
      intact.

      *"Just to say that you and me are OK. The teacher is also OK. He
      understands that you were having a wobble and is looking forward to
      welcoming you back into Maths tomorrow".*

If we don't make this kind of comment explicitly, we leave the pupil insecure and once
again at risk of his inappropriate behaviour escalating, because of his very real fear
of rejection or abandonment.

g)   We need to make an attempt to make connections ourselves as to why this difficulty might have happened.

"The level of work was too high. I need to make sure I give you work that generates success with only gentle challenges when you are feeling successful".

Remember we cannot expect the pupil to give us the answers to why they do what they do. Use a commentary, not a question. This considered process of attempting to understand and make connections in front of the pupil is going to be educative for him or her in communicating our empathy, building their self-awareness, and supporting them to know what triggers their anxiety and alarm systems.

WHAT HELPS US ...
"... friendly, approachable teachers"

Usually at times of difficulty, we will have to increase supervision and structure. Be ready to 'tighten the reins' as you would with a young child who had wandered off. If we as the adults can remain grounded at difficult times like these, our responses can have extremely powerful effects on the pupils in our care – more than we probably realise. David Howe (2005) describes this beautifully.

Strong minds keep you safe. Wise ones teach you how to understand the world and play your part in it. Only when children feel secure can they go on to explore – their own feelings, the reactions of others and how their behaviour affects those around them. Encounters with minds that are stronger and wiser often act as a turning point for maltreated children.   (p.275)

Additional strategies for specific situations

There are other more specific, supportive strategies that have proved useful in the school context. I need to highlight that 'time out' in its traditional sense (usually meaning separation from other pupils and activities, in a specified place) is not a strategy that I advocate for pupils who have experienced developmental trauma, because it tends to reinforce the internal messages we are attempting to challenge within our work (their beliefs that they are wholly bad and must/will be rejected/do not belong). If you do go ahead and use 'time out', you are likely to find that this strategy will precipitate deteriorated behaviour because of the shame, rejection, fear and panic it engenders for this particular pupil.

In every support case, it's crucial that our pupils need to know that reparative action is required to put things right; we don't just leave things undone and disturbed. The following has proved useful in attachment support work.

---

i   Disrespect

At the first sign of disrespect to a pupil's key adult, initiate the following procedure:

THE RESPECT PLAN – PRIMARY PHASE

- State *"No"/"Stop"/"Enough"*, in a neutral, matter-of-fact tone.

- The key adult leaves the room.

- The back-up adult or TA from the next classroom swaps in temporarily. There is no need to know the detail of what happened. The back-up adult will know by being called that there has been an incident of disrespect, and states that this needs to be repaired.

- The pupil is directed in a matter-of-fact way to complete a card to apologise for disrespect.

- If the pupil obliges appropriately, then the key adult can be reinstated.

- If the pupil refuses or continues to be disrespectful, then the back-up adult takes the pupil to a member of senior management where he waits until the staff member is ready to engage with the pupil.

- The senior manager then states how disrespect is taken very seriously in the school, and that all staff need to be communicated with respectfully – as do the pupils.

- The senior manager then decides on a more serious sanction, for example, detention in his room after school that day (with the manager present). It is important that all sanctions are implemented as close to incidents as possible – even in secondary schools.

THE RESPECT PLAN – SECONDARY PHASE

- The key adult states, *"No, enough is enough. I'm initiating the respect plan"*.

- The key adult leaves the room and heads for the Inclusion Department.

- The subject teacher knows that if she sees this happen she needs to approach the pupil.

- The subject teacher tells the pupil that she must leave the room and go immediately to the Inclusion Department.

- Once the pupil is in the Inclusion Department, another member of staff asks the pupil to complete a card to apologise for their lack of respect.

- The key adult only re-engages once the reparative task is complete.

- If any of this is not followed through, then the senior manager who is part of the TAC (Team around the Child) is contacted for outlining a more serious sanction - as above in the primary phase example. The incident would be talked through with the pupil with their key adult at a time when there was calm again. The key adult would quickly reassure the pupil that their relationship is still intact.

ii   Breaking/damaging property

If property is broken or damaged, then the pupil needs to be directed to repair it with adult support during their free time. In this instance, we need to make active and creative use of the Home/school partnership. It is essential to describe to the pupil's parent or caregiver what is happening and why in a way that will not increase the pupil's shame at home; for example, in the home/school book – *"Tom wants to put things right today as he broke Mike's pen. Overnight he's going to have a think about something nice he could bring in from home to share with Mike"*.

iii   Injuring another pupil (physical or emotional)

This needs to be treated extremely seriously. I am not an advocate for exclusion, but I believe that a firm boundary needs to be implemented at times such as these, for example, a detention or short-term exclusion as close to the incident as possible. It is helpful if parents/carers can be encouraged to complete a blanket consent form giving permission for any sanctions necessary to be carried out on the day of incidents, rather than waiting until a later part of the week. This is more common with younger children, but needs to be put in place for these vulnerable pupils to make more sense to them. We are attempting to make connections for them.

In my experience, if an incident is dealt with seriously and effectively, then there will be no need to progress to longer term/permanent exclusion. Exclusion, if used appropriately can be a communication of a boundary line.

- I must also stress though that *on no occasion must exclusion be discussed with these pupils as a threat*. If exclusion is deemed necessary it should just happen. Subtle or explicit threats to these pupils will have the *opposite* effect of increasing difficulties, not reducing them. A threat may leave the member of staff *feeling* more 'in control', but it is actually one of the most provocative actions we can take when relating to vulnerable pupils – who already feel on the edge, rejected and excluded, as I noted earlier in this chapter.

- These pupils are seeking out confirmation of their internal beliefs. Our job is to challenge these internal beliefs - not to collude with them! We need to stand strong and not do anything that might exacerbate the pupil's already low sense of self.

EXTRA NOTE

We really do not need to over-emphasise our upset, as if the pupil is more likely to 'get' it if we raise our voices. Pupils who have experienced developmental trauma will already be feeling dreadful, as I've described. Their feeling state may either be visible or hidden, but has the potential to overwhelm them. There is no need for voices to be raised, or for there to be shouts or threats. We need to maintain our self-control. We need to manage our own, mixed-up feelings by making creative use of our support mechanisms and networks *(and see Chapter 15, Self Care)*. It's understandable to have strong feelings, but it is not OK to use our communication with the pupil to manage our reactions, however overwhelming the feelings may be. We need to be firm, be matter-of-fact and most importantly, stay grounded.

If an exclusion is necessary, a debrief on the pupil's return is essential. The debrief should include both the pupil and his key adult. Be wary of having meetings with more than one/two adults present, as we want our pupil to be in a state where he can engage in reflective capacity. If the pupil experiences feeling threatened, he is more likely to retreat into primal responses again.

Together with his key adult, the pupil can create a card or letter – detailing the 'offence', an apology and what will now be different. After the exclusion, we'll need to provide increased supervision for a minimum of two weeks until the pupil is able to manage increased freedom responsibly.

Permanent exclusion must always be the *last option* and recommendations made by outside agencies and supportive measures *must have been put in place and followed through*. If this hasn't happened, exclusion isn't an ethical response. However, if it really does come to this, please read Chapter 13, *Moving On*, for more information on how to handle the process in a way that at least pays sensitive attention to a prepared ending, so that the pupil involved has more chance of succeeding in his next school placement.

iv Lying

- *Fantastical lying*   Relate to the pupil as if he or she were much younger. "Wow, wouldn't it be great if ..." "I wish I could have gone there too". "You're letting me now that you wish you were ..."

- *Serious lying*   If there is sufficient evidence that indicates that there are serious connotations as a consequence of the pupil lying, then:
  - speak firmly and clearly outlining the facts of what has happened in commentary style.

  - Be matter of fact, not using overtly emotive words if at all possible.

  - Be the pupil's mind. If there is opportunity to repair what has happened in any way, then make this clear. Otherwise it will be important to remove something from the pupil on a temporary basis, a special activity, a free time *(but not food, see p.159)* – as soon after the incident as possible.

"For now, we will put some supervision in at break times, as at the moment you are letting us know that you are not strong enough yet to stay on site by yourself".

- Always build in a reflective element to build up a pupil's self-awareness so that they can continue to develop their locus of control.

v   Stealing

- If there is sufficient evidence that indicates that the pupil you are working with stole an object from another student of the school, then the pupil needs to be given an opportunity to put this right. If there isn't sufficient evidence, then I would strongly recommend using a social story *(as in IIH, Bombèr 2007 pp.138-141)* about stealing at both home and school, so that we actively build up their capacity to understand and respect personal boundaries around personal belongings.

- Please note though, that many pupils will pick up things or find things that they simply take. I call this 'the magpie effect'! The pupil may naively believe that what they find, they keep! Finders, keepers. This is often a consequence of their early childhood experiences, especially in cases of neglect. It's not always necessary to use an over-the-top response to this, or to immediately call it stealing. Sometimes just a matter-of-fact intervention that communicates that something belongs somewhere else or to someone else is really all that is sufficient. The use of social stories are always helpful at these times too.

> ● Please remember that we can jump to conclusions too quickly.
> It's always important to check out the pupil's understanding of what just
> happened. As I have mentioned, my experience has been that these
> pupils are often interpreting what is happening in a very different way to
> the majority of us. In many cases, they just need some additional guidance
> and supervision – not severe discipline.

Getting back into the swing of things

Some pupils will feel toxic shame so acutely that it will significantly affect their ability to even re-enter rooms, meet particular staff again or continue with lessons. In these cases advocacy is needed by the key adult. Get in touch with the staff members that the pupil is feeling in shame around. De-brief them as to why this pupil might be finding it very difficult to re-engage. Encourage these staff members to approach the pupil through email or in person – rather than merely just waiting for the pupil to engage. This is too difficult for these particular pupils. They need the adults to provide the bridge. They are letting us know they don't have the capacity to do this. For example, you could encourage this kind of comments:

TEACHER

"I really missed you in Geography today. I was looking forward to seeing you. I know we had some difficult moments yesterday but today is a new day. We have lots of interesting material to investigate together".

This sensitive after-care is so, so powerful. Many pupils are shocked by this seemingly paradoxical approach, and this experience has been found to strengthen their respect for and relationship with the member of staff who took the time to do this.

To increase resilience, individual recovery plans like this one can be created and used with key pupils.

My recovery plan!

- I am a valuable and unique human being!
- I am meant to be here. I belong.
- I am going to notice what I'm good at
  - I can ...
  - I like ...
  - I'm proud of ...
  - I contribute by ...
- I am going to protect some special time for myself doing what makes me feel comfortable and happy, for example ...
- If I make a mistake or things go wrong I will forgive myself. Everyone messes up from time to time
- I will have a go at doing things that maybe feel a bit scary to begin with so that I move on to new ways of being and doing

- I will give myself a pat on the back or treat myself sometimes as I reckon I'm doing great
- When someone tells me I've done well or have tried hard I will say thank you and store that away in a special part of my memory
- I will hold my head up high as I'm proud to be me and I'm important
- I will let others know who I am and how I feel about things by telling them in a respectful way
- I will eat well, sleep well and look good
- I will try not to take things too seriously. I will have a go at laughing at myself sometimes!

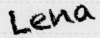

Finally ...

We need to be encouraging a greater awareness of the positive aspects of our pupils, in other words what makes them who they are, what they contribute and what they like and what skills they have *(see also 'parts' work, Chapter 6)*. We need to foster an appreciation of their individuality and facilitate opportunities to generate success so that they start to like themselves and view themselves as valued members of the school community. We can do this by using strategies outlined in Chapter 3, *Taking on the curriculum*. The Book of Success is an especially useful tool in helping these pupils hold onto their successes. The pupils themselves also need to also start taking responsibility for viewing themselves differently. We could encourage them both at home and school to work through a recovery plan on a regular basis!

FOR BEN

Jake tells Ben firmly that his comments are not OK. He tells Ben to follow him and instigates the respect plan immediately. Ben is taken elsewhere to complete a card to apologise to Mel. He strops about for a while but then does it.

FOR LENA

Ann immediately leaves the room after saying "No – enough". The class teacher tells Lena to go down to the Inclusion Department. Lena lets out a big sigh, muttering under her breath. The class teacher says, "No – enough. You know where you are meant to be". Lena reluctantly leaves and heads off for the Inclusion Department. Ann is in there beavering away. She nods at Lena, but doesn't engage verbally. Another member of staff takes over saying, "You know what you need to do. There's the card". Lena is left for a while. The member of staff checks in with her and asks if she is ready to put things right. Lena nods.

Ann looks up and smiles at her. Lena walks over with the member of staff keeping an eye and watches as Lena gives the card to Ann. Lena also says "Sorry". Ann says "It's OK", and thanks her for apologising. She lets Lena know that she doesn't like being disrespected but she's glad that it is now sorted. She reminds Lena that their relationship is still intact: "You and me are OK. This doesn't in anyway affect our relationship". She encourages Lena to go with her back to class to re-join the activity they left. They leave and return to class together.

Chapter 12

But I'm different …
Celebrating difference and diversity

Acceptance of and interest in the differences leads to the creation of a potentially unique and exciting landscape.   (Golding et al (2006) p.362)

PRIMARY PHASE

Some of Ben's classmates complain to the teacher that it's not fair that he is being treated differently.

SECONDARY PHASE

Lena arrives at the Inclusion Department and sits down on a chair away from everyone with her head in her hands: "What's wrong with me? Why can't I do what everyone else can?"

What Ben's classmates and Lena are struggling with is the feeling that difference means something negative or unequal. Difference in these examples is not seen as something positive or to be celebrated.

For a school to be truly inclusive, certain values need to be embedded at every level. In this chapter, I'll be looking at the importance of really examining the ethos of a school. Valuing and celebrating difference and diversity has to be a reality in order for this type of attachment support to be truly effective. This isn't an area we can afford to overlook, as the pupils in our care are going to need our guidance and direction. Reflecting on difference and diversity challenges us all to think about our own personal views and opinions, as well as the views and opinions of the school system in which we work. As schools are a collection of individuals, it makes sense that we will all play a part within the overall ethos created.

In order to illustrate the key messages that we need to take seriously with respect to difference and diversity, I'll be giving you an example of current good practice from a large primary school; proving that this can indeed be a reality, rather than some pipe dream! Good leadership seems to be the vital ingredient in terms of ensuring these values are integrated into school culture, so I'll be identifying what qualities this entails. We will then look in more detail at how we can utilise day-to-day opportunities in school to communicate the benefits of difference and diversity for everyone. These can include us engaging in:

i   Respectful communication between one another as education staff
ii   Respectful communication about the pupils with whom we work
iii Respectful communication about and with the families we work alongside
iv   Direct communication about difference
v   Indirect communication about difference

Older pupils who have experienced developmental trauma may be particularly interested in their early childhood experiences, and how these have made them different, so I've included some information on the science behind it all for discussions with them. Simply understanding why they do what they do can bring a sense of relief for some young people. For other pupils, knowing there are more children and young people out there who have experienced similar home environments can bring some sense of normality, as they come to realise they are not alone.

Finally, we will consider the implications for Ben and Lena, our two case pupils who we're following throughout this book.

WHAT WE NEED ...
"Knowing that every member of the team is committed to inclusion"
Headteacher, primary school

The message

The key message is that we are all different. This is reality, but as T.S Elliot points out, 'mankind cannot bear too much reality.' So many of us feel threatened by difference. Obviously some differences are more obvious than others, but the fact remains that we are all different and unique. We therefore need to be wary of using words that imply that 'one size fits all', as this just isn't true! Who are we kidding? Of course we need general policies in place as a starting point for all our work within schools. And we do need to promote equality; but equality doesn't necessarily mean more of the same. The value and importance of difference should never be compromised. Diversity and creativity are inherent in difference. It is crucial that we introduce the word 'flexibility' to both our staff and our pupils; I've found this to be one of the most empowering words for building towards greater inclusion in school. Every pupil deserves access to a good education, and we recognise it in the UK as a human right; if we don't move forward on diversity issues, I believe we run the risk of actually facilitating exclusion. As Glasser boldly states (2007):

> Until the mainstream classroom fully serves children with disabling conditions, many of the current learning environments would be appropriately termed 'exclusions'. Let's stop the bleeding and integrate a new level of inclusion.
>
> (p.234)

Let's use every opportunity within leadership, management, assemblies, primary classrooms, circle times, tutor group time, PSHE, citizenship, drama and other subjects to communicate clearly that it's OK to be different and OK to be related to differently.

For some pupils and adults this is going to be quite challenging, especially if personal attitudes, values and beliefs mean that particular people or groups are favoured over others. However, if our school states within its handbook that it promotes inclusive practice, then we have to be true to our word.

> It is up to us to examine our own core beliefs and to spread the word of the least dangerous assumption. We can no longer allow the justification of a prejudice that is so dangerous. Now is definitely the time to believe that all people are valued individuals with limitless potential.
>
> (Newton & Wilson, 2010)

WHAT HELPS US …
"I just want to belong"

In my role as a teacher/therapist, visiting and advising in primary or secondary schools and different authorities, I have visited and provided consultations to a wide range of schools, and there are many that are already truly inclusive. Here I want to draw particular attention to one school where I am consistently struck by their capacity to include and to respect diversity *(identifying details have been changed for reasons of confidentiality)*.

The school is above average in size, and an above average number of its pupils are eligible for free school meals. The number of pupils with special educational needs and or/disabilities is exceptionally high, at around eight out of ten pupils. Over time, the range of needs has become increasingly complex and many of the pupils now have significant speech, language and emotional or behavioural problems.

This is a school where their philosophy and vision is clear from the top down. There is an open permission for the teaching staff to be both flexible and creative in their approach with the pupils in their care. What is notable about this particular school is that there is a very definite interplay of both leadership and management skills and expertise taking place. The current leadership promotes a truly inclusive philosophy, inspiring and motivating staff and pupils to move ahead together, in the same direction. Leadership therefore encapsulates a longer term view than management. Management is more concerned with short term goals and objectives.

It's the leadership qualities of this school that have especially left a lasting impression on me, one that I feel inspired to pass on! To spread the word! This particular school includes all staff and all pupils despite the odds. They seem to have found a way to challenge the status quo. They focus on people – motivating, inspiring, aligning and attuning. They are innovative in their practices, sometimes changing the rules in response to the bigger picture. They ask the questions that need to be asked and by engaging in relationships that facilitate mutual respect, inspire trust. There is a genuine sense of both togetherness and clear direction.

How can the message of honouring difference be communicated?

This is a subject that we can tackle in all kinds of ways, but here are some ideas that have been particularly helpful in supporting pupils who have experienced developmental trauma:

i   RESPECTFUL COMMUNICATIONS BETWEEN STAFF MEMBERS

We are the pupil's role models. We'd better take this seriously, as we are being watched! Pupils always notice the way we relate to one another as colleagues. The following are some key principles that I have observed in schools that seem to make all the difference.

Key principles

- Let's relate to each other as valued individuals
- Let's speak about and to each other positively and constructively
- Let's relate to each other as equals, regardless of our position in the school
- Let's notice the strengths, gifts and abilities in one another by providing encouragement as we go along
- Let's view each other as significant team players, all necessary and all contributing in some way
- Let's see our differences as complementary to the school team
- Let's trust one another, assuming the best.

For example:

"It's great we've got Shona on the staff as she's so organised. Some of us creative types need some organising from time to time!"

"I really think that Mike should run a parents' group of some kind. Have you seen the way he gets on with them, even some of our harder-to-reach ones? He has a way of putting people at ease".

"Let's wait a few minutes before starting our staff meeting; Karen is just saying goodbye to Liam who needs additional care getting into his taxi, because of his wheelchair. We don't want to start until everyone is here".

WHAT WE NEED …
"Understanding that inclusion is determined by the strong relationships we build"
Headteacher, primary school

When this kind of healthy teamwork and staff collaboration is evident, the pupils experience a stronger sense of community. It is only with this 'real life' experience that they can begin to appreciate what inclusive citizenship might mean and look like.

ii   RESPECTFUL COMMUNICATIONS ABOUT PUPILS

Pupils pick up on how we relate to them and their peers, and will replicate (and build on) how we communicate in their own direct interactions with each other. So we need to be very self-aware, and mindful of our non-verbal and verbal communication; it's far more influential than I think we will ever realise. We are employed within education to engage in fair and non-discriminatory practice amongst pupils from all backgrounds, and what we say and how we say it has a profound effect. I think it's helpful every now and then to reflect on our own motives and intentions for working within education. What's our own value system? Why do we do what we do? Having a clear sense of purpose and remembering that we are working within a particular ethos will support us to feel part of the wider vision and team. This can only lead to a greater sense of job satisfaction.

When relating to the pupils in our care who have experienced relational traumas and losses we need to be mindful of certain areas of difficulty.

It is best to avoid ...	instead
sarcastic comments	Instead, be explicit and clear with your expectations, using a neutral tone
public reprimands	Instead, speak to the pupil individually when calm, using clear expectations as above. Use the word *"Let's"*.
aggressive reactions towards pupils	Instead, take some time out to regulate yourself first, seek advice, support, and then communicate assertively

shaming pupils	Instead, use 'parts' language to enable pupils to have a sense of who they are and the choices they can make. Remember they are often not aware of having choices, even though we talk about choices in school a lot.
criticising the pupil themselves rather than their actions	Instead, ensure that you openly communicate that you respect them as valuable human beings.
	Then, focus on naming what you would like to see more of, using parts language. Be sensitive, remembering that these particular pupils often feel that *they* are a mistake, rather than that they *have made* a mistake. There is a significant difference.
humiliation of pupils	Instead, allow pupils opportunity to mess up or make mistakes from time to time, seeing these times as opportunities for learning, providing reparative opportunities to put things right. Use language such as, *"Let's practise"*, or *"Let's get stronger at …"*
derogatory comments	Instead, only use words that build others up, engendering a sense of hope. Over time these are the kind of words that will bring the kind of change we are looking for.

Thoughtless words can wound as deep as any sword but wisely spoken words can heal   (Proverbs 12 v 18)

iii   RESPECTFUL COMMUNICATION ABOUT AND WITH THE FAMILIES WE WORK ALONGSIDE

We always need to be mindful of communicating respect to those with whom we work in partnership, and this of course includes our pupils' parents and carers. Of course, sometimes we are going to have different perspectives or different beliefs, but we can't allow these to interfere with our working relationships with families or with colleagues. If difficult dynamics arise, let's discuss these professionally in the appropriate context, such as a formalised meeting with another colleague, with a parent or together with outside agencies. Let's be mindful about not 'letting off steam' about specific individuals in public areas. Judgements often multiply and affect the work in hand; so let's not join the blame game as this will only worsen the situation. Let's find whatever support we need to stay grounded and professional, and work to strengthen our networks through our language and attitude to each other.

iv   DIRECT COMMUNICATION ABOUT DIFFERENCE

Staff de-briefs, focussed PSHE or SEAL lessons, circle times and assemblies are all important in communicating the facts about difference and diversity. As we all know, it's essential that the key message is communicated from the top down, so that this message can be fully embedded within the school values and ethos. It will then become the culture of a school.

Recently I ran a pilot project in a primary school amongst all the year 6 classes, called 'ConnectIn'. It involved class discussions, exercises and problem-solving around how to be engaged in the real task of community building. The young people were encouraged to discuss and explore topics such as those over the page. I'm sure you have other examples of topics that have helped explore difference and diversity and community building. These are the kinds of ideas that can be introduced and discussed early on in school, so that everyone can learn how to be truly inclusive citizens, and then, later on, contribute that approach within our communities.

v   **INDIRECT COMMUNICATIONS ABOUT DIFFERENCE**

There will be many informal opportunities to promote the benefits of difference as challenging moments crop up in school every day. Let's be prepared. Let's know our own values and beliefs, aware that they will be communicated through our words and actions. Let's take responsibility for making the most of these opportunities and communicate inclusive messages that celebrate difference and diversity. For example,

The teacher notices a couple of children laughing at Harry not being able to do up his shoe laces. "Harry might need some help with those, but one of his great strengths is football, isn't it!"

A key adult senses that Cadelia is checking out a peer's piece of written work, and looking sad. "We've got such a mix in here. Some pupils write stories we all enjoy listening to, some pupils can run really fast and have an eye for the ball in sport, and some have musical skills they love sharing. It's great to have such a mix".

Self reflection

How do you relate to those who are different to you?

Can you let yourself be aware of any prejudices you might need to challenge in order to engage in the real task of inclusion?

What support would you need to help you do this?

'The Science' behind it all

As pupils get older and more curious about 'who' they are, I find it important to let them have access to information about how they've developed and their additional needs. Many will have identity type questions, often around the ages of 9 to 13, but at other ages as well. It's always important to remember that pupils who have experienced developmental trauma are likely to have an 'emotional age' younger than their 'chronological age', so may ask questions out of synch with their peers. It may be that we want to gently encourage parents and carers to engage in some life story work together with social workers or therapists. At school we can support this process by being open and honest, and by using materials such as, *Blame my Brain* (Morgan, 2007) which explores everything that's going inside the normal adolescent. I find this a very helpful starting point.

Some of the key adults I work with have got into fruitful conversations about attachment difficulties and developmental vulnerabilities with the pupils they are supporting.   Both children and adolescents seem to be especially interested in the science behind all this, and so knowing some of the facts and the latest research is important.   Do check out the books listed in the references and background reading section.   Be mindful of sharing information sensitively – especially facts – at the pupil's pace – in partnership with the young person's parents or carers and other professionals.

Our case pupil Lena very clearly needs her key adult to get alongside her to help her with this. Her curiosity is growing. She is also becoming upset by her realisation of her own vulnerabilities and weaknesses. This is a perfectly normal response. Let's not deflect these feelings away, but work with them, supporting her into having a healthier, more integrative view of herself. The 'parts' language described in Chapter 6 can be helpful, and the science perspective will definitely help as well.

Many of our pupils really need us to encourage them by letting them know that practice (of the things they need to get stronger at) actually does make a difference! Some fall into despair, feeling that they have lost so much ground, so reminders such as using 'books of success' *(see p.65)* can be particularly helpful. Visual evidence of how far they have already come can be really helpful in providing reassurance and building the resilience to keep going.

Pupils really can be supported to have better self-awareness and to make the adaptations necessary in order to live well. It can be life-affirming to point out that some of the most influential leaders and visionaries in world history have suffered; look on the internet together to find some examples, track their life stories, and help the young person make a collage of what they find that inspires them. Creativity can be born out of suffering, though we may have to wait for our pupils to really know this for themselves. There is hope, and they can find it for themselves if we hold onto it firmly for them until they do. There is a future.

Finally ...

FOR BEN

As soon as the class teacher hears the comments that have been made in class about the special kind of support Ben is getting, she tells the class that they need some more work on being a community together. The class teacher suggests running a project over the next few weeks with her class, making it clear that the theme contains an explicit message that everyone is different.

Slowly and sensitively, the class examine their differences together, in terms of their vulnerabilities and strengths. They explore different types of support and how they are necessary and valued in school. The teacher is quietly confident in her philosophy, responding consistently to their questions and comments. Learning from her approach over time, the pupils start to realise that Ben receives the support he does because he needs it, just like other people. They are content with that and don't need to ask any more. The questions stop. In fact, Ben starts to be included a lot more as the empathy of the rest of the class seems to have increased. Difference seems to be far more honoured and respected by the class now.

FOR LENA

Ann seeks Lena out and suggests they find somewhere private to chat. They find a space in the Inclusion

Department. Ann asks Lena what's wrong. Lena then discloses how some girls had been making fun of her, saying she was stupid because she goes to the Inclusion Department. Ann lets her talk, engaging in active listening so that Lena feels acknowledged and listened to. She then says they need to come up with a plan, as she can see a few difficulties. Ann identifies three areas that need addressing:

- Increasing Lena's understanding as to why she has particular difficulties
- Increasing Lena's capacity to be assertive, so that she can manage stressful interactions such as these
- Advocacy on Lena's behalf to protect her until she is stronger to stand up for herself

i) Ann starts by offering to support Lena to have a go at identifying what she thinks are her weaknesses and vulnerabilities. Ann then suggests that she and Lena think together about where these patterns and difficulties might have come from, making it clear that some might be because of her personality, some might be because of the trauma and loss she experienced, and some might be because of adolescence – probably a mixture of all three. Ann says that if Lena has any questions she can't answer that they can ask Lena's social worker. She also mentions that she knows some good books they could use to support their investigative work

ii) *Ann suggests that they work on some role-plays together so that Lena can practise using some assertive scripts. Ann explains that it might be helpful to look at the differences between passivity, assertiveness and aggression in their 1:1 sessions together. She shows Lena some good workbooks they could dip into, for example, the Talkabout series (Kelly, 1997 onwards).*

iii) *Ann says that she is going to meet with the Head of Year (Lena's key senior manager who knows her well) as she would like to talk with the girls herself to find out what's going on and to make it clear that these kind of comments are not expected in the school. Ann makes it clear that she will stand up for Lena.*

Chapter 13

Will I stay or will I go?
Moving on – again

Lack of continuity in school will, however have undermined their progress, leaving them less able to make relationships with teachers or to trust in their guidance. Mistrust then acts as a barrier to the enjoyment of school and educational success. (Peake (2006) in Golding et al, 2006 p. 101)

PRIMARY PHASE

Because of difficulties between a number of pupils in year 4, staff are wondering whether to move Ben into another class after the holiday.

SECONDARY PHASE

Lena was involved in a series of serious incidents that left the school wondering whether to permanently exclude her. If they decide to do so, she would be moving to another school after the holiday.

There will sometimes be a need for a pupil to move on. We really do need to consider this extremely carefully, and only use it as a last resort, because, as I have discussed in previous chapters, change is highly anxiety-provoking for pupils who have experienced developmental trauma.

Wherever possible, I believe we should do all we can to keep these pupils in our schools, in their familiar classes, and in the same school environment. Pupils who have experienced relational trauma and loss need our support to learn what it's like to experience stability. The phrase 'fresh start' has been used far too often with our most vulnerable pupils, often contributing to regression and increased difficulty in the next context. We need to do everything possible to foster permanence – as are our colleagues within social care and health.

> Frequent changes of placement, discontinuity of caregivers and inconsistencies in care-giving all replicate the family environments that trigger attachment disorganisation.
> (Taylor 2010, p.40)

In this chapter, I'll look at the importance of staff care in ensuring stability for our pupils. I will then move on to thinking through the planning and preparation that needs to be in place for any kind of transition to be managed well. I will address this transition planning in two sections – that of *moving from* the familiar, and that of *moving to* the new setting, covering the following issues:

MOVING FROM THE FAMILIAR:
i   Communicating

ii   Remembering

iii   Preparing

iv   The exit interview

MOVING TO THE NEW:
v   Induction

vi   Follow-up

Finally, I'll consider the implications for Ben and Lena, our two case pupils who we're following throughout this book.

Staffing

Sometimes staff point out to me that the reason pupils are being moved about is because the staff involved need a break themselves, and it's true that our empathy can also be a source of our vulnerability (AKAMAS 2006). 'Secondary stress' symptoms are a reality when working with pupils who have experienced trauma, deprivation, abuse and neglect, and we mustn't undermine or overlook this. We all experience the *emotional* impact of this work to some degree.

However, if our schools are to be truly inclusive, our time and attention would be better invested in focussing on what we can do to look after our staff's mental health, rather than on moving specific pupils around, especially in the name of the 'fresh starts' that we're so accustomed to. We need to ensure our staff are well cared for, so that our schools can be freed up to do their job well; that is, to be 'pupil focussed' (*and please see Chapter 15, 'Staff Care' for specific attention to this important area*).

Transition planning

I will now outline the stages that I consider to be significant in transition work.

MOVING FROM THE FAMILIAR

i   Communicate

Say it as it is. Pupils need us to be upfront and honest. What is going to happen? Why does Lena have to leave? Tell the pupil you are working with the answers to these questions briefly and explicitly in a factual way, rather than adding any personal thought or judgements of your own. Remember to explain your motives, and sensitively check back her understanding. This is crucial; vulnerable pupils like Lena may experience rejection very deeply.

ii   Remember

Allow opportunity to reflect on what has happened – the successes and the failures during the pupil's time at this school, for however long that period has been. At this point, a memory book might be helpful.

iii   Prepare

Give as much information about the imminent change as possible, to prepare the pupil for the move to a new placement. As I noted in Chapter 5, preparation will reduce anxiety levels and thus keep behaviours more regulated and appropriate. Preparation could include:

- Creating a visual timeline/countdown to the imminent change
- Researching the new school and area
- Transition visit/s with a familiar adult
- Making a folder/book about the new school
- Preparing the new class for her arrival. What could the teacher and pupils do to welcome Lena and to help her feel included?

iv   The exit interview

Schools need to be robust enough to make time for some important questions to be asked, to be answered both by the pupils themselves and the staff involved. Let's open ourselves up to the possibility that maybe *we* didn't always make the wisest of decisions, and that maybe we too can learn from the experiences we have shared with this particular pupil. These interviews are essential. They will not only communicate to the pupil that their voice is valued, but that what they say might also enlighten our understanding. Our new learning can then inform future practice with the vulnerable pupils in our care at school.

This process will reinforce the message that this pupil is a combination of parts and is not 'all bad' as they often believe. Contributing in this way will honour and strengthen the pupil's helping part. Remember the importance of 'parts' language (Chapter 6). We do have a duty of care in terms of our pupils mental health, and how they leave school. Let's not neglect their well-being by overlooking the significant task of transition.

Let's protect some time so that the pupil who is leaving and the key adult with whom she has a good relationship can work through the following questions:

a)   What did we do that helped you to settle to learn?

b)   What do you now do differently, as a result of being at our school?

c)   What did we do that interfered with your ability to settle and learn here?

d)   What should we get better at?

e)   What would you like us to understand about vulnerable pupils?

Engaging in this type of discussion has impacted my own work considerably. I've been surprised by what I've learned from pupils along my journey in this work to date. Some phrases come to mind:

> "Teachers don't listen".
>
> "This school is too noisy".
>
> "You never wanted me here".
>
> "I felt so different".
>
> "No one ever asked how I was".
>
> "I feel crap most of the time".

> "I didn't have any friends".
> "I tried to tell you I wasn't
> happy but you just
> said you were too busy".
> "This school's too big".
> "Why should I speak to you?
> You don't really care".

Reading between the lines, I think you can join with me to think what might have been helpful for these pupils.

It is only when we truly listen that we become acutely aware of the misinterpretations and mistranslation going on within our schools, and the need for us to adapt our practice. We all need to make the effort to keep learning.

MOVING TO THE NEW

v   Induction

Ensure the class are prepared and ready to welcome this new entrant. Allow the pupil (Lena in this instance) time to settle in. A full timetable needs to be implemented over time, not all in one go. The time invested in the pupil's welcome really will be time well spent. The pupil will be especially vulnerable at the start of a new placement; so pair her up with other students who will be good role models and ask them to help her feel comfortable within her new environment. At the same time, be prepared for a possible 'honeymoon period', as difficulties usually arise once pupils feel more comfortable and settled, so we need to keep an eye on what happens so that we can increase support sooner rather than later – as a preventative measure, rather than merely engaging in crisis intervention.

vi   Follow-up

The previous school needs to continue contact with the pupil in person and/or through notes/cards. It's important that these pupils experience staggered endings – especially with their key adult (that is, not all endings happening simultaeneously). Many of our pupils have experienced several abrupt endings in their short lives to date. We don't want to exacerbate their experiences of unresolved trauma and loss. Like all of us, they need time to process endings, but they will need extra time because of what may be triggered for them. Staggered endings allow for this, and enable the pupil to experience sensitive care in this vulnerable area. Having experienced a thought-through transition with us, they will be able to manage whatever ending they next have to face with more resilience. Even an ending such as having to leave one particular school can become an educative opportunity for our pupil, if we manage it well. It doesn't need to merely leave the pupil with a sense of rejection and/or despair. I recommend at least three follow-up contacts, although some key adults may choose to continue with their relationship with the child or young person past this point.

WHAT HELPS US ...
"Getting help"

Some staff are concerned by this, perhaps worried that they may become 'over involved' or 'create unhealthy dependencies' with the pupils in their care, but I believe we've been far too cautious to date, to the detriment of vulnerable pupils. The benefits for pupils who have experienced developmental trauma of having continuity of significant relationships far outweighs any fear-driven consequences, in my view. As long as professional boundaries are maintained, I believe relationships can be continued and honoured, if this is what the pupil and the key adult would like.

WHAT HELPS US ...
"A 'safe' space/somewhere
to go outside of lessons"

Imagine what a difference it would make to a pupil with a fragmented sense of self, having experienced many different carers in their lives, to know that someone

WHAT HELPS US …
"Having close friends
I trust"

wanted to remain in contact, despite it not being their 'duty' or being 'paid' to do so. This after-care experience could prove life-changing for some, in terms of how they view themselves. So many pupils in this position are in the care system and have told professionals countless times that the only reason they think they are being related to is because we get paid, not for any other reason. Let's prove this internal belief wrong!

Finally …

FOR BEN

In Ben's case staff are asked if they would consider moving other pupils around, before moving him. He needs to be urgently flagged up as the one who must not be moved, unless there really is no other option. An external consultant suggests that the staff involved might benefit from additional support so that they could continue working with him. Only after these two options have been explored fully can the school feel comfortable about a move like this. The following plan could then be implemented:

Communicate

Jake explains what the plan is, that Ben will be moving class. He states that they both know Ben has had lots of problems with different children in the class. Jake explains that he will continue working with Ben, and his aim is to help Ben get stronger at managing stress.

Remember

Jake makes a memory book with Ben to identify all the things that he enjoyed and learnt whilst in that class. The book consists of pictures and words. Together, they find some photos to illustrate a class trip that Ben particularly enjoyed.

Prepare

Jake says that there are 5 more weeks until the summer holidays. He finds a calendar and together Ben and Jake colour in the weeks until the move will take place. Jake says that they are going to visit Ben's new class in a couple of weeks; that the other pupils there are looking forward to him coming, and because they have heard Ben is especially creative, they would love him to join their art lesson.

Exit

Jake asks Ben if there is anything he wants to do differently next time: in other words, has he learned anything from what has happened? Jake also asks Ben the difficult question about his class: "What do you think we should learn from this?"

FOR LENA

If a move is deemed necessary, as in the above case with Lena, we do need to be engaging in some essential transition work. I am concerned that some schools think that once a decision such as permanent exclusion is made, they no longer have responsibility for the well-

being of the pupil, still on their roll. We do: and we must act responsibly. The transition process must begin with communicating to Lena why a move is deemed necessary. Failure to attend to transition support at such a fragile time for the pupil does place him or her at considerable risk of experiencing profound rejection. The consequences of a pupil who has already experienced relational trauma and loss experiencing yet another profound rejection is toxic: toxic for both the pupils themselves, and their wider communities. Despair and isolation can lead to devastating effects, for example, blanking out the pain through drug taking, binge drinking, risk taking, compulsive addictive behaviours. Left without hope, these young people can become at risk of harming themselves, or others.

We must take this responsibility seriously in view of a pupil's mental health, future, and the well-being of their families and wider communities. The same process must be followed as in Ben's case.

Chapter 14

School's out!
The end of the day, weekends and holidays

Early, traumatic experiences have profound effects on their neurobiological development and strongly influence their beliefs about the world. Their sense of self, security and trust are severely compromised; often they continue to struggle with issues around separation and loss, long after finding 'security' in their adoptive families. (Archer. C et al, 2006, p.166)

PRIMARY PHASE

It's coming to the end of the day and Ben starts to become quite dysregulated. Jake steps in and stops him a bit before the end of the day to engage in his 'check out'.

SECONDARY PHASE

If the staff had decided to promote relational permanence by keeping Lena at the school and not permanently excluding her, we might see the following scenario. It is the last day of term, and Lena is on her way home from school. Other pupils are going hysterical around her shouting, "No more school!" Lena seems quieter than usual, and a little bewildered.

The end of the day – going home

Just as we started every day with a 'meet and greet' structure, it's advisable to have a check out at the end of each day if at all possible. This means we need to make space for the key adult and pupil to reflect together. How has the pupil found the day? It may be helpful to use a self-evaluation form of some kind with our pupils, as visual communication is often easier for them. We sometimes use comic strip conversations too, to support the pupil to tell us what has been happening. These are especially helpful for difficult dynamics. This tool was designed by Carol Gray (thegraycenter.org/socialstories/carolgray) and originally intended for pupils on the ASD spectrum. We gently get alongside the pupil, giving our feedback too, not in an intrusive or shaming way but merely highlighting any interesting similarities or differences between the two accounts.

If the pupil shared a special object with you during their 'meet and greet', *(see p.34)* give it back to them to take home. Let's make a point of reminding the pupil that tomorrow is a new day, and that we are looking forward to seeing them tomorrow! We sometimes use a transitional object or a note with the pupil, leaving it with the pupil or swapping items *(as described below)* to reinforce this message of us 'remaining' in a concrete way. Try and use repetition whenever you can to reinforce and strengthen new learning.

When pupils are picked up by parents and carers, it's helpful to be be part of the handover, giving a smile and a brief message about the day. Avoid using 'good' and 'bad' statements. Use specific language to describe events. We save the difficult conversations for private phone calls or email communications, so as not to humiliate or inadvertently shame the pupil, as we know they are so sensitive to this.

WHAT WE NEED …

"A belief and philosophy established into the school ethos that social and emotional needs are just as important as academic needs"
Assistant Head – primary school

Breaks and holidays

Like me, you probably really look forward to breaks – the weekends and the holidays – as do most pupils and education staff. However, for pupils who have experienced relational trauma and loss, a break is yet another transition to negotiate. Transitions, as we've seen, bring uncertainty. Uncertainty can increase anxiety. Some transitions are more difficult than others. The most stressful times for these pupils are the lead up to the big holidays. At these times schools are often off timetable, and there is lots of chaotic activity:

- furniture may be moved
- rooms may be used for different purposes
- classes may be doubled up
- expectations might change, for example non-uniform day
- timings can be altered, for example breaks, dinner time, and home time
- food can become irregular
- staff can take on different roles, for example becoming the production manager for the end of year concert
- staff can act differently, for example becoming more informal as they get excited about their own imminent release!

Fun for most of us. However, all this can be really difficult for pupils for whom routine is necessary to facilitate safety, security and stability. Powerful emotions can be aroused and the transitions create increased opportunity for anxiety triggers to occur *(see Bombèr 2007, pp.189-191).*

So we're going to need to think through how we can best support these pupils around these times.

First, I'll look at what might be in the pupil's mind at the end of the school week or term. I will then explore various strategies that have proved effective in supporting pupils like Ben and Lena. These will include:

i   The routine of a timetable

ii   Busy folders

iii   Visual countdowns

iv   Reflective time

v   Post-it notes

vi   Staggered endings

vii   Transitional objects

The pupil's concerns

For our pupils, thoughts such as the ones below are real and worrying

"Where will I sit? Where is my place?"

"I bet he is pleased to be leaving me. I bet he never really liked me anyway"

"Will I be remembered?"

"What is going on? What am I meant to be doing?"

"Will the school still be here after the break?"

"What's going to happen/what will I do through the holidays?"

"Am I coming back here after the break?"

"Will my new teacher in September know what to do when I get upset?"

"Will Mr Sparks still be there?"

"Will I have any friends?"

WHAT HELPS US ...
"Knowing where we stand"

So we must facilitate sensitive, attuned care to support the children and teenagers we are working with at these key times of heightened stress. If we don't do any thinking or planning in advance of the stress kicking in, our pupils may behave in such a way that they become at risk of being misunderstood, misinterpreted, and, at worst, excluded. It is not a co-incidence that many vulnerable pupils are either referred to Behaviour Support Services or excluded in the run up to a significant break. It really doesn't need to remain this way. We need to recognise their behaviour for what it really is – a communication about their distress. We need to plan, and we need to respond appropriately.

Possible tools for breaks

i   THE ROUTINE OF A TIMETABLE

Despite many changes to the types of activities going on at the end of term, I think we can still find creative ways to honour the routine of the usual timetable, even if it means doing a word-search for literacy and a puzzle for numeracy. It's important to predict for our pupils what will happen and when, insofar as we can. Uncertainty or surprises raise anxiety. Think about what it might have been like living in the kinds of places they have, where something unexpected happening could be an indicator that emotional and/or physical pain is just about to start. Relaxing our timetables or becoming more informal can frighten these pupils. Who knows what's going to happen next? Their defences are activated and the behaviours we see are often a reflection of their fear and panic. So, as far as possible, let's remain on timetable or create temporary timetables to reflect the content of the different term endings.

ii   BUSY FOLDERS

Some pupils benefit tremendously by having a folder of structured activities that they can take round with them, so that when their class is practising for the class pantomime or their class is engaging in a special themed day, they've got something

> **WHAT WE NEED …**
> *"Individual timetables supported by key adults addressing social and emotional needs as well as academic"*
> SENCO primary

predictable to do. They can then sit out from time to time to work through it. Just sitting around, not knowing what's going to happen next, is disconcerting for these pupils. My sense is that we don't always appreciate just how stressful it is for them not to know what they are 'meant to be doing' during unstructured times; they simply don't have the skills to manage themselves without the containment that structure brings. They still need us to model what to do, how to cope – as we would with a much younger child. It will be much easier if they have a specific task to focus on; the intensity of simply engaging in relationship with others in their class provokes too much anxiety.

So giving them something structured to return to as and when will be very supportive of our pupils, who, sadly, experience chaos and stress when other children and young people are enjoying the variety of activity the alternative day brings and the sense of freedom that comes from that.

iii   VISUAL COUNTDOWNS

Let's use visual countdowns to breaks. This can be as simple as highlighting the date each day on weekly or monthly calendars that can then be marked off. This will support the pupil knowing where he is in the process of time. We need to start these *earlier* for older pupils and *later* for younger pupils. For example, I'd start the summer break countdown a month before the last day for the secondary phase, and a fortnight before the last day for a young pupil in the primary phase. The older the pupil, the more time they need because of the increased complexity of meaning endings hold for them. However, we must also remember that chronological age does not equal emotional age: so as always, it's about attuning to the needs of your particular pupil.

iv   REFLECTIVE TIME

If we take time out to talk things through with our key pupil, we can go a long way to alleviating the kinds of worries I listed above. These worries can spring from:

- Developmental deficits – being much younger emotionally and socially, not understanding
- Getting mixed up between the past and now, for example, anticipating rejection at endings
- Not having the relational capacity to know how to manage unstructured times, which is a higher level skill

Let's protect some time to talk about and prepare for endings. Think and talk together about what has passed during the last week, half-term or year (whatever is appropriate) and what's going to happen after the up-coming break. You can look at what you're both pleased has happened, as well as the things you wish had happened, but didn't. Looking forward might mean including the things you hope will happen, as well as the things you're worried may happen, and preparing or planning for those as best you're able.

It's helpful to use drawing, writing and role-play to explore and prepare for transition. So often we presume that restricting information might actually prevent distress at these times, but the opposite is true for pupils who've experienced developmental trauma. So let's be explicit in our communications about transition. Coming alongside our pupils in this way will pre-empt or alleviate distress, by giving them plenty of time to prepare for and process imminent change.

v   POST-IT NOTES

I encourage all the key adults I train to stack up on these! Before a weekend, it can be really helpful to stick a post-it note on the pupil's book or inside their planner to let them know when you will see them next. This small gesture of sensitive care goes a long way.

> *"See you period 1 on Monday"*   Mr Dew
> *"See you in Maths on Tuesday"*   Miss Barber

vi   STAGGERED ENDINGS

If the pupil is due to move year groups or schools, ensure that he experiences staggered endings; this means that we divide up the tasks involved in preparing for a good ending into smaller, manageable steps that can be spread out over time. It isn't helpful for our pupils to experience all their endings in one go on the final day of term. So many goodbyes all at once can be too much for them to process, and lead to dysregulation. So, for example, to plan it better, Ann (key adult) might take Lena for a hot chocolate in the park a week before the final day at school to say her goodbye. Then, she might meet three days before the move to talk about the holiday and how Lena might use that time away. On the last day she might swap transitional objects with Lena, as described below.

Follow-ups are also necessary (once the pupil has changed class or school), as discussed in Chapter 13, *Moving on*.

vii   TRANSITIONAL OBJECTS

Let's use transitional objects to support the pupil. A transitional object is something that is a concrete, visual reminder of a continuing relationship: we could describe a wedding ring in this way. Let's support the child or young person we are working with to know that he can be 'kept in mind' (that is, that he can still be thought about and connected to emotionally) despite physical separation. Let's be explicit with our pupils about the fact that staff, space and the school itself will continue to exist and 'remain', despite a break or an ending. Some ideas for transitional objects might include: key rings, pencil cases/pens, postcards …

✔   *Key rings* It's helpful if as key adult, you have two key rings, with a picture of the pupil and you on them both. Give one to the pupil, and keep one yourself. As you give the key ring to the pupil, remind him that you will keep him in mind by looking at your own key ring during the holiday. You can tell him that the keyring will be a visual reminder for both of you that you will see each other again in September.

✔   *Pencil cases/pens* As above, but this time you and the pupil swap your pencil cases or a special pen, again with the use of the key scripts about 'being kept in mind' until the imminent 'reunion'.

✔   *Postcards* Sometimes it's appropriate in the longer breaks to send postcards to our key pupils. I encourage key adults to prepare them during term time and then just post them at regular intervals. Only brief comments need to be made. For example:

KEY ADULT

"Hope you are enjoying your holiday"

"Looking forward to working with you again in September"

"See you soon"

"Thinking of you during the school break!

Sometimes staff might be a little bit hesitant about engaging in the use of transitional objects, either because *a)* other pupils might object or *b)* because of the fear of creating dependency. However, this is an extremely important aspect of the work as I discussed in *Inside I'm Hurting* (2007, pp.94-95 *and* pp.166-7).

a)   Other pupils

Within my role of promoting inclusion in schools, I've found that other pupils need to know about two important facts:

- That you are a capable adult and know what you're doing
- That difference is honoured within the class and school

If these two facts are explicitly attended to, there won't be any difficulty with using transitional objects in the ways described above, as the pupils in your care will respect your judgement. If there is difficulty, I suggest the class or school spend time exploring the roles and responsibilities of education staff within school, or exploring difference in more detail *(see Chapter 12).*

b)   Dependency

As I've mentioned earlier within this book (and in *Inside I'm Hurting*) we need to challenge ourselves about this historic fear that has lasted generations! These specific pupils need *increased* opportunity to experience dependency, as it's within close relationship that many of the relational capacities that they need to manage school will develop and thrive. Dependency is the stepping stone towards healthy interdependence.

Self reflection

How do you prepare yourself for a big transition?
What helps you to cope?

Finally ...

FOR BEN

Jake puts his hand on Ben's shoulder and encourages him over to sit on the beanbags with him in the quiet area of the classroom. Jake gets the timetable out again and asks Ben to grade each lesson. Jake engages Ben in some reflective dialoguing offering his own reflections of the day too. Jake makes sure Ben has all his belongings back and packed up ready to go home. He swaps his pen with Ben and smiles. "See you tomorrow and we'll swap back!".

FOR LENA

Lena could have a staggered ending with her key adult Ann. She could make a booklet with Ann, outlining the successes of her last year, areas she wants to get better at next year, her hopes for her new year in September and any worries. Lena could either be allowed out earlier or kept back for ten minutes in the Inclusion Department, whilst she said her final goodbye to her key adult before the long break. Ann could send her two or three post cards throughout the summer holidays. Lena could be encouraged to keep a photo diary of her holiday away from school to bring in on the first day back.

Chapter 15

But what about ME?
Staff care

Caring for children who have experienced trauma, abuse, violence or neglect is difficult work that requires physical, mental and emotional labour, a deep emotional pool on which to draw, and adequate support from trusted others.

(Taylor 2010, p. 11)

FOR JAKE

Ben's key adult Jake starts walking home after school. Near his house, a neighbour greets him, and says "Are you OK? Haven't seen you for ages. You look like you've got the world on your shoulders". Jake says he's fine, but thinking about the comment later, he realises he does actually feel quite flat and run down. Reflecting on his week, Jake notices that he's been finding his work with Ben really upsetting.

FOR ANN

As Ann drives down the dual carriageway on her way to the gym after school, another driver cuts her up badly. Ann is startled and yells at him through the windscreen, something she never usually does. She is shocked by

her own reaction, and pulls off into a quiet road, where
she sit for a moment, shaking.

Secondary stress is a reality. This chapter is towards the end of this book, because I wanted to highlight the fact that the primary focus should always be the pupil, followed by ourselves, but in many ways it could be one of the first! Before you embark on working with a pupil who has experienced significant relational traumas and losses, please go through this chapter carefully and ensure you have appropriate and adequate support in place to see you through the long haul.

You can anticipate highs and lows. The pupil will experience times of growth and times of regression. Throughout the journey, it will be important to 'remain focussed.' What I mean by that is that we all have to work hard at holding on to the 'here and now', remembering the impact these pupils may have on us, because of their previous experiences of others relating to them in an unhealthy way. We are going to have to try our best to remain objective at the same time as entering into often unchartered territory – it's challenging! I know from my own work with pupils of many ages that *focus* enables us not to get knocked off course.

To begin with, I'll outline some defence mechanisms that we need to be aware of so that we don't become emeshed with our pupil's pain. I will then look at what I consider to be two key areas that need specific attention: that of *personal* responsibility for our well-being, and that of *corporate* responsibility for staff care. Let's commit to taking up both kinds of responsibility together. If we don't take care of ourselves and each other, we are putting ourselves at significant risk, and we are risking the well-being of the pupils in our care. We deserve good quality care. The pupils we are supporting deserve good quality care.

Defence mechanisms

Whilst engaged with this work, both I and my colleagues who work as attachment key adults have found it extremely useful to develop curiosity about our own internal experience at thinking, feeling and physical levels. I strongly recommend this kind of self-reflection in order to manage the work involved in relating to pupils who have experienced relational trauma and loss. We need curiosity to help us make sense of what happens between us and the pupils we are working with, what they may be trying to communicate to us through their behaviour. We must be so careful not to become either shut down or emeshed in our pupil's 'narrative' (the pupil's personal story of what they have lived to date). Shutting down, acting out or becoming enmeshed are three of the many ways we might protect ourselves from the painful feelings we may experience in the process of working alongside pupils who have experienced relational trauma and loss. Let's support one another to remain aware of this possibility, so that we can stay open and available for healthy and appropriate interventions.

> To defend against the humiliation of feeling impotent, workers can shut down their capacity to feel.   (Batmanghelidjh, in Perry, (Ed), 2009, p.185)

It may be helpful to think of the function of the key adult as being that of a 'compassionate companion'. To become and stay aware in that role, we need to develop our ability to be both objective and reflective. To support this reflection, I will outline four different mechanisms that need to be considered, preferably together with a professional who has therapeutic training. We will consider the possibility of clinical supervision later on.

i   PROJECTION

You may feel the effects of this interpersonal dynamic during or after you have been working with a specific pupil. So, for example, you might be left with very powerful feelings. These can be feelings that are provoked by similar emotions in the pupil, but were too painful for him to tolerate. Because the feelings seem overwhelming for him, they are unconsciously 'pushed out' onto the person who is trying to form a close relationship with the pupil. An easy way to understand this process is to imagine yourself at a party and talking together with someone who tells you about a problem in their lives, smiling while they're talking. Afterwards, you feel sad: you know you didn't arrive at the party feeling that way. Somehow something else the person might have been feeling has conveyed itself to you.

So it's important that you check in with yourself to find out how you are feeling at the beginning of a day or at the beginning of a particular piece of work with your key pupil, so that you can be clearer as to which feelings 'belong' to you and which to the pupil. If you can make this separation, and tolerate the feelings that the pupil is finding so difficult, then these unconscious communications can be reflected on as clues to what might be going on internally for him or her. Your awareness of these feelings will enhance your understanding and empathy. Projection, if used appropriately in this way, can direct our next steps and pace of challenge with a pupil.

Some examples of *unhelpful* ways of responding to projection are as follows:

✗ 'feeling' rubbish – *rubbishing something you've been part of*
✗ 'feeling' stupid – *being sarcastic to someone else*
✗ 'feeling' incompetent – *backing out of opportunities that might usually energise you*
✗ 'feeling' crazy – *going hysterical in front of the class*
✗ 'feeling' full up – *shouting at the next person who asks you about something*
✗ 'feeling' deskilled – *leaving the profession!*

We need to keep hold of our own reflective functioning.

ii   TRANSFERENCE

You may feel the effects of this particular form of unconscious communication during your work with a specific pupil. You will be able to realise that transference is occurring if you perceive that the pupil is acting towards you 'as if' you were someone else. The child or young person may seem to be expecting or anticipating a response or reaction from you that would be unusual or out of character for you. So, for example, as you lift your arm to get a book from the shelf, the pupil may wince. Where does that wince come from? It might indicate that the pupil is reacting to you 'as if' you were going to hit him. Maybe someone has made that movement before, and he has stored both what they did and how he reacted deep in his bodily response. This is a good example of transference, and important to notice.

iii   DISPLACEMENT

You may feel the effects of this during your work with a specific pupil. This is when you experience very strong emotional responses from the pupil which don't seem appropriate or proportionate to the current context *(and see Chapter 11, p.187)*. Basically, you have the sense that you're experiencing feelings that were '*not meant for you*'. So, for example, your key pupil has a complete melt-down when you make a simple correction in their book. This is very clearly an over-reactive response, indicating displacement.

iv   SPLITTING

You may feel the effects of this during and after your work with a specific pupil. Because of the nature of this defence mechanism, it's likely that more than one person will be affected. Splitting occurs when two or more people involved with supporting the pupil begin to have very polarised views, attitudes or beliefs to one another. This may start with a misunderstanding or even an argument. Powerful splitting is very common when working with pupils who present with more of a 'disorganised' attachment style *(see Geddes 2006, pp.103-126, and Bomber 2007, pp.35-9)*. The system around the pupil can start to replicate the chaos and polarisation inherent in the pupil's fragmented sense of self, sense of other people, and how they interpret the different contexts they find themselves in.

When this polarisation, animosity and blaming start to happen, the best thing we can do is to stop in our tracks and draw the attention of everyone in the team to the possibility of splitting. We need to work very hard at ensuring these splits are not allowed to grow. We need to work at being a tight team, trusting one another's competencies and working towards consistent, integrative support and practice. Please note that this defence mechanism can extend out into partnership with families/ carers at home and with other agencies such as, CAMHS, social services, the medical professions … no-one is exempt!

Now we have more awareness of what can happen for ourselves and others, we can reflect on what needs to be in place, at both personal and corporate levels, to support us in dealing with these dynamics. I will outline several strategies that help staff in these demanding roles. I must stress that these strategies do need to be integral to any intervention that goes on, and not an additional extra! Looking after ourselves and each other in this way has a powerful impact not only on us but on the pupils we're walking alongside. Let's not ever forget the powerful impact we have on one another.

Personal responsibility

As education staff, we need to take personal responsibility for caring for our own well-being, especially when engaging in this type of inclusion work. I often recommend that we actually map out the mechanisms we currently have in place on paper, so we can see where there may be gaps. It might be that we need to think up some more for ourselves, so I've included some ideas to initiate this process. None of them are rocket science! – but it's worth reminding ourselves of the basics.

→ **Take rest** We all know it's important to protect time just for ourselves to re-group and to ground ourselves – but do we do it?

→ **What do you do to truly relax?** What can you do to ensure this precious time is protected?
For example, every Thursday evening chilling out with a book and a glass of wine.

→ **Take exercise** We also know it's essential to exercise regularly. What kind of exercise are you most comfortable with? Exercise is a great stress reliever, especially when it's regular. *For example*, swimming every Tuesday

→ **Have a healthy diet** What kind of diet do you eat?
Is there anything that needs to be changed in order to have more balance in your diet? *For example*, eating less sugar, and including more slow-release carbohydrate

→ **Be connected** We know how important it is to be connected to close friends as well as to belong to wider groups of people. What do you do to maintain social relationships? Will you need to do anything to protect this?
For example, going out on Friday evenings with friends

→ **Express yourself** Expressing yourself as you go along can be of enormous benefit. Feelings that are allowed to build up can either leak out in inappropriate ways or have a detrimental effect upon our health. What do you find helps you to express your experience? *For example*, writing in a journal, painting, talking.

→ **Contain your own story** It is important to take time to resolve your own experiences of trauma and/or loss, if this has been your own personal background. All of us share an ethical responsibility to not allow our own 'baggage' to get triggered by or mixed in with the dynamics involved in supporting our pupils (****and see Riley 2010, below*).

→ **Link up with support networks** It is essential to be able to ask for help when you need it. There is no room for lone heros in this work. If we isolate ourselves, we can put ourselves at risk of burn-out. Sometimes the dynamics quickly get quite complex, and an objective view from an external specialist can be really helpful. Who would you approach if you needed support at any time? *For example*, CAMHS therapist, school counsellor, line manager.

→ **Engage in end of the day rituals** If you are working intensively with a pupil who has experienced significant relational trauma and losses, then it's helpful to build in some kind of ending ritual for yourself at the close of a school day. If you don't create something like this for yourself, you may well find that you experience intrusive thoughts at home.

Some ideas: *Talk* - find someone to offload to. *Write* – keep a journal of how you're left feeling. *Paint/draw* – whatever you are left with emotionally. *Wash your hands* – to symbolise ending, and rub some scented hand cream on! Think through what might be helpful for you individually.

***Riley (2010) has interesting findings in this area. He suggests that many difficult scenarios which occur in schools are contributed to by a teacher's own insecure attachment style. Up until now, we have been mainly focussing on what the pupil brings to class in terms of their attachment lens. Riley rightly challenges us to be curious about our own processes and why we do what we do. Some of us may have had unresolved issues of power and control from our own early childhood experience, whilst others amongst us may have rescuer tendencies often similary linked to what happened when we were very young. Perhaps at some point in the future, those of us working in schools will be expected to complete attachment style interviews, in order to assess whether we are psychologically fit for the role of supporting the pupils in our care.

Let's hope that if this happens, the people administering the interviews will be empathic, attuned individuals, capable of sign-posting candidates appropriately to additional services. For now, if you get the sense that that there is something that might interfere with you being able to be fully present with the pupil in your care: make a plan. If anything feels uncomfortable, is unresolved from your past or comes up during the work, what could you do to process this? Let's be prepared. You might, for example, be able to organise therapy, supervision and family meetings, as and when necessary.

Corporate responsibility

Schools need to think creatively about how to care for their staff, especially those who are working alongside pupils who have experienced significant, relational trauma and loss. As I mentioned earlier, there can be a very real risk of the key worker feeling or actually being isolated. We must find ways to actively resist this, in order to maintain the individual's well-being, and to invest in the long term health of our wider school systems. As we're all aware, a repeatedly high turnover of staff can reflect a lack of job satisfaction, and stress. Regular training and access to up-to-date resources and ideas are paramount in this work. As Riley (2010) states,

> Without an understanding of the raw emotions involved in teaching and adequate training in how to look after one's self and the students during moments of intensity, teachers are placed into intensely emotional environments ill-equipped to deal with the strong emotions when they inevitably arise.   (p.3)

Here are some additional ideas for best practice staff care, currently implemented in a number of the schools I've visited:

→ **Promote equality** Regardless of title, status, gender or responsibility, it's essential that all staff are given utmost respect and honour. Each should be valued for the contribution they bring and be entrusted with responsibility for their area of expertise. No-one benefits from a controlling environment or one where there is a culture of division.

→ **Have a clear, inclusive philosophy** Determine to ensure your vision is integrated in at every level, and only employ staff who agree with it. All staff need to know where they are going in terms of the school's shared goals. For example, from a hypothetical job advertisement: *"If you are only interested in national curriculum attainments, please don't apply. Our school is interested in the development of the whole pupil".*

→ **Protect breaks for staff** There a lot of key adults out there who are either not getting breaks or are not having enough time for a break. We are human! This is demanding work! Breaks are essential and lawful. Line managers need to ensure breaks are protected on behalf of their staff. Check up on those you manage. Insist on staff having access to breaks!

→ **Facilitate team building** We need to feel we belong to a team and are not isolated. We are working together. Plan team building opportunities into the academic year. Go raft building, mountaineering or orienteering and see what a difference it makes to your staff.

→ **Training** Give staff opportunities to receive good quality training. There is always more to learn. Learning is for everyone – regardless of status and ability. Inspiration and motivation is necessary at regular intervals to keep up the demanding pace of inclusion work.

→ **Peer mentoring** Match staff up from other schools who are supporting pupils presenting similar attachment styles. Shadow each other, and share strategies on a regular basis.

→ **Back-up adult** Sometimes it is necessary to have a back-up adult to support the key adult, especially if their key pupil presents with significant ambivalent or disorganised attachment difficulties and needs considerable adult support due to health and safety issues. This back-up adult can allow the key adult breaks, and can cover for meetings and courses.

→ **TACs (Team Around the Child)** Facilitate reflective groups that meet half-termly, to think through a pupil's impact on staff, from an emotional perspective. This group differs from an agenda-led staff meeting, in providing space to share sensitive thinking about the pupils in our care. A time to process this within the safe boundaries created and held by a facilitator (trained therapeutically) is a must.

→ **Line management** Regular, 'preventative' slots to meet and talk are important to find out how staff are doing – as well as checking targets and so on.

→ **The good ole cuppa!** Noticing that someone else might just need an extra break and some TLC is a great way to connect. Don't overlook your support staff or operate within hierarchies. We're all human. Why not encourage someone else by releasing them for five/ten minutes?

→ **Social events** Arrange regular, fun events - not just at the end of term, when everyone is exhausted and feeling pressure to turn up and 'show face'. Encourage positive relationships and a sense of being 'in this together'.

→ **Time out** Give staff the OK to stop and to take some time out sometimes. Facilitate staff going out for a walk around the block or to go to the staffroom to get a drink. Cover for them. Just 15-20 minutes can sometimes make all the difference.

→ **Wise allocations** Staff-pupil ratios need to be matched appropriately to the needs of the pupil. Make sure staff have balanced caseloads. For example, it wouldn't be appropriate for a key adult to be allocated a case load of all acting-out pupils! Ratios that are top-heavy can lead to shortcuts in practice and the staff member feeling overwhelmed. This can lead to burnout. We need to be responsible and think holistically.

→ **Access to specialist support** Be aware when what you can offer through your usual line management is not enough. Be prepared to refer staff on to counselling/ therapy interventions for themselves as provided for under the local authority. Sometimes staff will need specialist support. We cannot afford to allow complex dynamics to arise between staff members and pupils, so let's intervene and ensure that unresolved issues of trauma and loss and/or needs do not become emeshed.

→ **Supervision** Employ or use specialist, therapeutic staff based outside school. The school counsellor, a community mental health worker or a CAMHS therapist can all be clinical supervisors for this type of work where mental health issues are a concern and a priority. They can also provide consultations, so that staff have access to quality advice and expertise to inform their individual contact with pupils.

Supervision can be a very important part of taking care of one's self, staying open to new learning; and an indispensable part of the helper's well-being, ongoing self-development, self-awareness and commitment to development. We think that lack of supervision can contribute to feelings of staleness, rigidity and defensiveness.   (Hawkins & Shohet 2006, in Read 2009, p.85)

→ **Greetings** You may think it's daft to include this one, but I feel I have to! So many key support staff describe how other staff don't smile, say hello or enquire about how they are. We need to value our fellow colleagues. Let's create a working environment where everyone feels welcomed and included: mutual respect is essential.

→ **Encouragement** All staff need regular encouragement. Notes, cards, gifts and words are all appreciated. Let's notice one another and build each other up explicitly.

→ **Development** Notice the strengths and interests of individual staff.

Allow them room to grow in these areas. There are countless possibilities in the school context. Let your imagination flow!

→ **Let's celebrate successes** Please don't assume that staff realise you appreciate their efforts. Each one is valuable, so let them know.

→ **Rest room** Another one you might wonder why I've included! – but we all know that sometimes the staff toilet is our only private space in the whole school, somewhere to take some time out away from everyone and everything. So let's put a bit of thought into making them attractive and restful spaces. Invest in towels, hand lotions, fresh flowers, tiles, pictures and pleasant smells!

→ **Cultivate humour** Humour is good for us especially when working in stressful contexts. Let's facilitate opportunities for humour and laughter and not take ourselves too seriously.

→ **End-of-day ritual** Build in sufficient time to allow support staff to engage in some kind of debriefing/offloading at the end of each day. An extra half-hours pay (minimum) is an ethical response to the well-being needs of support staff in your care.

Finally ...

If as a practitioner we feel overwhelmed or isolated, like struggling mothers do, our care-giving capacity shrinks and we then tend to apply a care-giving style that is about 'one size fits all'. It is therefore important to receive nourishment as a professional, and regularly review your attachment relationship to your work.   (Read 2010, p.52)

HEALTH WARNING:
If you find your sleep, diet, social interactions or levels of energy are significantly compromised whilst engaged in this work, please seek professional advice ASAP. Your well-being is crucial.

FOR JAKE

Jake realised that how he was feeling was probably a response to his work with Ben, as other things in his own life are going well. In class, he's been very moved by the distress and sadness he's beginning to notice in Ben. Jake decides to talk about how he's feeling when he has his meeting with the other key adults next week. Even thinking about that meeting helps, and as he makes supper, and goes out into the garden to enjoy the evening light, Jake gradually feels more relaxed.

FOR ANN

Feeling a bit better after the gym Ann thinks about what's been happening at school; Lena immediately comes to mind. In fact it's been getting increasingly hard for Ann to stop thinking about Lena; there's something about her that touches Ann deeply. Ann realises she really needs some extra imput on how to work with Lena's sudden explosions of rage. Ann decides to arrange a consultation with the school counsellor, in one of her half hour 'time to talk' slots. She could also discuss this at the half termly TAC preventative meeting (Bombèr 2007, p.301). Once back home she makes a list of all the things she'd like to discuss. After doing this, Ann feels more able to leave school behind and concentrate on her own family.

Chapter 16

And us – the parents/carers?
Home/school partnership

FOR BEN

Jake has been engaging in weekly emails with Ben's adoptive parents. He is writing his latest one. Ben has been becoming so much more settled just recently. He feels that the stability of his relationship is having a powerful impact on him. Ben doesn't question as much now. It's as if he is starting to relax into the security of predictability that the key adult is providing for him.

Ben's adoptive dad responds with his weekly email after the weekend. He explains that Ben is very tired and a bit grumpy as he was away for a family party which involved travelling some distance. He says that he has sprayed some of his after shave onto Ben's collar this morning as he had seemed a bit clingy. He asks Jake to reassure Ben that dad will be keeping him in mind whilst he is at school today and all week.

FOR LENA

Lena's key adult Ann is determined to find some positives to bring to her first meeting with Lena's foster

Allow the pupil to sometimes witness you smiling, laughing or talking together. Seeing a positive relationship between the grown-ups will speak volumes to every Ben and Lena!

carer on Tuesday night, but is a bit worried about how many difficult things they need to discuss together. Lena's foster carer Pam really hopes this new school can actually understand that Lena's behaviour is all about trying to communicate her distress. Pam especially wants to let the school know that recently Lena's birth mother has made contact with Lena through Facebook, and that this has really upset Lena.

Parents and carers play such a significant role in supporting pupils who have experienced relational trauma and loss to settle to learn in school, and to ensure these pupils can make the most of all the opportunities on offer to them. In this chapter, I will outline a number of points that I've found particularly useful for the creation of a solid working partnership between us. I've separated out information for the education staff and parents/carers, since, despite there being many similarities in terms of advice to each party involved, and overlaps, there are also some distinct differences. This list has been devised using feedback from both education staff and parents/carers who have sought to work together. Both parties really want this partnership to become stronger and more effective: both parties realise that this really benefits the pupil's progress at school. The following supportive ideas have proved to be very effective in both primary and secondary schools.

Please follow the LEFT HAND PAGES for top tips for **parents and carers**

Please follow the RIGHT HAND PAGES for top tips for **education staff**

We'll all meet back together again on p.273 to consider what might work with the two pupils we're following throughout this book, Ben and Lena.

Top Tips for Parents and Carers for supporting pupils with developmental trauma at school

How to engage with education staff

✓ Make it a priority to meet together with education staff in person, at a mutually convenient time at the beginning of your child's time at this school.

✓ View yourself as an important member of the support team around this child. Remember you know your child so well and thus have so much to contribute to helping him to settle at school. Be determined from day one to commit to problem-solving together with school staff, rather than allowing blame to creep in.

✓ Be really patient with education staff who may have had limited access to the latest findings in this area. We, as education staff are responsible with what we know, but we all have a lot to learn (I hope all education staff will have access to more training in this area over time, but we are not there yet). It may well be that you know more than the education staff because of resources, trainings and meetings you've had access to or explored for yourself. Please be careful with the way you impart this knowledge. Let's be mindful of how this imbalance may make education staff feel, and gently signpost them to helpful resources, people and trainings that are now available.

✓ Please don't feel threatened by a member of education staff being allocated to your child to form a close relationship with, over a long period of time. This type of quality relationship will enable your child

Top Tips for Education Staff for supporting pupils with developmental trauma at school

How to engage with parents/carers

→ Arrange a mutually convenient time that you can meet up in person at the beginning of the work together. Protect some quality, uninterrupted time in a private space for this.

→ Facilitate a warm, responsive relationship. Be explicit about wanting to create a 'team approach' to supporting this pupil.

→ Be determined from day one to commit to problem solving together, rather than allowing blame to creep in.

→ Explain the importance of having one member of staff in school being allocated to the pupil, and that every effort will be made to ensure that this key adult remains constant throughout the pupil's time at the school. Refer the parent/carer to the evidence that relational permanence is essential for adaptation and recovery from developmental trauma and loss (Perry, 2011).

→ We can prepare parents/carers by explaining that we will be encouraging a relative dependency *(p.84)* between the key adult and pupil, and that over time, this key adult will become an additional attachment figure. Reassure the parent/carer that this support will in no way compromise their relationship (as the child or young person's primary attachment figure), but will be supportive over the long term as increased safety, security and stability are 'felt' by the pupil. Encourage the parent or carer by letting them know that other pupils have benefitted from this approach both in your school and nationally.

to become even more resilient in all areas of their lives. Relationship is the vehicle towards adaptation and recovery. Let's encourage schools to make the most of this very powerful vehicle, as these children are in school for a good proportion of time. The staff will honour your relationship with your child too.

✔ When staff ask you for background information about your child, please be as honest and open as you can be - even if you sometimes might feel awkward or uncomfortable or if the information is painful to you. The more you can share, the more likely your child is to be understood and supported more effectively to be all that he can be.

✔ Information needs to be passed on to key education staff about the pupil's history of trauma and loss — on a need-to-know basis. A confidential, A4 fact-file is especially useful, outlining the child or young person's history in bullet points on a top sheet, and summarising strategies that have been helpful to date. A couple of examples follow (on p.273):

✔ Please trust that any sensitive information will be treated confidentially and will only be shared on a 'need only' basis.

✔ Please remember if you are struggling in any way yourself that you need to actively access your own support network and not expect the education staff to do this. They may be able to signpost you, but you will need to follow the advice or support through. Education staff will work best if they are freed up to fully focus on your child 'in school'. Please do still share about what is going on in other contexts as this is so, so important. Just remember that whilst education staff may be empathic, they won't be able to focus on your other needs, as they

→ Some birth parents may experience considerable guilt or shame as a result of their shared history with the pupil. They may even feel threatened by you because of this. Be aware that very powerful feelings might well be around. Be empathic in your communications. Let these parents know that the 'here and now' has so many opportunities and possibilities and that this kind of working together will reap huge benefits. Encourage them by letting them know you are excited about the prospect of this work in view of all the progress that's possible.

→ Encourage them by letting them know that many parents and carers are beginning to come forward with numerous examples of their children and young people having settled to learn, of their making progress and of pupils being integrated into mainstream education because of attachment approaches being used in their schools. Draw attention to the fact that there is growing evidence that pupils who are related to developmentally, rather than chronologically, make quicker and more substantial progress.

→ Sensitively take a developmental history of the pupil, including any disruptions, by listing relational trauma and loss she has experienced to date. Include moves from her birth family and moves in-between different placements. Be mindful that for a number of reasons, this may well be emotionally painful for the parent/carer. Be sensitive to this, going at a careful pace, providing gentle encouragement along the way. Explain that the more they can share with us, the more we can then understand where the pupil might be developmentally, so that we can support her well and appropriately. Pupils we don't have as much information for are often misunderstood in our schools, sometimes just being seen as bad or mad. Anything that's shared needs to be recorded need to remain boundaried to focus on your child in school.

✔ If communication ever gets difficult, do feel free to either choose someone to go in and represent you, on your behalf, or ask someone to accompany you to meetings. Specialist teachers, social workers, therapists, psychologists and parent partnership organisations are best placed for this supportive role.

✔ Do ask what the school have learned about your child to date. Be curious about what works. What seems to settle your child to learn? What successes has your child had?

✔ Share what supports your child at home to focus, concentrate, rest/play and to follow your lead. This will give the school clues as to what might work in their context.

✔ When the school shares what works for them, try some of the ideas out at home. It may well be that they work at home too! Consistent strategies will really help, as these children need lots of repetition in order to organise areas of capacity in their brains (Perry, 2009).

✔ Do match the frequency of the school's communications with you. Life can become very busy, but this preventative style of working together is so, so important. It's important to arrange weekly contact with the child's 'additional attachment figure' – in other words, his key adult – the teaching assistant or mentor allocated. Such contact doesn't need to be extensive, but it does need to be planned, solution- and strength- focussed, and above all, regular *(and see Chapter 12 'Home/ School Partnership', in Inside I'm Hurting (Bombèr, 2007), for more detailed information on this).*

and stored in a confidential way. Any information should only be shared within school on a 'need to know' basis. Reassure the parents of this.

→ A confidential, A4 fact-file is especially useful, outlining the child or young person's history in bullet points on a top sheet, and summarising strategies that have been helpful to date. A couple of examples follow below *(see p.273)*.

→ Ask what the parent/carer already knows about what settles this pupil at school from previous experiences in the school context and/or from experiences shared at home. Engage in active listening to the parent or carer, as any clues will be so helpful!

→ Share what you already know about what seems to support this particular pupil, from your own experience to date. Share what you also know from reading or trainings that may well be relevant to this support work. This will instil confidence and trust.

→ If you do feel that the parent/carer knows more than you do about this area of specific difficulty, there's no need to feel threatened. See this as an opportunity for opening up further professional development. As education staff, we haven't had very much access to the research around in this area. Many foster carers and adopters have. They may well be able to point us towards helpful resources, organisations and any training that's available.

→ If there are difficulties at home, encourage the parent or carer to put the necessary, reparative opportunities in place, to put things right, as close to incidents as possible – as with a much younger child. You do not need to extend these at school. Just let the pupil know that you know. Remind her that we're all working together as a tight team.

✔ Let your child sometimes witness you smiling, laughing or talking with his key adult. Seeing a positive relationship between the grown-ups will speak volumes to your child!

✔ Do let the school know of any specific triggers that might dysregulate your child.

✔ Actively join in with contributing to individual planning and reviews in school for IEPs (individual education plans), IDPs (individual developmental plans), PEPs (personal education plans) and CAFs (common assessment framework). Your contributions are very important.

✔ In some cases it will be important that you participate in multi-agency forums, especially if your child is presenting with more of a disorganised/reactive attachment style of relating (Geddes 2006). When the education staff invite you, do go along if at all possible, as you have so much to contribute that will really help.

✔ If there are difficulties at school, encourage the school to put in place the necessary, reparative opportunities, as close to incidents as possible – as with a much younger child. You do not need to extend this at home. Just let your child know that you know. Remind him that you are part of the tight team around him. Let's keep toxic shame to a minimum, to ensure that these children stay open, not dispirited, and engaged in clear, reflective thinking.

✔ Attend parents' evenings, class assemblies, sports days and special events to communicate your interest.

✔ Show an active interest in the topics your child is covering at school

Let's keep toxic shame to a minimum, to ensure that these pupils stay open, not dispirited, and engaged in clear, reflective thinking.

→ Decide together on the frequency of contact and how you will communicate weekly: home/school partnership book, weekly emails, in person or a combination. It's important for the key adult in school to arrange weekly contact with the pupil's 'primary attachment figure' – in other words, their main parent or care-giver. Such contact doesn't need to be extensive, but it does need to be planned, solution- and strength- focussed, and above all, regular *(and see Chapter 12 'Home/ School Partnership', in Inside I'm Hurting (Bombèr, 2007), for more detailed information on this)*. Be mindful to set this up even if the pupil isn't worrying you at present! We need to be engaged in preventative, supportive work with our pupils.

→ Allow the pupil to sometimes witness you smiling, laughing or talking with their parent/carer. Seeing a positive relationship between the grown-ups will speak volumes to every Ben and Lena!

→ Do make sure to pass on to parents and carers any successes and positive changes you've noted with your key pupil, and share what you're enjoying about the work with her, so that your conversation with her family member really reflects all the parts of the child or adolescent you are getting to know

→ Make a point of inviting these parents and carers to attend parents' evenings, class assemblies, sports days and special events, and welcome any interest they express in the pupil's activities. A personal touch is really helpful.

by talking together, accessing supportive resources such as books and
DVDs and visiting related places of interest.

✔ Encourage reading at home by providing a wide range of materials
linked to your child's interests. Include magazines, comics, newspapers,
picture books, fiction books, pop-up books, reference books, story
tapes etc, and let your child see how quiet reading can give pleasure and
satisfaction. Whenever possible, and if you enjoy it, read out loud to
your child, whatever their age *(and see Signposting).*

✔ Keep an eye on activities/experiences planned during evenings and
weekends. Try to ensure that during term time, these children and
young people have plenty of time to rest and process everything that's
going on for them. Many are at real risk of sensory overload if we don't
monitor this.

✔ If the pupil is over-tired or ill, he is far more likely to engage in
regressed behaviours because his capacity to self-regulate can quickly
get undermined. Remember that if a child is in school, staff will be
assuming the child or young person is in a fit state to settle to learn.
So do make an assessment as to whether it's appropriate to send him
in to school. It may be that he needs an extra day at home to recover
fully and re-fuel before setting off again. Let's keep in mind that the
demands of school are particularly challenging for those pupils with a
history of relational trauma and loss *(see pp.29-30 for a description of the
numerous challenges involved).* Let's not set them up to fail.

✔ Do let the key adult know if there is something your child is particularly
concerned about, in and out of the school context, so that the key adult
can be supportive at school and take any action necessary.

→ If the pupil is over-tired or ill, she is far more likely to engage in regressed behaviours because her capacity to self-regulate can quickly get undermined. Let's encourage parents/carers to make an assessment as to whether it's appropriate to send her into school. It may be that she needs an extra day at home to recover fully and re-fuel before setting off again. Let's keep in mind that the demands of school are particularly challenging for those pupils with a history of relational trauma and loss *(see pp.29-30 for a description of the numerous challenges involved)*. Let's not set them up to fail.

→ Do let the parent/carer know if there is something the pupil is particularly concerned about, in and out of the school context, so that the parent/carer can be supportive at home and take any action necessary.

→ Pay a lot of attention to leaving the pupil with explicit, verbal and tangible messages that you are able to keep her in mind whilst separated. There will be separations during and after the school day or during weekends/holidays, when the pupil is not at school. For example, you might use post-it notes, swap pens or pencil cases, or send postcards *(see Chapter 14 for more ideas)*.

TEACHER, PRIMARY

"The attachment framework has just revolutionised my thinking about the pupils in my care. Since I have started using these strategies I have noticed a significant difference in the pupil I key work. He seems more calm, composed and he is at his desk working now!"

✔ Pay a lot of attention to leaving your child with explicit, verbal and tangible messages that you are able to keep them in mind though separate when he or she is in school. For example, you might show him that you have his photo in your wallet: you might swap an item of clothing: you might put a note in their lunch box, or a squirt of perfume/aftershave on their collar … *(see Chapter 12 in Inside I'm Hurting for more ideas).*

✔ If any opportunities arise in school for you and your child to work together, for example through the extended schools initiative, please join in. There are shared art groups, cookery groups, gardening groups and Theraplay opportunities out there in schools. This will have a significant, positive impact on your child's experience of school, and will have the additional benefit of strengthening your attachment together.

✔ Knowing you are alongside in a collaborative way will instil real trust and confidence in the education staff around your child.

ADOPTIVE MUM

"I never thought I would ever say this but my son is now settled and making good progress! Two years ago he was on the edge of exclusion and it was all a nightmare. It's just so reassuring to know that the staff know what they are doing and that he is getting what he deserves – a good education!"

Examples of fact files

FACTFILE: BEN
RELATIONAL TRAUMAS AND LOSSES:

- Severe neglect
- Physical abuse
- Emotional abuse
- Possible sexual abuse
- Move from birth family
- Short term foster care

Now adopted.

RESPONDS WELL TO:

- Intermittent eye contact
- Close proximity
- Transitional objects when apart
- Sport, construction
- Art, drawing
- Having lots of water to drink
- Chewelry
- Gym ball to sit on

FACTFILE: LENA
RELATIONAL TRAUMAS AND LOSSES:

- Birth mum very frightened during pregnancy – Domestic violence
- Lena born drug-dependent
- Hospital stay
- Severe neglect
- Move from birth mum
- Emergency foster care placement and left
- Foster care placement and left
- Foster care placement

Now in long-term foster care.

RESPONDS WELL TO:

- Close proximity
- Touch
- Tangles for calming
- Art and fashion
- Being read to
- Lavender and other scents on hankie
- Opportunity to use energy through movement, hockey, dance, yoga

Finally ...

FOR JAKE

Jake follows the advice of dad throughout the week and despite the shaky start on Monday, reports that Ben settled back into his routines of school well. Mentions there is a trip coming up but that he is unsure if Ben will manage all the transitions involved. Asks dad for his views.
Adoptive dad *Agrees with Jake about Ben being a lot more settled at school now. Says that Ben has even started talking about his lessons with some pride at home. He seems to really like Jake now even though he'd been resistant to help intitally. Jokes about all this taking time but that we will get there in the end!*

FOR ANN

Ann is really pleased that the meeting with Lena's foster carer Pam was so productive. They wrote up a factfile together and are now a lot clearer about the strategies each uses at home and school. Ann believes this will support Lena to negotiate inner conflicts and adolescence.
Foster carer *Pam feels Ann really understands Lena and is very relieved! She is impressed by Ann's sensitivity and insight into the impact of developmental trauma. She believes the email communications they've agreed will have positive impact on Lena settling better at school and on preventing splits from happening, as they had in the past at Lena's previous school.*

Chapter 17

Final words

> To make the best of ourselves and of each other, we urgently need to embrace a richer conception of human capacity.   (Robinson 2009, p.xiv)

Any given day at school holds countless possibilities for learning. Supportive opportunities provide the vulnerable pupils we've been following throughout this book with an alternative lens through which they can interpret themselves, others and their home/school contexts. For these opportunities to be maximised, we need to facilitate real relationships between both adults and pupils. We need to listen well and engage in reflective practice.

If we don't provide this kind of sensitive, additional care for these troubled pupils, we'll be wasting precious time. We all know that children in care are over-represented in exclusion figures. This really must end. Each moment is a moment never to be lived again. There are endless opportunities to challenge injustice! We can't do everything there is to be done, but we can each do something to contribute to adaptation and recovery, so that these pupils can thrive. Let's get alongside, engage and join in with our pupils. *Relationship will be their organising principle.* Yes, they do respond differently, and yes, they will challenge our existing way of 'doing school'. But if we choose to join together in this inclusive revolution, we will, over time, create a rich tapestry of opportunity in our shared journey.

So my new updated vision is for –

- **Developmental trauma and loss training** to be a core module in BEds and PGCES

- **One means of identifying vulnerable pupils** Let's establish and agree a common means of identification for pupils who have experienced developmental trauma and loss. Then no-one will be left off our radar, no-one's behaviour will be open to misinterpretation or, at worst, exclusion. Those currently identified as in need, at risk, vulnerable, looked after, on residency orders and adopted all share the same range of needs, so let's start viewing them as a shared community.

- **The provision of Attachment Support Services** offering specialist assessments, advices and support to key adults, teachers and schools. We need hubs in every authority whereby specialist support and advices can be obtained from time to time, as and when required

- At least one **Lead Attachment Teacher** in every school. This teacher would be at a senior level, so that they can affect all policies appropriately.

- **Lead Attachment Key Adults in every school** Teaching assistants and mentors would be trained up specifically in this area to key-work vulnerable pupils. In order for this to be effective work that is sustainable, these members of staff will need to be related to with a higher status than at present. They are essential staff in inclusive schools. They need to be given reasonable rates of pay, access to training and permanent contracts so that they can stay and provide pupils with the continuity and stability that they need.

- **Theraplay** to be incorporated into the national curriculum and into schools*

- **Integrating developmental assessments and tools** into usual, everyday classroom practice, in order to increase understanding around a pupil's starting point. We can then start to measure progress *developmentally,* rather than restricting ourselves to only using academic measures as indicators of progress in schools. Good models here would include the Boxall profile, NMT, Thrive, The Brief and the ISL's innovative, specialist developmental work in this area, *(please see Signposting, p.279).*

- **Safe spaces** to be set up in every school. These would be designated multi-sensory areas/zones/tents/rooms that pupils can access to engage in co-regulation together with their key adult, and to allow some 'downtime' or additional processing time to support our pupils' needs.

- **Break times/lunchtimes** to be viewed as significant parts of the school day. To incorporate increased structure and supervision. To be facilitated by those in senior positions and by those with play, counselling, mentoring and youth work experience and expertise

- **Accountability** around inclusive practice especially when working with children in need, at risk, vulnerable, looked after and adopted. We need staff outside schools working together with those in senior management to ensure that these pupils receive all they need in order to benefit from their experience of school.

*(An example of good practice can be found in 'Adoption Today' published by Adoption UK, Oct 2010 pp.19-21). We have waited for too long, to the detriment of many pupils, for clear frameworks backed by research which promote the use of touch and nurture. I view the use of Theraplay as essential practice for all our schools.

If we have the necessary commitment, passion and belief we can all make a difference – whatever our role. It can take courage to go that extra mile, to challenge our schools to be 'done differently', but together we can ensure this genuinely inclusive revolution gains momentum.

Our schools need to be places where all our pupils are integrated in and can thrive. As Margaret Dight MBE said at the *Faith In Families* national conference in November 2010, *"… an aspiration to excellence is infectious! Let's not inoculate ourselves against this infection by cynicism or depression"*. We must use our inner and outer strength to advocate for the vulnerable who are unable to create opportunity for themselves. Margaret went on to say *"I want to be thoroughly used up when I die"*. I am aiming to follow in her footsteps! Are you? Why not make your life count? Let's make a substantial difference to the way we 'do school'.

Finally, let's remember that:

> 'Human being' is more a verb than a noun. Each of us is unfinished, a work in progress. Perhaps it would be most accurate to add the word 'yet' to all our assessments of ourselves and each other. John has not learned compassion … yet. I have not developed the courage … yet. It changes everything. If life is a process all judgements are provisional. We can't judge something until it is finished. No one has won or lost until the race is over.
>
> (Remen 1996)

If you are already involved in promting attachment support in schools or would like to be, please do stay in touch on theyellowkite.co.uk. Make a pledge to be part of the inclusive revolution! Together we can make a difference!

Signposting – useful resources

KEY

📖 Book   ✂ Tool   📄 Handout   🖰 Website   💿 DVD

To facilitate calm/regulation/sensory integration

📖 *The Big Book Of Calmers* J. Moseley & R. Grogan
(2010) Positive Press Ltd: Wiltshire

📖 *The Scared Gang Books* E. Bhreathnach (2011)
Alder Tree Press: Northern Ireland
aldertreepress@yahoo.co.uk

✂ Theraplay   theraplay.org

🖰 Inspire Play   **inspireplay.co.uk**
🖰 Sense Toys   **sensetoys.com**
🖰 Sensory attachment intervention
sensoryattachmentintervention.com
🖰 Brain gym   **braingym.org.uk**
🖰   **heartmaths.co.uk**

To facilitate healthy development including 'learning'

📖 *Supporting Childrens' Learning: A Training
programme for foster carers*
C. Pallett, J. Simmonds & A. Warman (2010)
BAAF Adoption & Fostering: London

📖 *Billy Says … series* J. Alper (2002)
Fosterplus: Bedfordshire   **fosterplus.co.uk**

📖 *Draw on your emotions*
Margot Sunderland (1997)
Speechmark Publishing Ltd: Milton Keynes

📖 *The Velveteen Principles: A guide to becoming real*
T. Raiten-D'Antonio (2004) Health
Communications Inc: Florida   **hcibooks.com**

✂ Thrive   **thriveftc.com**

✂ NMT Neurosequential Model of Therapeutics
childtrauma.org

✂ The Brief   **4.parinc.com/Products/Product
aspx?ProductID=BRIEF**

✂ Catch up Literacy, Numeracy   **catchup.org.uk**

✂ Numicon for numeracy   **numicon.com**

✂ SEAL Social & emotional aspects of learning
**standards.dfes.gov.
uk/primary/publications/banda/seal**

✂ Boxall Profile   **nurturegroups.org**

✂ *The Emotional Needs of Children in Early Years
Settings: Observation checklist and accompanying
information* K. Golding & ISL, NHS,
Worcestershire Health Services (2010):
Worcestershire (unpublished manuscript)

✂ The Bear cards
incentiveplus.co.uk/bear-cards-14485

✂ *Sometimes I feel … (cards)* P. Jones (2005)
Speechmark Publishing Ltd: Milton Keynes

✂ *SEAL Social & Emotional Aspects of Learning*
standards.dfes.gov.uk

✂ *Wired For Health*
wiredforhealth.gov.uk/healthy.healsch.html

▤ *Keep the Cool in School*
    B. D. Perry   teacher.scholastic.com/
        professionalbruceperry/cool.htm
▤ *Creating an Emotionally Safe Classroom*
    B. D. Perry   teacher.scholastic.com/
    professional/bruceperry/safety_wonder.htm
▤ *Executive Function part 6: Training Executive
    Function*
    P. D. Zelazo Institute of Child Development:
    Minnesota   aboutkidshealth.ca

▤ *Improving the Attainment of Looked After Young
    People in Secondary Schools* (2009)
    DCSF–01048–2009 tel: 0845 605 5560
◌ Young Minds   youngminds.org
◌ Nurture Group Network   nurturegroups.org
◌ Theraplay   theraplay.org
◌ *Inclusion Development Programme Primary and
    Secondary: Supporting pupils with behavioural
    emotional & social difficulties* (2010)
        nationalstrategies.standard.dcsf.gov.uk

To facilitate healthy relationships with grown-ups

✂ Comic strip conversations   autism.org.uk
✂ Social stories   thegraycenter.org/socialstories/
                                    carolgray
✂ Circle of Security   circleofsecurity.org
✂ Catch up Literacy   catchup.org.uk
✂ Theraplay   theraplay.org

✂ Let's talk! Discussion cards   speechmark.net
✂ Top five! Discussion cards   speechmark.net
✂ Puppets   Good toyshops
◌ Child Trauma Academy   childtrauma.org
◌ Dads and Mums in prison reading stories
    for their children   storybookdads.co.uk

To facilitate healthy relationships with peers

▥ *Primary Playground Games* C.Weatherill (2003)
    Scholastic Ltd: Warwickshire
▥ *Talkabout series Developing social communication
    skills* A. Kelly (2003)
    Speechmark Publishing Ltd: Milton Keynes
▥ *The Incredible 5 Point Scale* K.D. Buron & M. Curtis
    (2004) Autism Asperger Publishing Co: Kansas

✂ Social stories   thegraycenter.org/socialstories/
                                    carolgray
✂ Comic strip conversations   autism.org.uk
✂ Puppets   Good toyshops
◌ Circle time   circle-time.co.uk
◌ Restorative Justice   restorativejustice.org.uk
◌ Tribes Learning Community   tribes.com

To facilitate focus/concentration/energy

▥ *The Big Book Of Energisers*
    J. Moseley & Z. Niwano (2008) Positive Press
    Ltd: Wiltshire

✂ Theraplay   theraplay.org
◌ Sense Toys   sensetoys.com
◌ Inspire Play   inspireplay.co.uk

To alleviate anxiety

▥ *Life Doesn't Frighten Me*
    M. Angelou (1993)
    Stewart, Tabouri & Chang: New York
▥ *Little Mouse's Big Book Of Fears*
    E. Gravett (2008)
    MacMillan Childrens Books: London
▥ *The Huge Bag Of Worries* V. Ironside (2011)
    Hodder Childrens Books: London

▥ *When My Worries Get Too Big!* K.D. Buron (2006)
    Autism Asperger Publishing Company: Kansas
▥ *Helping Children to cope with change, stress and
    anxiety: A photocopiable activities book* D. Plummer
    (2010) Jessica Kingsley Publishers: London
▥ *Sometimes I like to curl up in a ball*
    V. Churchill & C. Fuge (2001)
    David & Charles Childrens' Books: London

📖 *Supposing ...* F. Thomas & R. Collins (1999)
Bloomsbury Publishing Plc: London

✂ Make a box of worries
local stationers for box, paper

✂ Feelings Faces   feelingsfaces@hotmail.co.uk

To facilitate integrating loss

📖 *The Day The Sea Went Out And Never Came Back*
M. Sunderland (2004)
Speechmark Publishing Ltd: Milton Keynes

📖 *The Red Tree* S. Tan (2004)
Thomas C. Lothian Pty Ltd: Victoria

📖 *Badgers Parting Gifts* S. Varley (1992)
Picture Lions: London

📖 *The Original Velveteen Rabbit* M. Williams (2004)
Egmont Books Ltd: London

📖 *Falling Angels* C. Thompson (2001)
Hutchinsons Childrens' Books: London

📖 *The Wise Mouse* V. Ironside (2003)
Young Minds: London   **youngminds.org.uk**

📖 *Two of everything* B. Cole (1997)
Random House Childrens' Books: London

📖 *The Frog Who Longed For The Moon To Smile*
M. Sunderland (2000)
Speechmark Publishing Ltd: Milton Keynes

📖 *When something terrible happens* M. Heegaard
(1991) Woodland Press: Minneapolis

📖 *Remembering* D. Leutner (2009)
Child Bereavement Charity: Buckinghamshire

📖 *The Patchwork Quilt*
V. Flournoy & J. Pinkney (1995)
Puffin Books: England

📖 *Something Else* K.Cave & C. Riddell (1995)
Picture Puffins: England

🕯 Child Bereavement Trust
childbereavement.org.uk

🕯 Winston's Wish   **winstonswish.org.uk**

To facilitate a healthy expression of anger

📖 *How To Take The Grrrr Out Of Anger*
E. Verdick & M. Lisovskis (2003) Free Spirit
Publishing Inc: Minneapolis   **freespirit.com**

📖 *A Volcano In My Tummy*
E. Whitehouse & W. Pudney (2007)
New Society Publishers: Canada

📖 *What to do when your temper flares* D. Huebner
(2008) Magination Press: Washington

📖 *Seeing Red*
J. Simmonds & Family & Childrens' Service.
(2003) New Society Publishers: Canada

📖 *When Sophie Gets Angry – Really, Really Angry*
M. Bang (1999) Scholastic Inc: New York

📖 *Mad isn't bad* M. Mundy (1999)
One Caring Place: Indiana

To support separation or transition

📖 *Helping Children to cope with change, stress
and anxiety A photocopiable activities book*
D. Plummer (2010)
Jessica Kingsley Publishers: London

✂ Timers   good toy shops or pound shops
✂ Find it games   Amazon
✂ Key Rings   the local corner shop!
🕯 Dads and Mums in prison reading stories for
their children   **storybookdads.co.uk**

To facilitate inclusion

🕯 Inclusive Solutions **inclusive-solutions.com**
🕯 Tribes learning communities   **tribes.com**

🕯 The Yellow Kite Attachment Support Service
For Schools   **theyellowkite.co.uk**

To facilitate further understanding

📖 *Stop Wasting My Time!*
Post Adoption Central Support: Stirling
postadoptioncentralsupport.org

✂ The Wall   adoptionuk.org/information/
103254/thewall/

📄 *Understanding Why*   National Childrens Bureau
ncb.org.uk

📄 *Adoption, Attachment Issues & Your School* PACS
postadoptioncentralsupport.org

🖰 Circle of security   circleofsecurity.org

🖰 Nurture Group Network   nurturegroups.org

🖰 Presentation about effects of developmental
trauma and loss   healingresources.info
emotional_trauma_online_video.htm#int

🖰 Teachers in the know   thewhocarestrust.org.uk

🖰 A Home For Maisie *Please contact* bbc.co.uk *for
information on how to purchase this DVD*

🖰 Nowhere Boy film about John Lennon (2009)
Sam Taylor Wood (director)   Amazon

🖰 Looked After Children & Young People: We Can
and Must Do Better. J. Furnivall, G. Connelly,
B. Hudson & G. McCann (2008): The Scottish
Government

🖰 *The Nurture Room* (2010) True Vision North
Production.   thenurtureroom.com

🖰 Janine's story   familyfutures.co.uk

Useful organisations and addresses

Adoption Plus
Moulsoe Business Centre Cranfield Road Moulsoe Newport Pagnell MK16 0FJ   adoptionplus.org

Adoption UK 46 The Green South Bar Street Banbury OX16 9AB   adoptionuk.org

BAAF Saffron House, 6-10 Kirby Street London EC1N 8TS   BAAF.org

Barnardos Tanners Lane Barkingside Ilford Essex IG6 1QG   barnardos.org.uk

Caspari 53 Eagle Wharf Rd London N1 7ER   caspari.org.uk

Centre for Child Mental Health 2-18 Britannia Row Islington London N1 8PA   childmentalhealthcentre.org

Centre for Emotional Development
35 Clermont Terrace Brighton East Sussex BN1 6SJ   emotionaldevelopment.co.uk

Chrysalis Associates Ltd 48 Wostenholm Road Sheffield S7 1LL   chrysalisassociates.og

Coram Coram Community Campus 49 Mecklenburgh Square London WC1N 2QA   coram.org.uk

Family Futures 3+4 Floral Place 7-9 Northampton Grove London N1 2PL   familyfutures.co.uk

National Childrens' Bureau 8 Wakley Street London EC1V 7QE   ncb.org.uk

Post-Adoption Centre
5 Torriano Mews Torriano Avenue London NW5 2RZ   postadoptioncentre.org.uk

The Who Cares Trust Kemp House 152-160 City Rd London EC1V 2NP   thewhocarestrust.org.uk

Young Minds 48-50 St John Street London EC1M 4DG   youngminds.org

References

Archer, C. et al (2006) *New Families, Old Scripts: A guide to the language of trauma and attachment in adoptive families* Jessica Kingsley Publishers: London

Archer, C. & Burnell, A. (Eds) (2003) *Trauma, Attachment and Family Permanence: Fear can stop you loving* Jessica Kingsley Publishers: London

Aspelemeier, J. E. & Kerns, K.A. (2003) Love and School: Attachment/exploration dynamics *Journal of Social and Personal Relationships* 20(1) pp.5-30

Bannister, A. & Huntington, A. (2002) *Communicating with Children and Adolescents* Jessica Kingsley Publishers: London

Bannell, C. & Peake, A. (2004) *Attachment and the Consequences of Disrupted Childhood* Oxfordshire Local Education Authority

Barnardo's (2006) *Failed by the System: The views of young care leavers on their educational experiences* Barnardo's: Ilford

Barrett, M. & Trevitt, J. (1991) *Attachment Behaviour and the Schoolchild* Routledge: London

Bebbington, E. (2005) *"Stop Wasting my Time!" Case studies of pupils with attachment issues in schools with special reference to looked after and adopted children* PACS: Stirling, Scotland

Bennathan, M. & Boxhall, M. (1984) *The Boxall Profile Handbook: A guide to effective intervention in the education of pupils with social, emotional and behavioural difficulties* The Nurture Group Network: Wigan

Bennathan, M. & Boxhall, M. (2000) *Effective Intervention in Primary Schools: Nurture groups* David Fulton: London

Biddulph, S. (1997) *Raising Boys* Thorsons: London

Blackburn, C. *Foetal Alcohol Spectrum Disorder, Building Bridges with Understanding Project* Worcestershire County Council worcestershire.gov.uk/eycs

Bombèr, L. (2007) *Inside I'm Hurting: Practical strategies for supporting children with attachment difficulties in school* Worth Publishing: London

Bombèr, L. (2010) *What Makes You Think I'm Gonna Trust You?* Adoption Now: Banbury

Booth, P & Jernberg, A. (2010) *Theraplay: Helping parents and children build better relationships through attachment based play* Jossey Bass: California, USA

Bowlby, J. (1980) *Attachment and Loss Vol. 3, Loss, Sadness and Depression* Hogarth Press: London

Bowlby, J. (1988) *A Secure Base: Clinical applications of attachment theory* Routledge: London

Boxall, M. (2002) *Nurture Groups In Schools: Principles and practice* Sage Publications Ltd: London

Boxall, M, (2008) *Nurture Groups in School: Principles and practice* (Revised and updated by Sylvia Lucas) Sage Publications Ltd: London

Bradshaw, J. (1988) *Healing the Shame That Binds You* Health Communications: Florida

Bremner, J.D. (2004) Brain imaging in anxiety disorders *Expert Review of Neurotherapeutics* 4(2), pp.275-284

Burnell, A. (2011) Inside Out and Back to Front, Counselling Children and Young People *Counselling Children and Young People* BACP: Lutterworth p.2-6

Cairns, K. (2002) *Attachment, Trauma and Resilience* BAAF: London

Cairns, K. & Stanway, C. (2004) *Learn the Child: Helping looked after children to learn* BAAF: London

Chapman, L. & West-Burnham, J. (2010) *Education for Social Justice* Continuum International Publishing Group: London

Claxton, G. (2008) *What's the Point of School?* Oneworld Publications: Oxford, England

Clements, J. (2005) *People with Autism Behaving Badly* Jessica Kingsley Publishers: London

Connelly, G. (2007) Can Scotland achieve more for looked after children? *Adoption & Fostering* 31:1, pp.81-91

Cooper, G, Hoffman, K, Marvin, R. & Powell, B. (1998) *Circle of Security* Guildford Press: New York

Cooper, P. & Johnson, S. (2007) Education: the views of adoptive parents *Adoption & Fostering* 31:1, pp.21-27

Cooper, P. (2008) Nurturing attachment to school: Contemporary perspectives of special education and behavioural difficulties *Pastoral Care in Education* 26(1) pp.13-22

Cooper, P. (2002) *The Nurture Group Research Project* AWCEBD Newsletter, Summer 2002

Crittenden, P. M. (1992) Children's strategies for coping with adverse home environments: An interpretation using attachment theory *Child Abuse and Neglect* 16, pp.329-343

Daley, P. & Johnson, S. (2004) The vulnerable child in school in Phillips, R. (Ed) *Children Exposed to Parental Substance Misuse: Implications for family placement* BAAF: London

Davis, A., Kruczek, T. & Mcintosh, D. (2006) Understanding and treating psychopathology in the schools *Psychology in the Schools* 43, pp.23-417

Department for Children, Schools and Families (2007) *Social and Emotional Aspects of Learning (SEAL)* DCSF Publications: Nottingham

Department for Children, Schools and Families (2008) *Personal Education Allowances for Looked After Children: Statutory Guidance for Local Authorities* teacher.net.gov.uk/publications

Department for Children, Schools and Families (2008) *Social and Emotional Aspects of Development, Guidance for Practitioners Working in the Early Years Foundation Stage* DCSF Publications: Nottingham

Department for Children, Schools and Families (2009) *Improving the Attainment of Looked After Young People in Secondary Schools* teacher.net.gov.uk/publications

Department of Education and Skills (2001) *Promoting Mental Health with Early Years and School Setting.* The Stationery Office: London

Department of Education and Skills (2004) *Every Child Matters* The Stationery Office: London

Department of Education and Skills (2005) *Excellence and Enjoyment: Social and Emotional Aspects of Learning* DCSF Publications: Nottingham.

Department Of Education and Skills (2006) *Care Matters: Transforming the lives of children and young people in care* The Stationary Office: London

Department for Education and Skills (DfES) (2007a) *Statutory Framework for the Early Years Foundation Stage* DfES Publications: Nottingham

Doherty, J. & Hughes, M. (2009) *Child Development: Theory and practice 0-11* Pearson Education Limited: Essex

Douglas, A. (2006) Legacy of Separation *Community Care* pp.36-37

Egan, G. (2002) *The Skilled Helper: A problem-management and opportunity-development approach to helping* Brooks/Cole: Pacific Grove

Egan, K. (2005) *An Imaginative Approach to Teaching* Josey Bass: San Francisco

Egerton, J. *Foetal Alcohol Spectrum Disorder* Worcestershire County Council worcestershire.gov.uk/eycs

Elfer, P., Goldschmeid, E. & Selleck, D. (2002) *Key Persons in the Nursery: Building relationships for quality provision* Early Years Network: London

Ferguson, H. (2011) *Child Protection Practice* Macmillan Publishing Ltd: Hampshire

Flutter, J. & Ruddick, J. (2004) *Consulting Pupils: What's in it for schools?* Routledge & Falmer: London

Geddes, H. (2006) *Attachment in the Classroom: The links between children's early experience, emotional well being and performance in school* Worth Publishing Ltd: London

Gerhardt, S. (2004) *Why Love Matters: How affection shapes a baby's brain* Brunner-Routledge: Hove, East Sussex

Gerhardt, S. (2010) *The Selfish Society: How we all forgot to love one another and made money instead* Simon & Schuster UK Ltd: London

Gilligan, R. (2001) *Promoting Resilience: A resource guide on working with children in the care system* BAAF: London

Gilligan, R (2007) Adversity, resilience and the educational progress of young people in public care *Emotional and Behavioural Difficulties* 12:2 pp.135-145

Gioia, G.A., Isquithy, P.K., Guy, S.C., Kenworthy, L. The Brief® Behavior Rating Inventory of Executive Function® www4.parinc.com/Products/Productaspx?ProductID=BRIEF

Glasser, H. & Easley, J. (2007) *Transforming the Difficult Child: The nurtured heart approach* Worth Publishing: London

Golding, K., Dent, H., Nissim, R. & Stott, L. (2006) *Thinking Psychologically About Children who are Looked After and Adopted* John Wiley & Sons Ltd: Chichester

Golding, K. (2008) *Nurturing Attachments: Supporting children who are fostered or adopted* Jessica Kingsley Publishers: London

Golding, K., Fain, J., Frost, A., Durrant, E., Templeton. S. & Soni, A (2010) *The emotional needs of children in early years settings: Observation checklist and accompanying information* Unpublished manuscript

Golding, K., Fain, J., Frost, A., Mills, C., Worrall, H., Roberts, N., Durrant, T. & Templeton, S. (2011) *The emotional needs of children in school: Key stage 1 and 2. Observation and accompanying information* Unpublished manuscript

Goldschmied, E. & Jackson S. (1994) *People Under Three: Young children in daycare* Routledge: London

Gopnik, A. (2009) *The Philosophical Baby: What children's minds tell us about truth, love and the meaning of life* Bodley Head: London

Greenfield, S. (2001) *The Private Life of the Brain* Penguin Books: London

Greenhalgh, P. (1994) *Emotional Growth and Learning* Routledge: New York

Hardy, S. B. (2009) *Mothers and Others: The evolutionary origins of mutual understanding* Belknap Press: Cambridge, Massachusetts, USA

Hawkins, P. & Shohet, R. (2006) *Supervision in the Helping Professions* Open University Press: Maidenhead

Hare, A. & Bullock, R. (2006) Dispelling misconceptions about looked after children *Adoption & Fostering* 30:4 pp.26-35

Hoey, B. (1997) *Who Calls the Tune?* Routledge: London

Holmes, W. (2009) Catch up Literacy for Children in Care *Literacy Today* Issue 60 September 2009 pp.9-10

Howe, D. (1996) *Attachment Theory for Social Work Practice* BAAF: London

Howe, et al (1999) *Attachment Theory, Child Maltreatment & Family Support: A practice and assessment model* Palgrave: New York

Howe, D. (2005) *Child Abuse and Neglect. Attachment, development and intervention* Palgrave Macmillan: Basingstoke

Hughes, D. (1997) *Facilitating Developmental Attachment: The road to emotional recovery and behavioural change in foster and adopted children* Jason Aronson Inc: Northvale, NJ

Hughes, D. (2006) *Building the Bonds of Attachment: Awakening love in deeply troubled children* (2nd Edition) Jason Aronson Inc: Northvale, NJ

Hughes, D. (2009) *Attachment Focused Parenting* W.W. Norton & Company Incl: New York

Inclusion Charter (1989) *Ending Segregation in Education for all Students with Disabilities or Learning Difficulties* Centre for Studies on Inclusive Education (CSIE): Bristol, UK

Inclusion Development Programme Primary and Secondary (2010) nationalstrategies.standards.dcsf.gov.uk

Isle of Wight Council, (2003) *Policy for Inclusion of Children and Young People within Island Schools* Isle of Wight Council

Jackson, S (2001) *Nobody Ever Told Us School Mattered* BAAF: London

Jull, S. K. (2008) Emotional and Behavioural Difficulties (EBD): The special educational need justifying exclusion *Journal of Research in Special Educational Needs*, 8(1) pp.13-18

Kafetsios, K. & Nezlek, J.B. (2002) Attachment styles in everyday social interaction *European Journal of Social Psychology* 32(5) pp.719-735

Kluth, P & Dimon-Borowski, M (2003) *Strengths & Strategies Profile* inclusive-solutions.com/behaviour.asp

Kraemer, Sebastian (1999) Promoting Resilience: Changing concepts of parenting and child care *International Journal of Child and Family Welfare* 3: pp.273-287

Kranowitz, C (2005) *The Out-of-Sync Child: Recognizing and coping with sensory processing disorder* Penguin Group: New York

Lewis, R., Romi, S., Qui, X., & Katz, Y.J. (2005) Teachers' classroom discipline and student misbehaviour in Australia, China and Israel *Teaching and Teacher Education* 21 pp.729-741

Lively, K. & Kleine, P. (1996) *The School as a Tool for Survival of Homeless Children* Elementary and Early Childhood Education: New York, USA

Lynch, M. & Cicchetti, D. (1992) Maltreated children's reports of relatedness to their teachers *New Directions for Child Development* 57 pp.81-107

MacBeath, J. (2006) *School Inclusions can be Abuse* BBC News news.bbc.co.uk/1/hi/education/4774407/stm

Macnab, F. (1985) *Coping: How to bounce back and begin again* Hill of Content: Melbourne, Australia

Mcluskey, U. (2005) *To be Met as a Person: The dynamics of attachment in professional encounters* Karnac: London

Moran, M. (2007) Developmental Trauma Merits DSM Diagnosis, Experts say *Psychiatric News* Volume 42, Number 3 p.20 American Psychiatric Association

Morgan, N. (2007) *Blame my Brain* Walker Books Ltd: London

Morris, E. (2011) Every child still matters to teachers: What about the government? *The Guardian* 24/5/11 p.2

Mosley, J. (1996) *Quality Circle Time* LDA: Cambridge, UK

Mosley, J. (1999a) *More Quality Circle Time* LDA: Cambridge, UK

Mosley, J. (1999b) *Quality Circle Time In The Secondary School* David Fulton Publishers: London

Newton, C & Wilson, D. (2010) *Keys to Inclusion* (Book in process) Inclusive Solutions: Nottingham

Ocasio, J. & Knight, J. (2003) *Rediscovery of Trust: Erikson, Kaplan and the myth of foster care* Elementary and Early Childhood Education: New York

Orlans, M. & Levy, T. (2006) *Healing Parents, Helping Wounded Children Love and Trust* CWLA Press: Washington, DC

Owen, A. & Wilson, R. (2006) Attachment theory and its implications for psychotherapy with maltreated children *Child Abuse and Neglect* 18 pp.425-438

Pallett, C., Simmonds, J. & Warman, A. *Supporting Children's Learning, a Training Programme for Foster Carers* BAAF: London

Panksepp, J. (1989) *Affective Neuroscience: The foundations of human and animal emotion* Oxford University Press: New York and Oxford

Peake, A. (2004) *Moving on to Secondary School: A handbook for parents/carers* Oxfordshire Educational Psychology Service in conjunction with the Reach Up Team: Oxfordshire Local Education Authority

Pearce, C. (2009) *A Short Introduction to Attachment and Attachment Disorder* Jessica Kingsley Publishers: London

Perry, A. (Ed.) (2009) *Teenagers And Attachment: Helping adolescents engage with life and learning*
   Worth Publishing: London
Perry, B.D. Creating an emotionally safe classroom childtrauma.org
Perry, B.D. Keep the cool in school: promoting non-violent behaviour in children childtrauma.org
Perry. B.D. & Szalavitz (2010) *Born for Love* Harper Collins Publishers: New York
Perry. B.D. (2011) The Impact of Trauma and Neglect on the Developing Child Lecture given at Woburn
   Abbey Adoption Plus 24/05/11
Plummer, D. (2010) *Helping Children to Cope with Change, Stress and Anxiety* Jessica Kingsley Publishers: London

Read, V. (2010) *Developing Attachment in Early Years Settings: Nurturing secure relationships from birth to five years*
   Routledge: London *Reading remedy* Special Children Issue 190 Aug/Sept 2009 pp.39-40
   Regulation, regulation, regulation Adoption Today October (2010) p.19-21
Remen, R.N. (1996) *Kitchen Table Wisdom: Stories that heal* Pan Books: London
Riley, P. (2009) An adult attachment perspective on the student-teacher relationship and classroom
   management difficulties *Teaching and Teacher Education* 25(s) pp.626-635
Riley, P. (2010) *To Stir with Love: Imagination, attachment and teacher behaviour*
   Unpublished Thesis La Trobe Bundoora
Riley, P. (2011) *Attachment Theory and the Teacher-Student Relationship: A practical guide for teachers,*
   teacher-educators and school leaders Routledge: London
Robinson, K. (2009) *The Element: How finding passion changes everything* Penguin Books: London
Rothschild, B. (2000) *The Body Remembers: The psychobiology of trauma and trauma treatment* WW.Norton: New York
Ryan, M. (2006) *Understanding Why: Understanding attachment and how this can affect education with special*
   reference to adopted children and young people and those looked after by local authorities
   National Children's Bureau: London

Schofield, G. & Beek, M. (2006) *Attachment Handbook for Foster Care and Adoption* BAAF: London
Scroufe, L.A (2005) *The Development of the Person* Guildford: New York
Sharp, C, Fonagy, P & Goodyer, I (2006) Imagining your child's mind: psychosocial adjustment and mother's
   ability to predict their children's attributional response styles *British Journal Of Developmental Psychology* 24(1)
   2006 March pp.197-214
Slater, R. (2007) Attachment: Theoretical Development and Critique *Educational Psychology in Practice* 23(3)
   pp.205-219
Smyth, J. (2007) Teacher Development Against the Policy Reform Grain: An argument for recapturing
   relationships in teaching and learning *Teacher Development* 11:2 221-236.
Sunderland, M. (2006) *The Science of Parenting* Dorling Kindersley: London

Taylor, C. (2010) *Caring for Children and Teenagers with Attachment Difficulties* Jessica Kingsley Publishers: London
Tickle, L. (2007) Carers in the Classroom *Community Care* 10 May pp.26-27

Ungar, M. (2008) *Nurturing Hidden Resilience in Troubled Youth* University of Toronto Press: Toronto, Canada

Van der Kolk, B. *Trauma and Memory*, a video series cavalcadeproductions.com

Wilcox, P. (2010) *Trauma Treatment for Children* traumatreatment.blogspot.com
Wilkinson, M. (2006) *Coming Into Mind: The mind-brain relationship: A Jungian clinical perspective*
   Routledge: East Sussex
Wilson, P. (2003) *Young Minds In Our Schools* Young Minds: London
Winnecott, D. (1964) *The Child, The Family and the Outside World* Penguin Group: London

Index

abuse 18, 77, 124, 172, 225, 245
Action for Children 74
adaptive responses 4, **9**, 160, 161
addictive behaviour 11, 158, 163, 232
Adoption UK 5, 277
adoptive parent 77-79, 81, **258-73**
affect regulation 17-18, **22**
ambivalent attachment 7, 254
aggression 221
aggressive *language*, 176: *responses*, 190, 213
alarm system 130, 185, 196
anchors of safety 44, 48, 53, **55-6**
Archer, C. 157, 232
assertiveness 175, 176, 182, 184, 213, 220: *skills*, **188**
attachment *approaches*, 264: *difficulties*, 3, 14, 16, 28, 79, 124, 190: *-focussed support work*, 39, 86, 155, 197, 208, 276, 278: *formation*, 179: *framework*, 271: *-friendly opportunities*, 16, 19: *– key adults*, 247: *lead – teacher*, 276: *styles*, 6, 7, 91, 149, 250, 252, 254: *relationship*, 257: *representations*, 27: *-seeking behaviour*, 190: *system*, 14, 61-62:
attachment figure, *additional*, 263, 266: *primary*, 86, 269
attentive, 33, 43, 90
attune, attunement 31, 33, 38, 45, 46, 64, 90, 100
avoidant attachment 7, 22

Ball, C. 16
Batmanghelidjh, C. 247
beginnings, *of day*, 31-32, 39, 59, 102, 107, 248: *of lesson*, 52, 75: *of scanning process*, 35: *of school year*, 71
behaviour as communication 57
behaviourist approaches 8
Bennathan, M. 165
'big ask' **29**, 87, 95, 161

blame, blaming 13, 214, 217, 250, 262, 263
boundary, boundaries, 26, 37, 48, 86, 119, 142, 164, 199-200, *comfort –*, 22: *healthy –*, 99; *personal –*, 48, 78, 170, **172-7**: *task –*, 120: *time –*, 32
book of success 65, 218
Bowlby, J. 28
Boxall, M. 64
Boxall Profile 2, 276
Bradshaw, J. 124, 189
breakfast 41: *club*, 34, 40, 159
breaking point 184, **199**
break times 24, 40, 42, 102, **135-46**, 152, 174, 188, 202, 225, **235-43**, 254, 255, 277
brain 5-7, 11, 17, 18, 19, 34, 105, 122, 128, 153, 157, 158, 172, 187, 191, 216, 266
Brief, The 22, 277
bullying 170
Burnell, A. 17
busy folder **23**

calm box 117-18, **122**, 134, 185, 188
CAMHS 250, 252, 256
Catch Up 75
'checking in' 32-33, 47, 50, 52, 60, 90, 106, 108, 148
checklists 48, 52, 99, **105**, 107, 178: *developmental –*, 1-2
chewlry **120**, 136, 273
choice 78, 83, 119: *healthy –*, 119, 121, **123-4**, 137, 189, 214: *language*, 111, 114, 189
circle of friends 142
Circle Time 210, 214
Claxton, G. 16, 73, 111
collage 218
Commentaries 33, 35, 46, 66, 115, 116, 136, 196, 201
Compass Children's Services 75
compassion 10, 135, 247, 278
conflict 6, 8, 30, 99, 125, 140, 143,

153, 183-84, 188, 191, 274
ConnectIn 215
consistency 15, 49-51
constancy **25**
containing, containment 16, 37, 52, 59, 77, 120-21, 124, 238, 251
control 19, **24**, 28-29, 37, 84-87, 93, 103, 125, 135, 139-40, 147, 149, 173, 200, 202, 252: *emotional –*, **20**: *impulse –*, 20: *out-of-*, 111, 117: *self-*, **112-3**, 119, 200
co-regulation 64, **113**, 122, 149, 163, 271
courage 73, 278

defence, defences 7, 67, 89, 191, 237: *mechanisms*, 247-50
dependency **83-96**, 106, 143: *fear of creating*, 242, 244: *relative –*, 84-7, 85, 92, 120, 263
developmental stage, 76, 85, 136, 139, 176
developmental trauma 1-16, 73, 98, 119, 162, 262-63: *effects of*, **17-32**: *impact of*, 169, 274: *training in*, 276
deprivation 5, 19, 162, 225
difference, *between right and wrong*, 124, 189: *celebrating – and diversity*, **207-21**, 242: *educating pupils about –*, 174, 188: *making a*, 8, 59, 121, 143, 229, 254-55, 278: *noticing*, 14, 52, 234, 272
differentiate, differentiation 11, 63, 70, 102-03, 138-39, 170
Dight, M. 278
disappointment 149, *managing –*, **149**: *rituals*, **151-4**
discipline 9, 25, 73, 134, 190, 192, 203
disorganised attachment 7, 249, 268
displacement 249
diversity **207-221**
domestic violence 5, 71, 273
dysregulated, dysregulation 22,

35, 37, 57, 69, 100, 103, 109, 111, 113-15, 117-20, 123, 136, 233, 240, 268: *when a pupil remains –*, **133**

eating 22, 128, **159**, 161, **162-7**
emotional abuse, 5, 23: *age*, 24, 217, 238: *capacity*, 111, 176: *consequences*, 87: *control*, 20: *development*, 136, 183: *environment*, 253: *impact*, 225, 254: *labour*, 245: *limits*, 193: *needs*, 234, 238: *pain*, 5, 237, 265: *problems*, 210: *reactions*, 113: *resources*, 176: *response*, 249: *safety*, 55:
empathy 11, 17, 87, 94, 139, 140, 155, 182, 189, 194, 196, 216, 219, 225, 248
endings 107, 229, 236-40
enough food 54, 160, **162**, 166
equality 209, 253
exclusion 9, 86, 101, 124, 138, 165, 199, 200-01, 209, 231, 275, 276
executive function 17-18, **20-22**, 73, 98
exploration 61, 73
exploratory system 14, 29, 44, 62

failure 65, 226, 232
Family Futures 17, 18
Ferguson, H. 34
fight/flight/freeze response **18**, 71, 128, 149, 191
following, *the lead*, **24**, 29, 86: *part*, 93, 96: *– the leader game*, 93
Fonagy, P. 113
food 47, 54, 91, **157-67**, 202, 235
foster *care* 77, 158, 273: *carer*, 260, 267, 274
fresh starts 15, 49, 88, 224, 225
friends 24, 29-30, 47, 49, 118, 132, 148, 153-54, 157, 165, 172, 227, 236, 251
fun 33, 114, 118, 129, 152-54, 167, **180**, 220, 237
funding 11, 12
Geddes, H. 3, 27, 61, 90, 250, 268
Gerhardt, S. 10, 34

getting changed 171-79, 181
Gilligan, R. 88
Glasser, 9, 51, 209
Golding, K. 1, 136, 140, 147, 182, 192, 207, 223
Goldschmied, E. 65
good enough, *backgrounds*, 45: *care*, 2, 6, 9, 13, 15, 30, 85, **91**, 116, 158, 189, 195: *parents*, 115
Gopnik, A. 6
Gove, M. 117
Gray, C. 234
Greenfield, S. 6
gym ball **121**, 136, 273

hand of options 131, 181, 185, **186**
headteacher 32, 77, 88, 135, 142, 144, 166, 190, 212
hope 214, 218
Hughes, D. 83
humiliation 170, 189, 214, 234, 247
humour 127, 131, 134, 180, 257
hyper-vigilance 6, 33, 44, 46, 69, 149, 171-79
hyper-sensitivity 44

inclusion 9, 12-13, 16, 88, 121, 209, 216, 242, 250, 254: *Department*, 31-36, 41, 44, 70, 107, 135, 140, 145, 148, 155, 165, 167, 198, 204, 207, 220, 243: *manager*, 92: *mentor*, 59: *room*, 27, 48, 57: *policy*, 3: *team*, 165
inclusive citizenship 213, 215: *philosophy*, 211, 253: *practice*, 3, 10, 73, 210, 212, 277: *principles*, 17: *revolution*, 30, 275-8: *schooling*, 12, 225, 275-78
individualised learning development plans 62, 68
insecure attachments 7, 27, 91, 151, 252
Inside I'm Hurting (IIH) 1, 3, 88, 202, 241, 243, 268, 272
intentions 26, 29, 33, 38, 130-31, 139, 153, 173, 185, 186, 213
Internal Working Model 7, **27**, 28-30, 91, 190
interpretation 6, 8, 10, 28, 38,

49-50, 84, 91, 109, 129, 131-32, 152, 158-59, 192, 203, 250, 275

language, *body –*, 175: *choice –*, 115: *difficulties*, 210: *insulting –*, 176: *non-violent –*, 189: *parts –*, 66, 111, 115, **124**, 128, 214, 218, 227
laughter 180, 204, 268, 269
lead attachment teacher 276
leadership 49, 208, 210-11
learning friend 62, 119
literacy 23, 39-41, 61, 63, 75, 106, 138, 237: *emotional –*, 11
loss *passim*

mealtimes 160-61
memory cards 39, 84, **94**, 99, **106**, 107, 153-54
mentors 266, 276
modelling, *co-*, 34, 52, 65, 74-75, 94, 112, 114, 122, 162, 164, 166, 178-79, 182, 238: *role-*, 142, 151, 211, 228
motor skills 170, **179**

neglect 5, 18, 157, 158, **179**, 202, 225, 227, 245, 273
Newton, C. 310
NMT 277
noticing, *adults' behaviour* 34, 91, 211: *change*, 43, 249: *differences*, 14, 46, 110, 271: *difficulties*, 20, 109, 114, 130, 134, 137, 160, 173, 179, 185, 188, 192, 258: *hyper-vigilance*, 8, 33: *out loud*, 53, 93, 116, 152, 194: *parts*, 125: *strengths*, 204, 212, 256: *where energy is expressed*, 133
nurturance **83**, 84
Nurture Group 2, 15, 64, **165**, 166

observation 115, 121, 160, 176
Owen, Y. 37

Pallett, C. 72
panic 7, 26, 130-33, 148, 185, 187, 191, 197, 237
Panskepp, J. 62

parts, *of the body*, 174, 176: *of the day*, 52, 227: *language*, 26, 66-7, 111, **124-30**, 205, 214, 218, 227, 270
patterns, *of behaviour*, 160, 220: *sleep* –, 18: *traumatic memory* –, 157
pauses 62, **65**, 80, 82, 114
Peake, A. 147
Pearce, C. 27, 73, 188
peer, peers 7, 23, 24, 29, 30, 94, 99-100, 111, 136-37, 142-43, 170, 174, 185, 188, 213, 216-17: – *mentors*, 52, 254
permanency **25**
Perry, A. 3, 247
Perry, B. 43, 61, 90, 151, 172, 263, 266
pizza game 118
Place2Be 143
play 64, 266, 277: *games*, 153-54, 165, 192: *indoor* –, 148: *times*, 135-46, 152: *sport*, 40, 178: *wet* –, 152
playful part 127, 129, 180, 266
Plummer, D. 97
primal *responses*, 191, 201: *system*, 172
projection 193, 247-48
proximity **34-49**, **64**, 91, 133, 142, 171, 273

rage 25-26, 258
Read, V. 31, 64-65, 257
reading 20, 66-67, 270: *minds*, 36: *mis-*, 26, 153
reflection 36, 46, 73, 116, 149, 191, 243, 247
reflective *capacity*, 128, 133, 191, 201: *dialoguing*, 111, **115-17**, 243: *functioning*, 248: *groups*, 254: *part of the brain*, 128, 187: *practice*, 19, 202, 275: *time*, **102**, 236, **239**
rejection 153, 192-93, 195, 197, 200, 226, 229, 232, 239
relational trauma and loss *passim*
Remen, R. 278
reparation 183-206
respect 57, 58, 91, 94, 116-17, 170, **175-6**, 180, 202-03, 208, 210-11, 219, 242, 253, 256: *dis-*, 182, 184, **197-99**, 206

Riley, P. 251, 252-53
Robinson, K. 1, 275
role-play 52, 175, 181, 185, **188**, 221, 239
rules 48, 54, 211

safe space 32-44, 48, 52-53, **57-59**, 107, 122, 133, 189, 203, 229, 277, 235
safety features 44, 53, **47-49**
scaling 130
scanning 35-36, **44**, 46
school community 35, 143, 146, 205
SEAL 215
seating 69, 121: *plan*, 24
second chance learning 4, 166
secondary stress 225, 246
secure attachment 7-8, 24, 28-29, 44, 88
secure base 14, 27, 32, 44, 86, 90, 155-56,
self-awareness 94, 111-13, 121, 129-30, 137, 171, 187-88, 196, 202, 213, 218, 256
self-control 94, 112-13, 119, 200,
self-consciousness 30, 171
self-esteem 124, 138, 171-72
self-reflection 38-39, 46, 69-71, 81, 94-95, 101, 113, 130, 133, 217, 242, 247
self-soothing 22, 111-13, 120, 121
senior management 15, 26, 50, 54, 57, 88, 135, 139, 173, 198, 221, 276
sensitive care 51, **155**, 170, 229, 239
sensory integration 109, 170, 180
separation 25, 29, 64, 197, 233, 240, 271
sexting 172
shame 32, 44, 48, 52-3, 55-59, 107, 122, 133, 189, 203, 229, 235, 277: *toxic* –, 25, 80, 100-01, **124-25**, **189-90**, 203, 265, 269-70
social story 52, 202
splits, splitting 249-50, 274
staff, *care*, 224, **245-58**: *stability*, 49: *support*, 5, 124, 191, 193
staggered *breaks*, 138: *endings*, 229, **240**, 243

stress 7, 19, 30, 62, 100, **109-34**, 136, 163, 180, 183, 185, 186-8, 191, 220, 230, 237-38: *for staff*, 245-58: *relief*, 172
stressometers 187
Sunderland, M. 135, 183, 194
supervision 54, 136, 139-40, 163, 195, 196, 201-3, 247, 252, 277

tangles 119, 273
Taylor, C. 10, 14, 38, 87, 98, 109, 190, 224, 244
Theraplay 15, 180, 272, 277:
timers 48, 52, 80, **104**, 106, 164, 179
timetable 37, 47-48, 52, 58-59, 82, 104, 179, 228, 235-37, 243: *individual* –, 37, 40, 42, 105-06, 118, 238: *off-*, 57
touch, *appropriate* –, 22, 34, 64, 272: *brief* –, 34: *firm* –, **117-18**, 122: *need for in exploratory system*, 62: *sensory* –, 23, 111, 180
toxic shame, see shame, *toxic*
transference 249
transitional object **37**, 234, **240-42**, 273
transitions 15, 96-107, 148, 235, 274
translation 4, **8**, 28-29, 84, **90-93**, 115, 131: *mis-*, 185, 228
trauma *passim*
Trauma Tree 17-19
Thrive 277
trust *passim*

uniform 35, 181, 235

Van der Kolk, B. 4
violence, 18, 245: *domestic, see domestic*
visual countdown 238
visual planner 37, 104

Wall, The 5
Walsh, C. 11
weather report 118
Wilson, D. 37, 210
WISE UP 78-79, 177
wondering aloud 35, 110, 115, **117**, 150